GESTALT THERAPY
INTEGRATED

ERVING POLSTER, PH.D., has long been a leader in the training of gestalt therapists and an active spokesman for gestalt therapy through his extensive writings, workshops, lectures, and courses. He has contributed to a number of volumes, including *Gestalt Therapy Now; Recognitions in Gestalt Therapy; Encounter;* and *Twelve Therapists.* He led his first of innumerable gestalt workshops in 1955, and in the early 1960's, through a series of his courses and practicums, founded the Postgraduate Training Program of the Gestalt Institute of Cleveland, where, until recently, he was Chairman of the Training Faculty.

MIRIAM POLSTER, PH.D., is a member of the Training Faculty at the Gestalt Institute of Cleveland and has taught psychology at Case-Western Reserve and Cleveland State Universities and at the Cleveland Institute of Art. Her gestalt training includes work with Fritz Perls, Laura Perls, Paul Goodman and Isadore From. Trained also as a musician, she has led workshops in which music served as a point of departure for exploring personal experience. She has also developed a method of using story-telling and allegory as a means for self-discovery.

The Polsters are now in private practice in San Diego where they are continuing to develop training programs in gestalt therapy. Dr. Erving Polster is also associated with the Western Institute for Group and Family Therapy, and both he and his wife are on the staff of the California School for Professional Psychology.

Gestalt Therapy Integrated

Contours of Theory and Practice

By
ERVING POLSTER, Ph.D.
and
MIRIAM POLSTER, Ph.D.

BRUNNER/MAZEL, *Publishers* • NEW YORK
BUTTERWORTHS • LONDON

To

ISADORE FROM

Teacher and Friend

Soon he was softly breathing the no-geography of being at a loss. He tasted the elixir of being at a loss, when anything that occurs must necessarily be a surprise. He could no longer make any sense of his own essential things (that had never made him happy); he could feel them fleeing away from him; yet he did not snatch at them in despair. Instead he touched his body and looked around and felt, "Here I am and now," and did not become panicky.

PAUL GOODMAN—The Empire City

Introduction

Our society is witnessing an ongoing struggle between the forces for humanism and the forces for alienation and dehumanization. Gestalt therapy, a significant force in this struggle, has been developing and presenting its method of personal growth along two pathways. One is through working towards liberation from *psychopathological* unfinished business. The other direction is through its support for catalyzing and nurturing undeveloped or unrealized *human potential*. Under the leadership and stimulation of its main proponent and developmental genius, Fritz Perls, a number of gestaltists have dedicated themselves as professional mental health specialists and humanists to efforts aimed at spreading the theory and techniques of gestalt therapy. The authors of this contribution to the growing body of publications on gestalt therapy, Erving and Miriam Polster, have here brought their clinical experiences and acumen to the task of creatively enlarging the understanding of gestalt therapy by professionals, paraprofessionals and other serious students in the mental health and growth movement scene.

New light in any field requires an openness to reviewing long-held theory and practices, implying possible abandonment

—or at least revision—of currently popular theories. Gestalt therapy is both a way and a challenge to long-standing psychiatric and psychoanalytic assumptions, though not all of them, to be sure.

We see here that these authors have fortunately not "discarded the baby with the bathwater." They repeatedly emphasize the importance of theoretical orientation among therapists so that current "action" methods become more than gimmicks, mimicry or glib oversimplifications. They also acknowledge their ancestry when they say, "The integrative energy of psychoanalysis in our social development during the first half of this century is well known and impressive. It is the foundation upon which all psychotherapeutic theorists have built." In the inevitable movement from the psychoanalytic base, they see gestalt therapy as a major integrative force in contemporary social development. The authors are at their most eloquent in struggling with the paradoxes inherent in their differences from Freud—especially when they elaborate their view of *meaning*, comparing it with that of the Freudians. They picture the search for meaning as a human reflex, but also show how the *compulsion* to meaning can drown out experience itself.

In recent years, the subject of gestalt therapy has often been brought to our attention alongside behavior therapy, transactional analysis and the encounter movement. Lumping these new developments together has served none of them well and produced mystique and confusion. This mystique has both attracted and repelled serious students and workers in the field of psychotherapy.

Today's gestalt therapy—as developed by Perls on the basis of Köhler's work—is currently recognized as a major force in the stream of avant-garde influences in psychotherapeutic approaches. As more and more gestalt techniques are understood and used successfully for psychotherapeutic interventions with individuals, couples and groups hung up with "unfinished business" and an excess of psychopathological introjects, there is an increased demand for an articulation of gestalt therapy principles which is readily understandable and relevant to the demands of therapy today. The authors have responded to this demand ably, in an erudite yet clinically comprehensive and practical fashion. Gestalt concepts which have needed to be more clearly defined and which are elaborated on in this book include contactfulness, resolution of polarities, behavioral experiments and the undoing of crippling, growth-retarding introjects. Moreover, they show how gestalt therapy—an action oriented therapy—calls forth a new kind of creative and free-flowing involvement from the *therapist* as well as the patient.

The authors of *Gestalt Therapy Integrated*, like Perls himself, do not present gestalt therapy in terms either of instant joy, instant sensory awareness or instant cure. They obviously subscribe to Perls' statement in his introduction to *Gestalt Therapy Verbatim* that, "The growth process is a process that takes time. We can't just snap our fingers and say, 'Come on, let's be gay!' Gestalt therapy . . . is no magic short-cut. You don't have to be on a couch or in a Zendo for twenty or thirty years, but you have to invest yourself, and it takes time to grow."

This book is provocative as well as timely, inserting its principles and their ramifications into the contemporary scene within which gestalt therapy is to be experienced and understood. The authors say, for example, "Since it is inevitable that perspectives change, theoretical integration must subsume the new spirit which these perspectives both reflect and create. Some of the most persuasive of the new perspectives which are the foundations for gestalt therapy—and indeed for a large part of the humanistic movement—are the following: 1) power is in the present; 2) experience counts most; 3) the therapist is his own instrument; and 4) therapy is too good to be limited to the sick."

The authors do not perpetuate the rigidities of those who literally allow only or exclusively for here-and-now data while derogating all else as mere "aboutism" or "archeology." Instead they present a view of the here-and-now experience which broadens the gestalt therapy experience so as to include common human concerns which a narrow view of here-and-now might otherwise exclude.

Erving Polster is one of that group of second generation gestaltists (including, among others, Joen Fagen, Abraham Levitsky, Irma Shepherd and James Simkin) who learned from and have further developed and refined the work of Fritz and Laura Perls. He and his co-author, Miriam Polster, are well equipped to bring us a unified vision of gestalt therapy as well as the possibilities for integrating it both within itself and into the more commonly used varieties of analytically-oriented individual, family and group psychotherapy. Their workshops in gestalt therapy have attracted many students, including both old and new practitioners.

There is a timely, scholarly, holistic and humanistic viewpoint expressed throughout this book. This sits well with me, particularly since I have been actively espousing similar views for many years, not only in individual, couples and group therapy, but in many areas of community psychiatry as well.

To the serious participant in the development of new and better approaches in psychotherapy, it is obvious that gestalt therapy is not a fad but occupies an important place in the growing repertoire of valued ways of undermining psychopathology and promoting growth.

I predict a wide acceptance of this volume among psychotherapists of varying backgrounds.

MILTON M. BERGER, M.D.
Director of Education and Training
South Beach Psychiatric Center
New York

Contents

Preface

The main purpose of this book is to convey the breath and breadth of gestalt therapy in one coherent unit, integrating the theoretical perspectives and therapeutic choices open to the gestaltist. In doing this, we present the fundamentals of gestalt therapy as well as developing new concepts and reformulating familiar ones. We have tried to evoke a sense of new dimensions in gestalt therapy which encompasses the rhythm between rationale and excitement, humanity and technique, personal horizons and universality.

For those workers in the psychological arts who are at the border of recognizing and experimenting with gestalt methods, we hope this book will provide a stimulus for further gestalt experience and training and for exploring personally the power and scope of these principles.

We would like particularly to acknowledge the lively colleagueship of the Training Faculty of the Gestalt Institute of Cleveland, all the more precious to us as we prepare to leave Cleveland. They have been our companions in the search for gestalt action and perspective—some for as many as twenty years. They are more than a "Faculty." They are: Marjorie Creelman, Rainette Fantz, Cynthia Harris, Elaine Kepner, Ed

Nevis, Sonia Nevis, Bill Warner and Joseph Zinker, joined recently by Frances Baker and C. Wesley Jackson. Absented from this roster by his untimely death is our dear colleague, Richard Wallen.

We also want to testify to the prodigious work of our secretary, Harriet-Carole Senturia, whose efficiency, humor and lovability have made the communication of what we wanted in this book as much of a delight as it could be, begrudging us no error or confusion and allowing a deep sense of mutuality to develop between us.

And last—and most—we want to express our love for Sarah and Adam, our children, who have happily turned our preoccupations into live encounters with their irreverence and simple perspective. Sarah has edited parts of this book with pungent and loving amusement and Adam has accepted with shaggy grace and humor the times we were unavailable for his purposes. Furthermore, they have dreamed up countless riotous titles, mary of which were either unprintable or irrelevant but a lot more fun than the title we wound up with.

ERVING AND MIRIAM POLSTER

Cleveland
March, 1973

GESTALT THERAPY
INTEGRATED

1

The Now Ethos

The old symbols are dead, and the new reign.
But it is perfectly certain that the new will die in
their turn of the same disease.

JOYCE CARY

Children have a chant that helps them start when it becomes important for them to get moving. It goes:

One for the money
Two for the show
Three to get ready
And four to go!

Right now many people feel stuck in stage number three,
bogged down in an age of getting ready—of preparing for
events that either never come off or take so long before they
finally do that one comes to them worn out and already disappointed. One works in drudgery all year for a glowing two
weeks' vacation—like the light at the end of a long, dark

1

tunnel. One scrimps through a lifetime anticipating an ease-
ful retirement. An endless sequence of classrooms, lecture
halls, churches, museums, concert halls and libraries promise
to teach one about living. Frequently learning itself is not
even presented as an act of living *in its own right*. Real living
is to begin at some time in the future—after we finish college,
after we get married, after the kids grow up or, for some,
after we finish therapy.

Preparations for the real event, whatever it may turn out
to be, are dangled in front of a person who buys speculative
shares in a glowing future. He pays for future happiness by
deadening or denying the impactful presence of current sensation. But even when he arrives at the promised land, an unwelcome by-product of his bargain is that the habits of
downgrading present experience have accompanied him into
that future which has finally become his present. Now, when
he could begin to *live*, according to the terms of his contract
with society, he still holds back! He has been duped by the it's-
good-for-you con game.

The times are ripe for change. The magnetic force of immediate experience is hard to beat and the promise of future
success or payoff has to compete with the punch that sensation and immediacy deliver right now.

Not too long ago, little attention was paid to immediate
experience under the assumption that personal involvement
while learning disrupted the objectivity essential for clear-
headed conceptualization. Learning *requires* a sense of personal immediacy however, as well as theoretical perspective;
like one hand washing the other, they are inseparably linked.

Such splitting off is no longer tenable in psychological activities either. The emergence of the word "relevance" has become almost a code name for getting things together in life,
relating all experiences to some central core issue which matters deeply. Until recently, psychotherapists were among the
headmasters of the school of irrelevancy. Cloistered and ex-

clusive methodologies, combined with the medical model of sickness, kept psychotherapists withdrawn into their own offices, isolated from direct impact on the community—almost like the contagion model of illness—entering their views into the cultural lore primarily through lectures or consultations or weighty papers directed mainly at colleagues. With the advent of existentialism and the recognition of the commonality of man's basic problems,* the range of concerns of the psychotherapist expanded. People began to care not just about whether they were sick or not, but also how they might exercise their power, how they might experience a sense of belonging, how they might get up-to-date with their actual needs and wishes, how to create an environment where people could develop new institutional forms centering around marriage, birth, death, loss of a job, divorce, family integration and other human concerns. Furthermore, they brought these concerns into their psychotherapy and expected that they would be able to find some answers and directions there. All of these questions then, when assimilated into the psychotherapeutic ethos, resulted in the burgeoning of a psychotherapy which was humanistically oriented.

Now, with the exciting proliferation of new behaviors and values, people are caught in mid-air. They are fascinated by the fresh liveliness possible in first-hand experience, but they lack the integrative cohesion which theory provided by giving meaning and perspective to the things they needed to do and feel. Theory and knowledge remain suspect, not because of inherent worthlessness, but because of their historic isolation from action. Without theoretical orientation, however, action is vulnerable to oversimplified and glib imitativeness—even mimicry—and to the use of the gimmick.

Until the 1950's, psychoanalysis was just such an integrative force. In the face of a hostile society, it had created what

---

* Polster, E., *Encounter in Community* in *Encounter*, Burton, A., Ed., San Francisco: Jossey-Bass, 1969.

was then a compelling portrait of human nature and it had provided new perspective for many behaviors which had previously remained largely incomprehensible. The integrative energy of psychoanalysis in our social development during the first half of this century is well-known and impressive. It is the foundation upon which all psychotherapeutic theorists have built.

But Freud protected the inviolability of his views; he was intolerant of deviation and its disintegrative possibilities. To maintain the integrity of his own system, he disavowed the new theoretical developments even though they may have come from original formulations which had been essentially inspired by him. Because he experienced divergencies from his principles as threats to the *real* truth, he was unwilling to permit some brilliant perspectives to add dimension to his system.

Since these perspectives remained alive anyway—as will any theory which speaks to the needs of the society—they did become a base for much of the contemporary ethos. Although the deviations from Freud had less impact than the views of Freud, their vitality could not go unfelt.

NEW THEORETICAL PERSPECTIVES

It is plain that no theory has a monopoly on the *real* truth, but in those early days, when psychoanalytic theory was being formulated for the first time, it was as difficult for those who split from Freud to tolerate the limitations of their own methods as it was for Freud himself. One theorist, however, Otto Rank*—who did split with Freud—nevertheless was able to transcend parochialism when he commented:

> . . . theories of psychology change, one might almost say, like fashions, and are perforce compelled to change in order to express, as well as make intelligible, the existing type of man in his dynamic struggle for maintainance and perpetuation.

---

* Rank, O., *Beyond Psychology*. New York: Dover Pub., 1941.

With such a view, new theoretical developments need not harden into polemic and perpetual self-justification. They can resemble paintings, which are the expression of one man's view of his experience; they are *his* perspective, after all, but not to be taken as life itself. Theories, too, illuminate our way. We need them to tie our behaviors and our views together, so that what we do for now will make sense to us and will have some continuity. But they are not the *real* truth; there is no such thing. Hall and Lindzey* define what a theory is:

> . . . theories are not "given" or predetermined by nature, the data, or any other determinant process. Just as the same experiences or observations may lead a poet or novelist to create any one of a multitude of different art forms, so the data of investigation may be incorporated in any of countless different theoretical schemes. The theorist in choosing one particular option to represent the events in which he is interested is exercising a free creative choice that is different from the artist's only in the kinds of evidence upon which its fruitfulness will be judged.

It is a healthy sign that many people are not taking established theory as seriously as they once did. Nevertheless, what they lack now is a theory which can reflect practical concerns. They need ways to orient themselves articulately about what they and their contemporaries are thinking and feeling and wanting. Gestalt therapy provides such an orientation. It is a creative composition assimilating the Freudian dissidents almost unrecognizably within the gestalt perspective.** Its major premise is that the therapeutic experience is not merely a preparatory event, but a valid moment *per se,* needing no external referent to confirm its inherent relevance to the patient's life.

---

* Hall, C. S. and Lindzey, G., Ed., *Theories of Personality.* New York: Wiley, 1965.
** Nevertheless, it is important to acknowledge who and what some of these influences have been. See Appendix A for a brief summary.

Our truth in gestalt therapy is only a temporary truth, one which is currently serviceable and responsive to the vital stimulation of the times. To say that gestalt therapy is a temporary truth does not mean that what is described in this book, and other books like it, will no longer be true 40 years from now. Rather, 40 years from now what we are teaching may be a stale way to look at life then. For example, consider a core psychoanalytic concept, transference. This concept was a magnificent stroke, illuminating, as it did, our knowledge about distortion. Nevertheless, in the minds of many psychotherapists, this concept has gone stale. It emphasized the as-though quality of the psychotherapeutic relationship, but this emphasis is inadequate for those people who want to go beyond the depersonalization which is rampant today. What is needed now is more than a recognition that many current relationships are re-hashes of significant earlier relationships. The emotions which can occur between psychotherapist and patient are authentic in their own right, and it is possible to deal with present distortions on their own merits. It is too simplistic to think of all happenings as though they were elementary imitations of a relationship to one's parents.

Echoes though they may be, gestalt therapy focuses on the present relationships *qua present*. If the patient is angry at the therapist, it might be important, for example, to know how the patient accepts this feeling now, or what he intends to do about it now. The transference interpretation deflects the individual from the accumulated results of his experiences in life, explaining away the powerful force of present action and feeling, substituting once-upon-a-time for right now. This is not to imply that the concept of transference did not make a valid point about people reacting presently in terms of what they learned in their relationships with their parents. It is simply no longer the point we are interested in. A contemporary painter will find a Rembrandt painting absorbing, but he wouldn't be caught dead painting that way seriously.

Though he surely accepts the verity of Rembrandt's vision, he must follow his own visions of the world he is inhabiting and his own techniques for making contact within that world.

Since it is inevitable that perspectives change, theoretical integration must subsume the new spirit which these perspectives both reflect and create. Some of the most pervasive of the new perspectives which are the foundations for gestalt therapy—and indeed for a large part of the humanistic movement—are the following: 1) power is in the present; 2) experience counts most; 3) the therapist is his own instrument; and 4) therapy is too good to be limited to the sick.

POWER IS IN THE PRESENT

A most difficult truth to teach is that only the present exists now and that to stray from it distracts from the living quality of reality. Since this seems so obvious and is so widely accepted among people in the so-called third stream of psychology, it always comes as a surprise that an emphasis on the present as providing great therapeutic leverage is vigorously opposed by a large number of psychotherapists. Two basic paradoxes obscure the dynamics of the present as the pre-ordinate power base of life. The first paradox is that gestalt therapy recognizes the *acts* of remembering and planning as present functions even though they *refer* to the past and future. The second paradox is that we also deal with topics which are *about* concerns which extend beyond the scope of direct interpersonal confrontation and *refer* to many authentically important issues, such as Vietnam, city planning, friendship, government, racism, ecology, etc.

Since these paradoxes are a prime source of confusion about the power of the present, a discussion of them may be necessary to clarify and extend our boundaries as to what constitutes the present. As many have realized, a rigid view of the present—one which permits none but literally present experiences to enter into any engagement—is stultifying. Only through arbitrary exclusion is it possible to wipe out stories concerning events which have happened or may happen outside the here-and-now setting. Some of these events form the most poignant and rich drama of a person's existence and for these stories to be off-limits is a great loss to both the teller and the listener.

Past and future—The dimensions of past and future give recognition to that which once was and that which some day may be, thus forming psychological boundaries for present experience and a psychological context which provides the figural present a background upon which to exist. The paradox is that, while a concern with past and future is obviously central to psychological functioning, to behave as though one were indeed *in* the past or future, as many do, pollutes the lively possibilities of existence. Only in the present can the individual's sensory and motor systems function, and it is from the perspective of these functions that present experience can be palpable and lively. When, for example, a patient is remembering a past event and stiffens up while telling about having been spanked by his father, if he treats that incident merely as a past event, he is only minimally present. Were he to become aware of his stiffened quality, his present experience would be heightened greatly. Then, if he could further allow his stagnant tightness to build into a live tension system, he might well tell the story with the rage, let us speculate, which is inherent in his tension. Tension has its own directional power and—memory or not—moves into the present by erupting into verbal eloquence, crying, screaming, flailing, berating, pounding and other expressive actions. What had previously been choked off, cast into the past, becomes reborn now through the currently available sensory and motor realities. Completion emerges through recognition, enhancement and continuing focus until motor discharge—available *only* in the present—finally releases the person from living *in* the dead past.

The discrimination required to gauge the presence-quality of any experience requires connoisseurship rather than a system of rules. Grammatical edicts which require people to speak only in the present tense may be interesting experiments for people who need this particular discipline, but to require this across the board is a great sacrifice of the range of human communication. Overstylization, which mistakes a poetic moment or experience for a way of life, loses the pungency of relevant content and invites the stereotyped and cultist behavior of the imitator. That gestalt therapy is as vulnerable as it is to overstylization is ironic, since telling people how they *must* talk to each other is an exact contradiction to the anti-should orientation that gestalt therapy espouses. A person who is learning how to be in the present cannot be required to be in the present until he discovers how. If he is legislated into the present by grammatical edict—or some other imposed form— he may comply, but it will be a stereotyped compliance, an empty form rather than a vital presence.

Aboutism—The second gestalt paradox centers around how to talk *about* something without sacrificing the immediacy of experience. The trouble with aboutism is that it can become a poisonous addiction; one is likely to get stuck in it, like getting caught in a revolving door. As Fitzgerald says in the *Rubaiyat*:

> Myself when young did eagerly frequent
> Doctor and Saint, and heard great argument
> About it and about: but evermore
> Came out by the same door as in I went.

Crying poison is not enough, though. People *are* natively interested in much that stretches beyond any arbitrary limits of the here and now; they *will* talk about what moves them— a movie that turned them on, who should start as quarterback, will the mayor be reelected. However concernful topics like these may be, they are also major carriers of depersonalization. They may be merely attempts to make conversation, to distract from distrusted feelings, to show off one's knowledge, to have a ready-made engagement, to avoid fight, sex or confusion, and all the other maneuvers which may make life safe but uninteresting.

As a reaction against this kind of depersonalized communication, insistence on staying in a closed-off world, bounded by the narrowly defined limits of present experience, is only slightly less poisonous. Many people, especially those who are experienced members of therapy groups or encounter groups, will say that concern with Vietnam, contemporary architecture, how to build a hi-fi, favored vacation spots, etc., are not "group material." This is patently absurd, because operating within such limits erases the substance of people's lives.

One man talked to his group *about* Vietnam but eventually moved into his own impassioned view of the conflict, developing considerable grief about the holocaust and discovering his own personal terror about the coming prospect of his son's involvement. In another group, the topic of old age in our culture was batted around for awhile until one member began telling about her own experience when she placed her mother in a nursing home instead of taking her into her own home to die *en famille*. This soon developed into a fantasy conversation with her mother, where she told her what she never could in actuality. Through this dialogue, she recovered her own sense of priorities and got unstuck from her stereotyped shoulds about mothers.

Learning to make something personal and engrossing out of primarily topical raw material is a major challenge not only to those in the personal growth movement, but to all people trying to get messages across. Lectures, unfortunately, are still a favored medium, but the general fruitlessness of low-yield communication is well known. Still, people come, and they do learn even through depersonalized media. Habits are strongly ingrained and inventiveness has not yet carved out enough new forms of communication which could tie information and topic into individual participation and action. The effort is on, though. More and more teachers and students are developing live action in their pedagogical encounters. Contract education is one example where teacher and student work out an individual design and negotiate what is to be learned. Work-study programs and independent study projects are designed to give education a sense of immediacy in place of the familiarly distant aboutism. Beyond education, architects are involving clients in a personal work-through of environmental needs as an organic factor in the design of houses, buildings and offices. Police are learning about their relationship to people through role-playing and other techniques. Conference planners are building more and more personal interaction into their designs. Writers of textbooks include more action problems which require the immediate involvement of the reader and engage him in personal reactivity.

It is plain that our whole cultural system—shot through as it has been with sterile aboutism—needs new designs which will arouse people to experience their present action while they are communicating and learning. It is no wonder that the expulsion of aboutism from therapy and encounter groups has become almost ritualistic. However, such phobic-like excommunication of all that is topical makes the process vulnerable to involutions of self-awareness, so narrow in scope that they twist inward into ever-decreasing smallness. By the time this inbreeding runs its course, we could become our own grandfathers.

Presence itself—The weight of gestalt therapy swings toward simple presence in the face of these paradoxical complications. That is, the therapy experience—individual or in groups—is an exercise in unhampered living *now,* where topics or past and future activities are no longer of prime consequence. Since neurotic living is basically anachronistic living, any return to present experience is in itself a part of the antidote to neurosis. A person must learn that there is no predetermined contract in the present interaction for feeling that he might not fidget, tell bawdy stories, see through another person's obfuscations, holler, sit passively, criticize, embrace, develop a mad fantasy, giggle and all the other behavioral possibilities in existence. If he is in a group, he is in a new community, defined in its function by the *actual* natures of the people in it and the implicit consequences of the interaction. Thus, someone might well squawk when he giggles and that is a reaction he must take into account. The opportunities for growth then come through actual abrasions and the work-through to resolution comes in actual meeting of people in the present. When residues from the past intrude, he must learn to set them aside and to experience the actuality of his behavior right there within this group of specific people.

One patient was asked how he thought his life would be different if he were healthy but had amnesia. At first he was delighted at the prospect of being free from his current entanglements, but then he ruefully observed, like a person caught in his own practical joke, that he himself was the only person keeping the past alive. Indeed he was.

EXPERIENCE COUNTS

Almost inextricably tied to the primacy of the present is the primacy of experience. The need to make sense out of experience has been so strongly imprinted culturally that it has covered over the experience itself. Experience has come to mean either more or less than it seems and cannot thus be taken on its own merits.

Freud saw both the experiential and meaning aspects of the therapy interaction. But his way of handling this split left psychotherapists focused on the meaning of events in therapy and everyday life rather than on the quality of the immediate experience. His Janus-like view of transference clouded the basic issue of direct experience. On the one hand, Freud's view of transference has a bare, as-though quality, deflecting all present interactions into nothing but disguises which front for the past. On the other hand, the transference contact with the analyst *was* a central factor in therapy, even though it was ultimately explained away. Despite admonitions about the blank-wall nature of the analyst, he *must* become a personal presence for patients who legendarily refer to my-analyst-this or my-analyst-that. These two possibilities appear in Freud's writings* where he described both the deflective qualities of transference and its potential for intensifying experience. At one point, speaking of neurotic and dependent attachments to the analyst, he says:

> . . . the danger of these states of transference evidently consists of the possibility of the patient *misunderstanding* their nature and taking them for *fresh* experiences instead of reflections from the past. (*emphasis added*)

Of course, this construes the ongoing relationship with the therapist as merely a red herring, convenient only to distract from the real scent on the trail of the unconscious. In contrast, however, Freud also says, in the same reference:

> Another advantage of transference is that in it the patient produces before us with plastic clarity an important part of his life history, of which he would otherwise probably have given us only an *unsatisfactory* account. It is as though he were acting it in front of us instead of reporting it to us. (*emphasis added*)

Here Freud clearly shows his preference for the present fresh moment over stale historical reminiscence. He recognizes the dramatic, symbolic nature of the therapeutic scene. What he fails to acknowledge is that instead of looking for symbols from the past to illuminate present experience, present experience *itself* produces symbols which are valid statements and

---

* Freud, S., *An Outline of Psychoanalysis*. New York: W. W. Norton & Co., 1949.

which extend beyond the limits of the therapeutic interaction. The symbolic quality of an event projects it forward because of its power to take on newly created meaning for the individual. When it acquires such meaning, it assumes its place in the context of his life and does not remain restricted and encapsulated only in those interactions which occur in the therapy scene.

One woman, Alice, had developed an extended fantasy in which she wound up walking in the woods with her mother, arm-in-arm, feeling her mother's warmth for the first time. When the session ended, Alice walked over to me,* kissed me tenderly, said to me, "I love you" and left the room. She really did love me then; not her father or anyone else, as the transference people might believe. In the gestalt perspective, such expression is taken at face value, leaving aside all questions of the causes of her behavior or feeling. Instead, a trust of the natural flow of the relationship is invoked, not pinning this flow down by resorting to symbolic connections to the past, or looking beyond this incident to whatever psychologistic vectors might explain her present behavior. This symbolic "I love you" leans into the future so that love itself becomes more generally assimilable. The event, as all events with force in them, will affect this woman's sense of herself, her world and her directions in it. It has natural microcosmic relevance: representing, crystallizing, summarizing and dramatizing live issues which dominate her current experience.

When the patient kisses her therapist, as in the above illustration, and tells him she loves him, the meaning which she attributes to this experience may be, "I am now open to love and to express it when I feel it and in any way that feels right to me." Such a characterization gives leverage to the therapeutic event, projecting it into new stimulation and a

---

* In order to avoid cumbersome grammar, couching personal experiences of the therapists in third person, we intend to use first person when talking about an event.

new moral context for her future behavior. It is not indispensable to verbalize this, and often to do so would give the experience a stamp of meaning which may be premature. The danger of assigning meaning to experiences is that it stamps into a mold that which is still in process, thereby leading to behaviors which may become subservient to the meaning and establishing only another base for stereotyped behavior.

Meaning and experience, therefore, have a complex interrelationship and an excess of either can block out the necessary function of the other. The arts illustrate this problem well. Some works of art, like the paintings of Hieronymus Bosch, have developed systems of symbolism so intricate and compelling that it is easy to lose sight of the painting itself and focus more centrally on what it *means*. Other artists, especially contemporary writers like Albee, Pinter and Beckett, deny the symbolic import of their work, insisting that the spectator just *experience* the play. The audience, though, is so accustomed to the search for meaning that, when the playwright doesn't provide it, they will fill the gap with their own speculations. Nevertheless, the reflexive need for meaning* is not merely capricious, and nobody knows it better than these writers. They intend that whatever meaning may come out for the audience will form from a fresh life process where each person is simply affected by his experience of the play. The meaning of the experience then unfolds uniquely, appearing either during the play itself or appearing later, but having a different significance for each person according to the context his life provides.

Picasso** says about understanding painting:

Everybody wants to understand painting. Why is there no attempt to understand the song of birds? Why does one

---

* The parallel between the need for meaning and the figure/ground phenomenon which is a central concept in gestalt therapy is explained in Chapter 2.

** Ghiselin, B., Ed. *The Creative Process.* New York: The New American Library, 1955.

love a night, a flower, everything that surrounds man, without trying to understand it all? . . . Those who try to explain a picture are most of the time on the wrong track. Gertrude Stein announced to me joyously some time ago that she had at last understood what my picture represented: three musicians. It was a still life!"

Picasso's impatience is common among artists who have long been frustrated by the primacy of meaning blocking out basic aspects of existence, as though the discovery of meaning were merely an intellectual pursuit. His impatience, though, seems directed against the native experience being *replaced* by the search for meaning, because even he gave the painting meaning by saying it was a still life. This was his meaning. To Gertrude Stein it was three musicians. Harold Pinter refuses to be drawn into explanations about the meaning of his plays, believing that he has already said as much as he could right in the body of the play. Yet, so strong is the search for meaning, that even Pinter, when he directed a play of Robert Shaw, questioned Shaw repeatedly about what he meant by this or that event in the play.*

We are in the same boat in gestalt therapy, having been burned by meaning-searches which have characteristically wiped out actual experiences. Since the search for meaning is accorded a central place in gestalt theory, the real question boils down to ascertaining its rightful place. We want to hear the story first and let the meaning unfold, rather than to be present with expectations of a certain significance into which all behavior is then fitted. Though the search for meaning is a human reflex, the *compulsion* to meaning frequently drowns out experience itself. Meaning evolves out of the sequentiality of life and the natural rhythms between experience and the attribution of meaning. In psychotherapy, the symbol is most powerful when its meaningfulness arises out of experiences which exist first for their own sake and *then* project them-

* From an interview in *The New York Times Magazine*, Dec. 5, 1971.

selves into a natural and evident meaningfulness which helps tie experiences together. In this process, the patient participates as an equal, giving each new experience a place in a new context and with new applications of his own, uniquely transcending the therapeutic present without the stereotyped search for causes, history, and meaning, meaning, meaning.

This emphasis on experience itself rather than on the interpretation of experience reflects the spirit of protest against the authoritarianism that entitles one person, who presumably knows more, to put something over on another person, who presumably knows less. Instead of playing intellectual guessing games, we prefer that a patient get inside his own experience, trusting that when he gets a clear sense of what is happening inside him, his own directionalism will propel him into whatever experience is next for him. His internal dynamic needs recognition and re-awakening. Usually, people are only tangentially aware of what supports or adds to the richness of their own existence. If one were to ask someone, for example, what he is experiencing as he tells of his boss's latest demands or a friend's kindness or his trip to Africa, he would probably be startled, perhaps even turned off, and unable to say. Yet, whenever people are able to describe, or at least be in touch with, their own experience, conversations take a turn upward toward increased absorption. Such awarenesses are often considered either private or distracting, so we are frequently left with flat interactions. These interactions are flat because the personal and human detail has been omitted or covered up. Correspondingly, not long ago, buildings were designed to conceal or disguise basic structural necessities. Visible supporting steel beams, uncluttered walls, open kitchens, were all avoided and considered unlovely. Now we want to see them. If the comparable structures within the individual's experience were to be revealed, we would hear such remarks as, "I'm scared by your question" instead of someone ignoring it or lying; "I'm awed by your knowledge" instead of playing one-upmanship; or even, "I'm thrilled that you like me!" instead of playing it cool.

THERAPIST IS HIS OWN INSTRUMENT

Joyce Cary* has said that all art is a combination of a fact and the feeling about the fact. The therapist also plays from his own feelings, like the artist, using his own psychological state as an instrument of therapy. Naturally, just as the artist painting a tree has to be affected by that particular tree, so also must the psychotherapist be tuned in to the specific person with whom he is in touch. It is as if the therapist becomes a resonating chamber for what is going on between himself and the patient. He receives and reverberates to what happens in this interaction and he amplifies it so that it becomes part of the dynamic of the therapy. Using his own reactivity, when the patient's voice grates harshly, he may say, "You make me feel like a naughty child." Or a twinkle in the patient's expression may set off a fantasy about the kind of playmate the patient might have been, or is. Sometimes the therapist is bored, confused, amused, angered, amazed, sexually aroused, frightened, cornered, interupted, overwhelmed, and on and on. All of these reactions say something about both the patient and therapist and they comprise much of the vital data of the therapy experience.

These experiences may be fed in simply by the therapist describing his own experience and following through on whatever effects these remarks may have on the interaction. The therapist says he's bored, for example. The patient may respond by saying he is not there to entertain the therapist or he may say he feels squashed by the remark. Whichever happens is grist for the therapeutic mill. In the first instance, the therapist may ask what the patient's objections would be about entertaining the therapist—calling forth a whole range of pos-

---

* Cary, Joyce, *Art & Reality*. New York: Doubleday and Co., Inc., 1961.

sible responses which would bear on how interesting the patient is willing to be in therapy or in life outside therapy. The one who is squashed by the therapist's boredom may deal with his own hypersensitivity about being uninteresting or he may be taught how to be interesting, by changing his language, for example, or by getting better breathing support for his voice, or by telling what is really on his mind rather than the worked-over junk he was talking about.

At other times the therapist may not feed his own experience in by articulating it, but instead by acting on it. He may hold his patient's hand while the patient is crying, refuse to answer questions that make him feel tricked, lend his patient money when he needs it, become sympathetically enraged when the patient has been wronged, tell a funny story when amused or tell the patient he or she is beautiful when the therapist sees it. Or the therapist may let his feelings develop into metaphorical fantasies which confront the patient and illuminate one of his important characteristics.

For example, a 27-year-old man, Charles, regarding himself as a homosexual but seeking the heterosexual, was finally courting a girl. He talked a lot about it, in a special dilatory way, not quite making the point, leaving gaps in his account, and seeming to be waiting out his story instead of telling it incisively. I leaned back and allowed a visual fantasy to come to me. In my fantasy, Charles was a devil with flowing cape, alternately green and red, quite sinister. As the fantasy scene developed, a woman materialized. She was undressed and sexually ready for Charles. She had become ready through his devil's magic rather than through any activity which he actually experienced. I saw the woman as a combination of my own wife, my mother and his girlfriend. Charles, the devil, would have to take his cape off for a human screw. Then he would be a man. But he also wants to continue to be a devil so he hesitates about what to do. In this period of vacillation, I go in and screw the woman. The fantasy ends. As I finish telling

him my fantasy, I open my eyes and see that Charles' face has
swelled in absorption. He begins to talk about his father, whose
memory my story has evoked. He had found his father disgusting, an irresponsible man, who had been married three
times. He does not find me disgusting, though, and in fact
Charles suddenly realizes that his father, marrying three times
as he had, was a man of considerable activity who didn't fuss
around when he wanted to do something! He was, by now,
delighted with this new view of his father and equally delighted by my audacity. Soon after this session, he met a second
woman with whom he experienced sexual glories he had never
foreseen. Though there were, of course, many other experiences in his therapy that affected his sexual development, this
one was at least as important as any other.

The range of interaction within which the therapist's experience is pertinent—even indispensable—to full therapy engagement is very large. Recognition of the centrality of the
therapist's own experience exists not only within gestalt therapy, but also within Rogerian work, experiential therapy,
sensitivity training, and among the psychological workers who
are existentially oriented and who see therapy as a two-way
human engagement. Within this frame of mind, to include
the therapist's experience is as simple as one and one equal
two.

However, the advantage of using the therapist's own experience goes beyond the additive quality of including everything
available in the therapy encounter. When the therapist enters
himself, he is not only making available to the patient something which already exists, he is also taking a hand in making
new experiences happen which are based on himself as well as
on the patient. That is to say, he becomes not only a responder
and a feedback giver, but also an artistic participant in the
creation of new life. He is more than a catalyst which, though
affecting chemical transformation, does not itself change. The
therapist does change; he becomes more open to the range of

experiences which he can know first hand, discovering with the patient what it is like to engage in the many ways which become open to them. Suppose, for example, the therapist discovers in himself a broad streak of hard-nosed demand, yielding little to pleas for compassion and repeatedly throwing frustrating roadblocks in the path of any soft interactions. It is the therapist's business to become aware of this characteristic and to accept this awareness as part of the therapeutic stream. If he neglects to do this and concentrates only on the so-called sick patient's nature, he encourages personal distance. In doing so he sacrifices the vitality of a mutual engagement between two humans and he gives himself little opportunity for personal growth. When he acknowledges his toughness as a part of his humanity, he may unblock the sources of his own compassion. Or, instead of becoming compassionate, he may recognize the fruitfulness of his frustrating behavior, as Perls did. Perls spoke often of skillful frustration,* even though he could also welcome his own tenderness. Acknowledging and supporting one's own hardnosed nature and letting it be a living part of a new confrontation for the patient as well as himself may be a greater source of engagement than conventional therapeutic permissiveness. If the therapist ignores this quality in himself, he may, nevertheless, do good work with many people, but he becomes a technician, ministering to another person and not living the therapy with the full flavor that is available.

Furthermore, it is important for the therapist to work freely, because otherwise he risks dulling his prime instrument —himself. Occasionally, he may need to block out his native function temporarily, almost as a gift to the patient whose own movement could not bear the therapist's reaction. Though the therapist may say he is bored when he is, there are also times when, as a gift, he permits himself to be bored, knowing

---

* Perls, F. S., *Gestalt Therapy Verbatim*. Moab, Utah, Real People Press, 1969.

he will end the boredom if the patient doesn't. However, he can only afford a limited amount of such tithes and should offer them sparingly. The taxes become too high, though, when he risks losing the easy effervescence which he senses when he is functioning best. Like a cat preening himself or a safecracker who sandpapers his fingertips, the therapist has to keep himself honed.

Obviously, this view about the usefulness of the therapist's inner experience contains seeds of trouble. First of all, he risks taking the free flow of his experiences as in itself a *sine qua non* of excellence, which it is not. To say one is bored, for example, even when one is bored is hardly a high quality statement, authentic though it may be. The most puerile engagements can become hallowed when one gratuitously assumes that just because it happened inside him, it is the eternal verity. Spontaneity is no guarantee of excellence, although it is one of its hallmarks. Taste and talent are needed to work out the resolution of flow between patient and therapist which gives recognition to their purposes and continuing interests. Otherwise, theoretical orientation—meant as a guide, not a guarantee—can be traduced into a certification of excellence merely by slavishly adhering to its precepts.

Free expression attains its fullest meaning primarily within the behavior which accepts responsibility for what follows. Whatever we do, there is always a next moment. Evading responsibility in the next moment is a way of depersonalizing. Although it allows a surface freedom, it also puts up a wall through lack of genuine concern between any two people and certainly between patient and therapist. The result is not a free association system, but rather what Perls has referred to as "free dissociation."* This is somewhat like the adult equivalent of what Piaget** describes in childhood where two

---

* Perls, F. S., Four Lectures, in Fagan, J., and Shepherd, I., Eds., *Gestalt Therapy Now.* Palo Alto, California: Science & Behavior Books, 1970.
** Piaget, Jean, *The Language & Thought of the Child.* New York: The World Publishing Co., 1955.

individuals ramble on, each authentic within his own frame of reference, but neither affected by what goes on in the other. As an exercise, free association has generative power. Ultimately though, free associations must help orient one to his need to make free choices. The main difference between free association and free choice is the difference between passive receptacle or active creator. The first person is at the mercy of his free associations, the second has a hand in their creation. The emphasis on free association, which is common among many spontaneity cliques, is often a copout from the natural law which insists that one thing follows another. To make choices freely, even though one must stay with the consequent concatenation of new developments, is the way to discover how one creates his own life.

THERAPY IS TOO GOOD TO BE LIMITED TO THE SICK*

A new question for the psychotherapist to ask is whether a theory can go beyond mere effectiveness in achieving either a so-called cure or even personal growth into its implications for the nature of an evolving society. What, for example, might it be like to live in a gestalt society?**

This question is relatively new to psychotherapy because psychotherapists have until recently remained confined to their offices. Now psychotherapists are moving into the foreground in orienting people to new values and behaviors while religion, the historical mentor, appears to be fading as its principles collide with the more timely ones which form out of the contemporary milieu. Psychotherapists who have been used to thinking of the individual, the dyad, and the small group have recently glimpsed the vast opportunities and the great social need to extend to the community at large those views which have evolved from their work with troubled people.

---

* Some of the material in this section appeared originally in E. Polster's paper, "Stolen by Gypsies," in *Twelve Therapists*, A. Burton, Ed. San Francisco: Jossey-Bass, 1972.
** Note B. F. Skinner's *Walden II* (New York: Macmillan, 1960) as one fantasy relating a theory to a society based on its principles.

We no longer limit ourselves to working with the sick, and the concept of cure has long been an anachronism. The traditional psychotherapist's view of the therapeutic cure was a naive one. Presumably, according to this view, the society had such range within it that anyone who was in sound psychological form could find a rightful place for himself. Only those who resorted to distortion and obsession could fail to fulfill the opportunities of their own directions.

It is apparent now that this was pure pollyanna and that the reality is closer to the graffiti sentiments of young people who write *Horatio Alger eats shit!* We wanted only to "cure" people, until it became clear that "sick" was obviously an inadequate label to pin on most of the people we worked with.

So the term "growth" became current. New people came along, more of them than ever and more who were seeking better forms of living, thinking little of cure and a lot about self-improvement and personal discovery. Excitement became more central than ever as a motivation. The forms of interaction did induce great excitement, leading to experiences of primal familiarity, deep and warm, among people who might otherwise have remained strangers or mere acquaintances.

Given this emphasis on common human needs and on the group as a mini-community based on therapeutic principles, the next sociological step moves not only beyond "cure" but also beyond personal "growth" into the development of a new communal climate. Since no one can escape the psychological pollution of his surroundings until we, in our groups or therapy, germinate the psychologically necessary changes in our communal climate, we live a two-world existence, straddling the atmosphere of the encounter group and the world in which we live our everyday lives, reconciling neither to the other. New ways of communicating, new values, new priorities in changing over institutions such as marriage, schools and government, new vocational requirements, new reward systems—all are parts of a necessary change in the spiritual atmosphere of our society.

At this time in history, the psychotherapist and his kindred workers are feeding their perspectives and wishes into the sociological stream. In an article in *The New York Times* Book Review, Marshall Berman* observes:

> Where our parents and grandparents once turned to novelists, we find ourselves more and more apt to turn toward sociologists, anthropologists, psychologists, for light on the way we live now.
> Thus we might imagine Erik Erikson as our Tolstoy; Oscar Lewis could be our D. H. Lawrence; Margaret Mead might be our George Eliot, our culture's matriarchal sage. Claude Levi-Strauss has given the anthropologist's field trip the spiritual urgency of a Mellvillean or Conradian quest. David Riesman could be our Thackeray—though it once seemed that he might become our Flaubert. R. D. Laing, who in his youth seemed intent on becoming our Dostoevsky, seems now, in his middle age, to have settled into being our Hesse.

Although these views are currently having great impact, they are hardly assured, at this moment in time, of having the most effective voices. The greatest challenge comes, as always, from materialistically oriented people who, sometimes through greed, sometimes through habit, and sometimes through the most fundamental need, believe that a chicken in every pot will give all of us what we need. Materialistic needs, like eating, to name one, *are* so primordial that they do seem to outweigh all other considerations and draw the attention of people and their governments. The psychological facts of life, of course, recede into the background, only a slight homage being paid through the workings of faded religion. It is, therefore, from a position of poor leverage that psychotherapy makes its mark. Perhaps our foray into materialism has already begun through the

---

* Berman, Marshall, *New York Times* Book Review, February 27, 1972.

extensive work of psychologists in industry and the growth of consultations with governments and other social institutions.

In the meantime, through a concern with climate as well as personal growth, a more fully holistic view of man is evolving as not only whole within himself, but inseparable from his community. The loosening up of poisonous taboos is happening all around us. Boys are wearing very long hair, young men and women live in the same dormitories, black people appear on TV commercials as consumers, not servants, peace-niks influence the conduct of a nation at war, nude people are seen on stage and in movies and clothes have become a riotous delight. Psychotherapy has had an important place in all of these creations, having sent out the message for years for people to experience their own actuality rather than swallow the stereotypes and distortions which have previously made deviations from the norm seem like pathology.

Input is continuing at an increased rate nowadays. One can hardly keep up with the new technological prospects that are emerging. Large-group innovations lead the way, adding the concept of *design* to the interactive illuminations which were discovered in the open-ended small groups. The designs have supported leaderless experiences—valuable where need continues to outstrip staffing—and have allowed interchanges between as many as 1,000 people in a room. Large size groups have been used in setting up new designs for interaction in conferences, coffee houses, growth centers, housing projects, industry, universities, welfare agencies, town meetings and other normal groupings of people. Technology now also includes recordings, TV and self-administered programs. Furthermore, a sociological architecture is developing as reflected in new-town movements, in the study of the psychological effects of environments, planned and unplanned,* and in new humanistic design philosophies.

---

* Proshansky, H. M., Ittelson, W. H., and Rivkin, L. G., Eds., *Environmental Psychology*. New York: Holt, Rinehart & Winston, Inc., 1972.

Obviously, these brief words about new channels responsive to the populist message are only a lick and a promise. But they may perhaps be enough in this context, however, to suggest how widespread innovations in humanist technology will inevitably affect the society at large, moving it further into directions which people within the psychotherapy milieu have inspired.

2

The Lively Figure

Once I tried to convince a Behaviorist that when, in speaking of a male bird, he referred to a female as "a stimulus" he ignored the problems and facts of organization.

WOLFGANG KOHLER

Years ago, one of our colleagues playfully began a collection of "laws." Rueful bits of wisdom these were, codified out of homey surprises about man's peculiarities: A bruised shin always knocks twice, a piece of buttered toast will always fall on the side so as to do the most damage, things you like to play with grow on you, and finally, the law that concerns us here, there is more to visual perception than meets the eye.

The simple perceptual experiments of the early gestalt psychologists* opened the way for studies showing how motivation

---

* Kohler, W., *Gestalt Psychology*. New York: New American Library of World Literature Inc., 1959.

affects perception* and still later to the therapeutic insights of Perls,** who synthesized laws of simple perception: first into a system of psychotherapy and further into a humanistic view of man's existence.

BACKGROUND OF EXPERIENCE

The gestalt psychologists investigated the dynamics of the act of perceiving. They theorized that the perceiver was not merely a passive target for the sensory bombardment coming from his environment; rather, he structured and imposed order on his own perceptions. Basically, he organized perceptions of the incoming sensory stream into the primary experience of a *figure* as seen or perceived against a background, or *ground*. The figure might be a melody as distinguished from a harmonic background or it might be a visual pattern emerging as a coherent entity against a grouping of extraneous lines. A figure, whether it is simply perceptual or consists of a higher order of complexity, emerges from the ground in the manner of a bas relief, advancing into a position which compels attention and enhances its qualities of boundedness and clarity. The figure appears richly detailed and it invites scrutiny, concentration and even fascination.

Another important characteristic of perception is the individual's movement toward closure. A figure is seen as a complete, bounded image—in some cases the perceiver even visually compensates for gaps in outline as, for example, in seeing these separate dots as the figure of a circle:

---

* Beardslee, D. and Wertheimer, M., Eds., *Readings in Perception*. Princeton, N.J.: D. Van Nostrand, 1959.
** Perls, F. S., *Ego, Hunger & Aggression*. London: George Allen & Unwin, 1947; Perls, F. S., Hefferline, Ralph and Goodman, Paul, *Gestalt Therapy*. New York: Julian Press Inc., 1951.

More than a perceptual reflex, this surge toward completion of experiential units is also a major *personal* reflex which is frequently thwarted by the social facts of life which interrupt people who are in the process of doing many of the things they want to do. These incomplete actions are forced into the background, where they remain—unfinished and uneasy— usually distracting the individual from the business at hand.

Peggy realized during a therapy session that she never again sat on her father's lap after, at a very early age, her mother screamed at her for sitting there. She accustomed herself to distance, even choosing a husband, as she suddenly realized, who she knew would not want physical closeness. Peggy accomplished this accommodation in many ways, including muscular blockage of her sensations of warmth—a physiological defense—and by believing that one only gets into trouble if one gets close to men—an ideological method. Nevertheless, the surge toward completing that early interrupted act—probably a whole series of them, since sitting on your father's lap only begins a sequence of closeness—is a force about which she must remain vigilant. The gestalt view is that Peggy will feel dissatisfied until she has the opportunity, perhaps several opportunities, to allow that surge to take its course and reach completion. This prospect she is not yet ready to allow. But until she can, it will probably be a central issue in her growth from a child intimidated by the neuroses of her parents. When Peggy can respond to the fascination of getting close to men, her need can become figural and compelling and she can become a grown woman who appreciates her own needs and lives them.

The ground, on the other hand, has no such magnetism. Unbounded and formless, its main function is to provide a context which affords depth for the perception of the figure, giving it perspective but commanding little independent interest. The power of the ground is in its fertility. Ideally, the division of experience into figure and ground is a transitory one, even fleeting at times, and the ground is a source of continually new figural formations. You have only to glance out of your window to experience how freely the flow of your attention can dart from one part of the panorama you see there to another. First, a tree just starting to bud captures your eye and you attend to it. Suddenly, a bird launches itself from a branch and you follow its flight against the sky. A cloud of intriguing shape distracts you from the bird's flight and sets off a train of associations. A milk delivery truck pulls up. You no longer see the bird or the cloud, but instead you hear the grating of the gears, the clank of bottles. You watch the curve of the milkman's shoulders as he trudges up a neighbor's driveway with his wire basket of milk, eggs, cheese. Unimpeded, this is how experience flows. At any moment that which is figural may recede into the background and something in the background may become figure.

However, this innocent flow is only part of the story. In studies which investigated the influence of motivation on perception, it became clear that the perceiver not only structures what he perceives into economical units of experience, he also edits and censors what he sees and hears, selectively harmonizing his perceptions with his inner needs. For example, a hungry individual proved more likely to perceive an ambiguously presented stimulus as food.* Thus does inner experience color and determine current experience. Just as a hungry person perceives food, even when it isn't there, so does another unsatisfied person continue to work out, in his current activities, unfinished business from his past. What we are calling either figure or ground is grander than the simple perceptual activities which the early gestalt psychologists were talking about. Extrapolating from these basic perceptual activities, it becomes apparent that all human concerns reflect organizational require-

* McClelland, D. C. and Atkinson, J. W., The projective expression of needs: I. The effect of different intensities of the hunger drive on perception. *Jour. Psych.* 25:205-222; 1948.

ments which are holistic in nature. One's whole life is, in a sense, background for the present moment—even though many of the specific events in this background may disappear like a single bubble in boiling water.

Three elements compose the background in an individual's life. They are:

1. *Prior living*—Characteristics of kindness, knowledge-ability, ambition, and so on, are qualities which give orientation in living and which influence the experiences which emerge into the foreground of the present. Being characterized essentially means just this: that the acts or thoughts which fit or blend with this characteristic will emerge into figural prominence more readily than others which are less compatible with such a background.

If one's background contains kindness, it will be easier for a soft word or an expression of sympathy to emerge as figure than if the background is colored by sadism. If, for example, a person cannot abide his own homosexuality, all behaviors which require homosexuality for a ground will be either neutralized or confusing or anxiety-inducing. Whatever fulfill-ment might accrue will be diminished by the separation be-tween his act and the background of his "nature" which could give it dimension and context. Thus, if the word or concept, homosexuality, is a "taboo" term, the experience of some be-haviors which might be subsumed within it—such as tender-ness in a male, toughness in a female, etc.—are also less likely to surface. A sexual moralist will have a harder time permitting sexual thoughts or feelings to emerge. When they do, trouble begins, ranging from mild discomfort to panic.

The job of psychotherapy is to alter the individual's sense of his background so that such new experiences may be har-monious with his nature, *now*. He must discover that the ex-periences are not what he thought they inevitably were, that they are indeed welcome and, through these experiences in changing, his background alters and consonance is possible in his life. When a figure pops up from deep in the background where it previously received little or no recognition, the whoosh of excitement is great. This may be either exhilarating for the adventurous, or it may create anxiety and shock for those whose backgrounds are obscured from their own ken or the view of others. The covering-up of parts of the background represents a careful effort on the part of the individual *not* to tap into these deactivated funds of characteristics or experiences. The background, then, is not freely available as a source of new figures.

Figure/ground reversibility is at the root of fluidity in life. Ideally, there would be no experience from the ground of existence which, under the right circumstances, could not become figural. During therapy, one can come into touch with all the varieties of one's madness, ranging from paranoia to psychopathy. One can, in addition to knowing one's kindness, also come to know one's cruelty. One can reach into the reservoir of experience for gullibility, vindictiveness, competitiveness, perversion, nausea, caginess, passivity, stubbornness and all those other characteristics which may enter into deep union between figure and ground. The clarity and effervescence of one's life are profoundly affected by how richly *figural* material from the background may become, because it is only in *full* figure, ardently perceived against accepted background, that ease and vitality may exist together. Excitement that cannot be tolerated is transformed and experienced as anxiety. Where background contains shadowy pockets, it cannot provide the basis for the effervescence in experience that makes excitement possible. People whose figural flow is compulsive or whose figures are perceived unsupported by background lose the quality of depth which is sensed in those whose figural development seems to spring up naturally and gracefully from a rich experiential background.

The same is true for what may be called the repertoire of personal experiences related to the present moment, like a background of swimming in a person who, wanting physical activity, goes swimming. The conditions for figure/ground interrelationship here are similar to those which influence the individual's personal characteristics. When a person has swum, traveled, run a lathe, planted flowers, ridden a motorcycle, made wine, painted a picture, parachuted, he has increased the fund from which he may draw for new figural developments. In other words, as the background of his experience becomes more diversified, it also becomes potentially more harmonious with a whole range of happenings. The resulting diversity is more likely to ensure relevant background for anything that might be happening in the present.

This is a rule of trumb implicitly subscribed to by parents who, risking dilettantism, see to it that their children have dancing lessons, music lessons, travel experiences, visit museums, learn about flowers. The wisdom of expanding the range of one's background because it makes one more susceptible and responsive to experience has been beautifully described by poets. Keats, for example, has written the following poem which shows the luminous excitement and meaning aroused in him when he read Chapman's words against the background of his own experience:

> Much have I travell'd in the realms of gold
> And many goodly states and kingdoms seen;
> Round many eastern islands have I been
> Which bards in fealty to Apollo hold.
> Oft of one wide expanse had I been told
> That deep-browed Homer ruled as his demesne:
> Yet did I never breathe its pure serene
> Till I heard Chapman speak out loud and bold:
> —Then felt I like some watcher of the skies
> When a new planet swims into his ken;
> Or like stout Cortez, when with eagle eyes
> He stared at the Pacific—and all his men
> Look'd at each other with a wild surmise—
> Silent, upon a peak in Darien.

Or even more simply, stating relationship of figure to ground, Aitken writes:

> Music I heard with you is more than music,
> And bread I broke with you is more than bread.

Though the relationship of figure to ground is inevitable and basic, there is no guarantee that this relationship will be a vibrant one unless the movement between one and the other is facilitated by the accessibility of the whole repertoire of characteristics and experiences of the individual.

Also in one's personal background is a general orientation in life, such as provided by certain philosophies, religions, particular creeds or one's own view of what life is about and how it may best be lived.

For example, Helen, who had been reared by a perfectionistic mother who had emphasized moralistic precepts to the exclusion of human considerations, was having great trouble resolving her own ambivalence about how to be a good mother. She wanted to be free and unjudgmental with her children, but still felt that she had to maintain unrealistically high standards for herself about how her home should look and how much work she should do during the day. This left Helen frazzled and irritable with her children and guilty about her shortcomings. The rub between allowing herself and her family to live freely and keeping her home neat was chronic and abrasive. How to decide which to give higher priority? One day in a therapy session, I suggested to Helen that she might resolve such conflicts by putting "people values" above "property values." Her face lit up, and she recognized immediately that, when the struggle was viewed in these terms, she had no problem about deserting her mother's standards—which Helen deplored but had acknowledged as correct—and following her own evolving standards, which she sensed were right for her. Against this context, Helen's own warmth and loving could emerge much more effortlessly as figural.

2. *Unfinished business*—There is an apocryphal story, variously attributed to Bach, Handel or Haydn, wherein the aged maestro prepares for bed and hears a friend playing the clavichord downstairs. The friend plays beautifully and the music builds but ends abruptly, on a *dominant* chord! Now, in those days dominant chords were inexorably resolved by leading into the tonic and final chord. The maestro, restless, tossed and turned in his bed but could not fall asleep until he tramped downstairs and banged his resolution into the clavichord. All experience hangs around until a person is finished with it. Most individuals have a large capacity for unfinished situations—fortunately, because in the course of living one is fated to be left with plenty of them. Nevertheless, although one can tolerate considerable unfinished experience, these incompleted directions *do seek* completion and, when they get powerful enough, the individual is beset with preoccupation, compulsive behavior, wariness, oppressive energy and much self-defeating activity. If you don't tell your boss off at work but would really like to, and then come home and give it to your children, chances are that this won't work because it is only a feeble or partial attempt to finish off something which still hangs around as unfinished anyway. Similarly, the nymphomaniac who screws over and over again, presumably trying to develop sensations which may lead to release and completion, and the person who tells the same fact over and over again because he never feels that he has been heard or that he has said it just right, are both living out their unfinished business. Furthermore, uncountable conferences and conversations have been sunk because there was a hidden, incompleted agenda which interfered with fresh interactions.

So also with the familiar varieties of unfinished business which the psychotherapist has historically observed. I never told my father how I felt, I was humiliated when I wanted attention, I wanted to be an artist and they made me become a doctor, are proverbial complaints. Until closure is brought about, if these unfinished circumstances are powerful enough, the individual, no matter how successful he is in deflected directions, can never be satisfied. Closure must come either through a return to the old business or by relating to parallel circumstances in the present. Thus, the person who has never been able to sit on her father's lap may find closure through doing it with someone else, where it becomes possible to experience comforts and delights which would have been the natural completion in the earlier situation or perhaps through fantasying doing it again. Once closure has been reached and can be fully experienced in the present, the preoccupation with the old incompletion is resolved and one can move on to current possibilities.

Whenever unfinished business forms the center of one's existence, one's effervescence of mind becomes hampered. Ideally, the unencumbered person is free to engage spontaneously with whatever interests him and to stay with it until this lively interest subsides and something else draws his attention. This is a natural process and a person who lives according to this rhythm experiences himself as flexible, clear and effective.

There are two polar hindrances which may interfere with this process. The first is the obsession or compulsion which constitutes a rigid need to complete the old unfinished business and which leads to rigidity of figure/ground formation. The opposite interference is the labile mind, which leaves little opportunity for the person to experience what is happening because the focus is so fleeting as to prevent closure from developing and being experienced.

In the first instance the individual may be obsessed, let us say, with sex or success or stamp collecting. Much of the data of his life becomes immediately related to these obsessions, thereby reducing the effervescent richness which naturally occurs when life is experienced as variable as it is. He keeps his own unfinished business the center of gravity toward which attention is indiscriminately drawn with almost magnetic attraction. The person focused on sex wonders whether the woman at a party asking him to bring her a drink wants to go to bed with him. The success-oriented person wonders how he can strategize to get professional support from a powerful figure who smiles at him. The obsessed stamp collector gets a warm letter from an old friend living in Zambia and is thrilled only by the prospect of having a new stamp. These figural rigidities prevent discriminate excitement from developing and therefore restrict the range of openness in one's life. While these interests are not necessarily pathological, and may sometimes even be the source of considerable personal satisfaction, these people are all too frequently vulnerable to sterility in their lives—and they are often terrible bores.

At the other end of the spectrum are the labile people who do not permit a stable relationship between one moment and the next. There is little opportunity within them, therefore, for any figural development to achieve either completion or meaning, since each direction is quickly abandoned. It is as though they were free-associating through life, which is akin to being the victim rather than the creator of one's flow of actions and thoughts. One then becomes a soul wanderer, never finding peace or rest. At the pathological level, of course, this is a manic psychosis. At the more common level, one sees people who receive only little fulfillment even though they appear to be engaged in worthwhile activities. One may even be surprised that something is wrong with such people, who appear flexible, inventive, and even joyful. But they cannot light long enough to feel a sense of completion, so they get purgatorially pinned right in the middle of everything. They are left without the boundaries which exist when one has a sense of beginning and end; they are stuck, without the consequent sense of identity which develops through completing the small sequences of one's life.

It might seem as though one would inevitably *know* when a sequence of events represents a completed unit. Actually, this is not the way completion works; it takes considerable artistry in life to know when something is finished. We are not talking here about the stereotypes of completion which affect all of us, like the end of a day's work, or the end of vacation, or graduating from school, or a divorce or the end of a book. According to such norms of completion, once having started one should, for example, finish college or finish moving the lawn. However, when the individual's unique sense of completion is paramount, he may rightfully leave the lawn mower in the middle of the lawn and go off to bet on the races. Whether this action qualifies as completion depends on his own good focus and his artistry in knowing when his life feels right to him. On the other hand, a capricious sense of completion may be nothing more than a copout on an essentially fitting task, whether it be to finish college or to finish mowing the fucking lawn. No formula can do the job in life anymore than it can tell a painter or novelist when his painting or novel is done. In fact, nowadays completion in the arts is quite different from what it has been in the past. Many who are governed by the familiar expectations for closure wind up confused and disappointed by the inconclusive endings they encounter in novels, music, paintings. The artists have different units in mind, and when one is oriented to the old units, he may well feel as though he has been left hanging.

3. *The flow of present experience*—Where purposes, interactions and topical developments are complex, they create great difficulties in coordinating one's own flow of figure/ground relationships with those that are going on continuously outside oneself. Suppose you are a participant in a staff conference and a colleague is reporting on the activities of his committee. You have a lot of associations and thoughts concerning what he is talking about and perhaps some suggestions and exploratory ideas. What do you do about your own flow of mind while he continues with his report? Usually, if you have learned your lessons well, you keep your mouth shut until he is done,

hoping you can still remember your brilliant reactions then, or hoping that it will still fit the mood you had or others had, or hoping that it will still be relevant in the face of the later ideas which developed. The same process, though admittedly less complex, goes on even in one-to-one conversations where, although it is easier to interrupt, you are taking the chance of disrupting the train of thought of the person you are talking to.

The process of interruption is especially difficult to deal with when communications have a specified purpose and differ from the wanderings which are more acceptable in simple conversations where contact and talking are more important than purpose. When purpose intervenes, meandering conversation becomes less tolerable. A conference on how to improve the water supply will not allow much tolerance for nostalgic tales about how someone's aunt liked the water that came out of deep wells in the country—though it is quite likely that, ultimately, the meandering style could show a relationship between the thirsty aunt's habits and tastes and possible solutions to current water problems. The concept of brainstorming takes meandering into account, but it is primarily used as an exploratory catalyst for ideas rather than a common style of communication. Virtually all of our purposive communications require a sense of timing, holding back commentary until the right moment arrives.

Perhaps we can never amend the requirement for timeliness in our thinking and talking, although surely we could do better than some of the present authoritarian structures permit. Wait your turn and stick to the subject are guidelines so rigidly insisted on now that they impoverish the mind. Fertility as a natural process springs from generosity of mind, not parsimony. And generosity of mind includes an acceptance of the ground of experience from which figural development can emerge. If we are to loosen up the current system of intercommunication and return to a more native process than is presently acceptable, there are two contingencies we have to take into account.

One is that the time required for good communication must be extended drastically—not an easy requirement in the time-bound culture we all know. In a culture where time, every moment of it, is at a premium, we wind up speaking in symbols and formulae which condense large hunks of experience, as when we refer to the "domino theory" of the U.S. involvement in Asia. Or, we wind up saying only what is already completed and worked through in our minds, issuing position statements on how to expand birth control or what the democratic party is likely to do about welfare policy in this country. This system of taking policy positions is tempting even in the elemental levels of communication: whether watching TV is good for people, or whether to go walking instead, or whether to read aloud to each other of an evening. Now, obviously, this has healthy aspects—it is useful to have some sense of clarity about beliefs and tastes, and people would surely become paralyzed if they approached all of life with a completely open and unformed mind. Policy positions communicate fast even though considerable discussion has gone into their formulation. That's why board meetings can be stultifying, as they repeatedly are. Committees thrash out topics and report summary conclusions and recommendations to which the board is to respond yea or nay without much communication among them. Each board member might have as much to contribute as the original committee members did but, of course, if they fed in their individual ideas, it would require a new work-through process which would gobble up even more time.

The second element is that we are phobic about chaos. The movement from chaos to clarity is inherent in creativity. Chaos is frightening, though, because there is no assurance that completion of any theme will follow. The prospect of anything which requires completion remaining incomplete is natively frustrating and painful. Furthermore, in the absence of controls, there is no telling what threatening words or acts might occur during the chaotic phase. This is also a serious source of threat to those people who are engaged. Chaos is disruptive of any system which is already set. It reaches beyond current moral standards, beyond the familiar means of coping and invites new solutions, new configurations and new viewpoints. When people are struggling to get out of their old bags, chaos can sometimes provide the opening, even though it is scary. We have occasionally experimented with chaos in groups by asking members of the group to be altogether ungoverned by any considerations other than what each individual wants to say or do, even though there would be a period of chaos. This suggestion is usually resisted like the plague. When it has been accepted and tried, it has almost invariably resulted in one topic eventually becoming so central to the whole group that they all become fascinated with it and can then participate freely without a sense of holding back at all. When a person becomes raptly attentive, chaos leaves and unity begins.

In psychotherapy, individual or group, the tolerance for chaos can be greater than in any other institutional form of communication, except perhaps in art forms. Through the reintroduction of chaos it is possible to restore to the individual a more free relationship between figure and ground than a blocked and programmed person may allow himself. Cary* knows how this process goes:

> . . . the concept is always the enemy of the institution. It is said that when you give a child the name of a bird, it loses the bird. It never *sees* the bird again but only a sparrow, a thrush, a swan, and there is a good deal of truth in this. We all know people for whom all nature and art consists of concepts, whose life, therefore, is entirely bound up with objects known only under labels and never seen in their own quality.

---

* Cary, Joyce, *Art & Reality*. New York: Doubleday and Co., Inc., 1961.

In addition to the restrictions imposed by time and chaos, there is also the valid lack of synchronicity between the needs of one person and another at any given moment. So what is needed is the development of skill in managing these temporary but inevitable incompatibilities—through a process we call *bracketing-off*. In bracketing-off, the individual holds some of his own concerns in abeyance in favor of attending to what is going on in a communicative process. This is a risky technique because it borders on suppressing oneself. There is a difference, however. The distinction is that in bracketing off, one is establishing priorities as to what is most important at that time and not allowing interfering concerns to immobilize him. He does not wipe out the concerns which seem irrelevant to his temporary engagement, but will return to them later on. For example, if he is in conversation with a colleague with whom he has only tangential personal relationships and if he has come there to discuss a new program they are both trying to work out, he may choose not to talk to him about a violent fight he just had with his wife. He holds his feelings about the fight separate because he would find it aesthetically troublesome to pour his heart out to this particular man and also because he knows he wants to work out the details of the new program. He holds these feelings out then—not because he is ashamed or because he does not feel his problems are worthy of attention or for any of the wide range of justifications the self-suppressed person may provide himself. Squashing himself is not in his mind; he is confident that at the right moment he will deal with the issue that he is troubled about. But he can wait, just as the person who feels a pang of hunger in the middle of an absorbing drama in the theater knows that he has the tolerance within himself to bear the hunger and still remain interested in the play. To behave otherwise is to become victimized by irrelevancies and to lose all sense of personal choice in life. Human beings have range—their ability to set something aside for later attention is quite remarkable.

One night I was scheduled to demonstrate publicly, using my own flow of awareness, how in gestalt therapy we may describe the here-and-now experience. Unfortunately, on that very afternoon I had received some shocking news, news which I did not want to bring forth at a public demonstration. Although there was no need to hide the content of the news, to speak of it to a large group of people I didn't know was aesthetically intolerable to me. I was very anxious about the dilemma; it was clear to me that I must bracket-off my concerns, but then I wasn't sure if I could remain authentically in tune with my actual experience in the here-and-now. As it turned out, when I got up before the audience, my previous concern disappeared and I went on without the slightest need to block anything out. By setting up my own priorities, I was able to stay with my original intention, freely describing my awarenesses at that moment. There is no sure formula, but it is clear that in many situations the bracketing-off process is fundamental to a sense of choice and purpose and, furthermore, that without it mere honesty becomes a puerile imitation of innocence.

The problems brought on by competing experiences in figural developments resemble those in the bracketing-off process. Ideally, such competition is easily resolved so that what emerges as figural would be in harmony with one's own background and with the need to communicate it to another person.

Kierkegaard, in *Purity of Heart Is to Will One Thing*, describes complete absorption in God as the deepest unity in life. All ambivalence would disappear and competing interests would be reconciled. For most of us, this singleminded purity is hard to achieve, since what emerges in our minds has variable force and variable primacy. Some thoughts, wishes and images are like a blip on the horizon and to give them expression is a paltry and indiscriminate yielding to the flow of the moment. Minds are not so tightly organized that any occurrence within them is equal to any other. Each person must develop within himself a sense of which events have the force to come into expression and which are only mild appearances not ready for birth. Foetuses are not brought into babyhood by arbitrary fiat; they must grow into it. So also with any human experience including thoughts or wishes—they may either become stray wisps in one's effervescent system or they may move into the centrality which calls for expression.

ACCESSIBILITY OF GROUND*

It is evident that in postulating figure/ground formation as the basic dynamic of awareness, we are addressing ourselves to the familiar issues of how accessible our experiences are to us and what composes the context for the events in our lives. If there is *any* psychological principle which many theorists share, it is that there are dynamically powerful forces within the individual which may be inaccessible to his awareness but which, nevertheless, influence his behavior. The most prominent of these, of course, is the psychoanalytic view of the unconscious, to which figure/ground formation is the gestalt counterpart. The concept of the unconscious contributed much to twentieth century man's knowledge of his own nature by dramatizing the power of that which was not available to his awareness. Since it is a good wind that blows no ill, it is not surprising to find that, in spite of its eminent position as an orienting principle, certain drawbacks have become apparent.

First, this view of man creates a conscious-unconscious split, dichotomizing him and ignoring the holistic view of his nature. The free flow between the accessible and the inaccessible, although paid some slight notice in the concept of the pre-conscious, went largely unrecognized and unused. The unconscious became the core concern in determining a psy-

---

* Some of the material in this section appeared previously in a paper by E. Polster, *Trends in Gestalt Therapy*, distributed by The Gestalt Institute of Cleveland, 1967.

chotherapeutic methodology whose search for unconscious meaning created such great leaps from one psychic reservoir to another that these mental gymnastics overshadowed any trust in consciousness. People become deflected from immediacy, once removed from overt experience, so that they might discover what was *really* going on.

The figure/ground concept, on the other hand, supports the individual's surface experience as a source of great therapeutic leverage, as we shall show throughout the course of this book. Life *is* as plain as the nose on your face when you are willing to stay with that which is presently clear, moving from one moment of actual experience to the next, discovering something new in each, something which moves forward, developing the theme of its own movement and culminating in illuminations which were inaccessible in the beginning. Thus, the *sequence* of actualities tells the tale rather than a clever diagnostician. Interpretations and symbolic equations are bold attempts at divination, exciting drama for the divine knowers. This is a special game, ingeniously played, offering challenge and self-confirmation for excellence in psychological marksmanship. For the person observed it may offer illumination and sharp surprise. Aha! When the interpretation reaches its mark, it will tie together one's consciousness with the new data from the unconscious and one will experience the unity which makes him whole again. The risk is that one learns to mistrust the foreground and to depend on an external authority to explain reality. To interpret the nature of a person's unconscious neutralizes his own developmental process. This process is more firmly established when it is based instead on his own awareness from moment to moment, each new awareness riding on the momentum of previous experience.

Here is an example of how the sequence of figural formations may unfold in a therapeutic session, working without interpretation of the unconscious process. Cleo was a 35-year-old woman, long divorced, classically unsatisfied in spite of successes in her work and easy sociability. She chronically maintained her aloofness, fixing into the background those feelings without which she was left in a vague state of longing and incompleteness. One day Cleo became aware of her fear that if she got close to people she might fall in love. For her, this position would be unbearable if she weren't loved in return and Cleo feared she would wind up in purgatorial need of the other person. The experience of her fear was a new figure for her, one she had not previously allowed to emerge. As she spoke I asked her to describe how she felt. She said there was a twinge of sensation which she could not describe and which she also felt afraid of, only this time the fear was palpable and specific—another new figure. As she focused her concentration on this sensation at my suggestion, Cleo began to feel that if she really yielded to it, the feeling would get so strong that she would *have* to do something, a sense of inexorability which Cleo was not accustomed to allowing—another new figure. I asked her to close her eyes and allow a fantasy to come to her. She fantasied the scene in my office—another figural step. Then I asked her to visualize what she would like to do there. She saw herself coming into my arms and then she saw herself crying. The color rushed to her face and, although she didn't actually carry out her fantasy, she felt great warmth inside herself and none of the fear which she would have imagined would accompany such full sensation. She said she felt whole and surprisingly independent, not at all vulnerable to unrequited experience. A new configuration had been formed. She could talk seriously and warmly with me from the support of her inner sensation and, from this point on, her relationships outside of therapy began to take on greater and greater warmth and Cleo's security with people was dramatically increased.

This illustration shows how the non-interpretive movement from figure to figure may happen in a therapy experience. In it, the patient is going her own route, having her own choices to make at each stage of the game. Her present experience became pivotal in the resolution of her unfinished business about permitting deep sensations.

The process of moving from moment to moment reflects the existential view that whatever exists, exists only now. Flux is basic to experience, so if one can allow each experience the reality it seeks, it will fade into the background in its turn, to be replaced by whatever next has the force to appear in the foreground. Only psychological hanging on can maintain the semblance of sameness in life. For example, once Cleo was able to experience and give up her belief that warmth and closeness would make her stay purgatorially in love, the flow of her awarenesses was restored. Each figural moment contributes only its share in the whole experiential process, much as a single film clip contributes one fleeting image to the uninterrupted flow of a moving picture. If the film is stopped, even though the figure is sharply in focus, the quality of liveliness disappears and we are left with a stagnant version of what might have been a vital process. The restoration of this movement through time is a pervasive theme of our therapy. Where this movement has gaps or when it is interrupted, life becomes awkward, disconnected or meaningless because one has lost the support of the constantly rejuvenating cycle of development and fruition which is native to the ongoing life process.

The gestalt perspective puts a premium on novelty and change, not a pushy premium, but a faith-filled expectation that the existence and recognition of novelty are inevitable if we stay with our own experiences as they actually form. Beisser* has described this as a paradoxical theory of change because of the fact that change rests on the full, albeit temporary, acceptance of the status quo. Paradoxical games are

---

* Beisser, A., *The Paradoxical Theory of Change* in Fagan, J. and Shepherd, I., Eds., *Gestalt Therapy Now*. Palo Alto, California: Science & Behavior Books, 1970.

not easy to play since they require profoundly artful discriminations. In accepting the status quo, that is, staying with experience as it unfolds in its own way, the individual runs the
danger of hanging on to the status quo. This is the poison
inhaled by those who don't sense when to let go and let the
native process of change take over. If the letting-go process
is forced, we abort the continuity which each moment naturally
has with its next moment; if the letting-go process is delayed,
we are interrupting this continuity.

It is important to learn the difference between staying with
an experience until it is completed and hanging on, trying to
get something more—anything more—from a situation which
is either finished or barren. The basic clues are whether attention to the issue is a loose, unfixed, mobile attentiveness or
whether it is an attentiveness which feels glued to its object.
The people with the bug-eyed stare, the clinging grasp, the
insistent preoccupations, the sense of desperation, the ready-
made sermons, the unwillingness to leave when conversations
are finished, the quoting of authorities, etc. are all hanging on.
When an individual remains in any situation which is causing
him great trouble and doesn't promise to improve, he is hanging on. Twenty years on the job and no rewards, ten years of
marriage with someone he doesn't even like to be with or
clearly can't make it with, maintaining a desired self-image
in the face of all kinds of indications to the contrary, are all
further signs of hanging on. For all of these circumstances, as
well as innumerable other instances, when the immediate situation is persistently out of harmony with the context for the
individual's needs, he is hanging on.

Ken, who had been beguiled by the status and security he
felt were represented in academic life, was miserable with the
actuality of his role as college professor. He felt oppressed
by the need to publish, the endless committee meetings mad-
dened him, and there were countless other ways he would have
preferred to spend his life. Ken was an excellent businessman

and dreamed of running a resort community. He even had some innovative ideas about how he might do this and still maintain some professional connections through lecturing and consulting. But he hung on doggedly to his college appointment, ignoring his current needs, and clinging to his image of the secure academician whom everyone looked up to and respected. When disharmony persists and no efforts are made to change the circumstances, someone is hanging on.

Open attentiveness to alternatives and the individual's sense of his having a choice among these possibilities are hallmarks of staying with it. Obviously, staying with it when the experience is a pleasant one is an easy choice to make. But staying with it even though this may involve considerable unhappiness and pain still retains the flavor of a decision made through choice rather than through self-coercion. Thus, a painter working through difficult contradictions in his painting may laboriously search for solutions through painstaking sculptures, as Matisse once did. A student hating graduate school but knowing that he wants the training for support in his future work is staying with it if he experiences his decision as valid in the context of his life's needs. A man who is married to an invalid wife but who chooses to stay with her and remains fresh and loving in the process is staying with it even though the pain may be extensive.

Though all these examples have some aspects in common, it is clear that in each instance the individual's personal judgment and the deep absorption with which he continues his engagement are crucial. There are no hard and fast rules to govern the distinction between hanging on and staying with it. It is the unique responsiveness to each event which determines the quality of a person's life. What is hanging on for one person is staying with it for another. The job is to stay in touch with one's self and one's needs.

3

Resistance and Beyond

"... You are an exceptional amalgam of vehement forces. ... We do not speak in blame terms. So many factors are mediating. Fomenting. Promulgating. Everyone is different. A billion small things unperceived by the object of their influence. ... Negative and positive elements strive, and we can only look at them and wonder or weep. You may sometimes see a clear case of angel and vulture in collision."

SAUL BELLOW

The concept of resistance has far-reaching implications for the therapist who wants to go beyond the endemic "shoulds" of our culture. Traditionally, resistance implies that a person has specific goals which can be identified, like visiting a friend, doing homework or writing a song. Any intrapersonal interference to moving in these directions is called resistance, a stubborn barrier, alien to the person's natural behavior. The barrier must be removed, according to this view, so that the

51

"right" goal may be reached. Thus the resisting force is seen as the saboteur among the varied forces which exist within the individual and, in fact, as an agent not of the self but rather of the anti-self. This is reminiscent of the medieval superstition of possession by demons or malignant spirits.

The resistance merits equal billing. What usually passes for resistance is not just a dumb barrier to be removed but a creative force for managing a difficult world. A child learns to prohibit his own crying when it brings on unwelcome reactions from his parents. Since his arena of action is restricted to the environment he can navigate, he takes conditions as he finds them and does the best with what he has. Later on, he becomes less limited, ranging farther from home, developing a new sense of freedom and power. Now if he retains the childhood image of the awesome consequences of tears, he is hooked indeed to the past and it will take some new force to unhook him.

Instead of seeking to remove the resistance, it is better to focus on it assuming that, at best, a person grows through resisting and, at worst, the resistance is nevertheless a part of his identity. Labelling the original behavior merely resistant is misleading. To remove the resistance in order to return to the pre-resistant purity is a futile dream because the person who has resisted is a new person and there is no way to return. Every step in the development of resistance becomes part of a new formation of the individual's nature. He does not become the old person plus a resistance which can be removed as soon as he gets brave enough to remove it. He is a new person altogether.

We can see, for example, that the person who resisted crying because of the pain which it brought on when his parents spanked him, left him, surrounded him, or hollered at him, has done a great deal more than just to block his crying. He has exercised his perceptions of his parents, thereby extending his sensitivity; he has discovered what life can be like when crying is an unacceptable alternative; he may have become toughened and durable; he may have developed tenderness about the needs of others; he may have expanded his powers to assimilate sensation without having to release it, etc. Naturally, he may also have developed a cold nature so as not to be tempted to cry or he may have developed a chronic whine or a thousand other unpleasant characteristics.

In any case, though, the only course open to the therapist is to take the person as he is, accentuating what exists so that it becomes an energized part of his character rather than a depersonalized dead weight. Suppose, for example, John says he cannot talk to Mary, a woman in his group, because there is a wall between them. This is his form of "resistance" to talking to Mary. John needs to *experience* this wall, not to remove it; to be the wall or to talk to the wall or to describe the wall—anything that will lead John to be rid of the stagnant stereotypes of wall and to discover its living reality. Here is an idealized dialogue showing the basic process, purer than actuality perhaps, but validly illuminating.

John is asked to play the wall, and says:

"I am here to protect you against predatory women who will eat you alive if you open yourself up to them."

John says in response to the wall:

"Aren't you exaggerating? She looks pretty safe to me. In fact, she looks more scared than anything."

W: Sure she's scared. I'm responsible for that. I'm a very severe wall and I make a lot of people scared. That's how I want it and I have even affected you that way, too. You're scared of me even though I'm really on your side.

J: I *am* scared of you and I even feel you inside me, like I have become like you. I feel my chest as though it were iron and I'm really getting mad about that.

W: Mad—at what? I'm your strength and you don't even know it. Feel how strong you are inside.

J: Sure, I feel the strength but I also feel rigid when my chest feels like iron. I'd like to beat on you, knock you over and go over to Mary.

Therapist: Beat on your iron.

J: (Beats his chest and shouts) Get out of my way—get *out* of my *way!*

(Silence)

My chest feels strong—but not like it's made out of iron.

(Another silence . . . John's mouth and chin begin to tremble. For a moment he fights the upsurge of feeling, then yields to sobbing. He looks up, and then says to Mary)

I don't feel any wall between us anymore and I really do want to talk to you.

This illustration shows the strengths inherent in the wall as well as its interfering quality. When the wall becomes assimilated within the individual—when John can accept how *he* is "wall"—it becomes a part of his purposiveness, contributing its strength, and adding to his life rather than subtracting. The characteristics which re-entered John's awareness extend his sense of valid identity and recharge him. His behavior reclaims the juice from the static vitality which had been bound up in the stalemate.

In many therapeutic events the same factors are present but with complications added. For one thing resistances are of manifold nature. While the wall, in the foregoing illustration, was a solid and unambiguous representation of resistance, resistance can take many forms: verbal, metaphorical, or behavioral—either simultaneously or sequentially. So staying with resistance requires an artful choice where the therapist's own selectivity becomes a transcendant force, moving beyond an exclusive focus on the simple identified resistance.

For example, in one workshop, there was a huge bear of a man who looked the modern equivalent of Falstaff, a gigantic frame, a large belly, a ruddy face, and a hearty manner. In spite of his huge bulk and a physical power so grand that he dominated the visual quality of the workshop scene, Hal was silent most of the time. When he did speak, he spoke with darting glances, a great self-protective hunching of his shoulders, and addressing no one in particular. A look of fear was in his face and a sense of vagueness and nondirection in his demeanor. Hal looked as though he feared an attack at any moment. When asked about his silence, he said that he had great difficulty in dealing with bossy women, especially when they are in the role of authority. He said he would not turn his back on one, that he wouldn't trust one to be behind him. Thus, Hal expressed his resistance in his silence, his distrust, and his hunched shoulders. I let him use his hunched shoulders, his silence and his distrust. First, I got up and walked behind Hal and asked him what it was like for him now that I *was* behind his back. He was sitting on the floor. When he turned around to confront me, he put his hands down, as though crouching. So, the resistance moved into a crouch. I walked around again, searching for a way we could use his silent, distrustful crouch. This time I climbed on top of his back, crouching on top of him, and I asked Hal what he could do with me. He was free for a whole range of reactions, including flicking me off like a cigarette ash. If I had sensed that was the direction in which his energized resistance would go, I would not have gotten up on him. But he said, "Well, I could ride you around the room." He had chosen his own medicine. Riding me around the room put *him* in control. Even though it looked like the woman was on top, Hal had flipped the sense of dominance over to himself. He also proceeded to turn a threatening situation into a playful one, using his strength, developing great delight and a sense of union within himself, with me, and with the group, which had become aroused by seeing him ignited. The roars and the fun confirmed his power. For me it was like a jolly ride on an elephant. Hal was the mover, determining much of the speed, direction and playfulness. By the time we got back to our original places and I got off his back, he was able to laugh and say in new freshness that he no longer felt cautious with me and expected he would be heard from during the rest of the workshop, which indeed he was, becoming a central figure in the group. Thus through accentuating and mobilizing his resistance, Hal unharnessed its power, making it unique and timely to our interaction instead of staying stuck in his anachronistic expectations. Instead of being dominated by a woman, *he* could dominate; instead of threatening combat, we developed playful union; instead of maintaining a stalemate of inaction, filling it with suspicion and projection, he entered an actual contest which had its own rich detail and unpredictable outcome.

Hal transformed aggressive energy, potentially disruptive, into socially acceptable behavior. According to the concept of sublimation, this man played *instead* of controlling or hurting. When resistance is viewed as creative, however, we would assert that *no substitution* took place. Among the infinity of directions he could move in, he made a choice. The resulting acts were the culmination of a combination of forces, each one valid in its own right and including aggression, playfulness, suspicion, trust, affection, anger, etc. To infer sublimation requires a judgment between what is *really* true and what actually happened, a distinction which we are unwilling to make. Whatever combination of suspicion and hostility may have previously interfered with playfulness or trust was no *more* basic than the present behavior which included playfulness and trust. To view original motivations as more generic to current behavior than present experience is to downgrade much of the surface of behavior. This view risks reducing manifest events into mere tickets to the true event, an entry into the real but latent mysteries of life.

On this dimension, where the reality of manifest life is returned to respectability, gestalt therapy has made a major contribution. By keeping the focus empirical rather than abstract, we attend to each experience on its own merits without needing a classification of what a person is really like. We are delineating a new view of man, not a view of man against himself but rather a view of him as a composition, where each of the components is vitally *for* itself. This view is without prejudice about the real nature of man as a class—or even the real nature of any particular man. There is no real nature of man *as distinct from* the totality of his experience. His so-called resistance is no less a part of him than the impulse he may be resisting. So we can move from one experience to the next without enshrining any particular aspect of an individual. His story will unfold through following its own directedness.

COMPOSITION

Viewing man as a *composition* of characteristics rather than merely a resister leads to a picture of man in trouble when he is divided *within* himself rather than *against himself*. The war within, frequently either stale or stalemated, is a war for existence waged by each aspect of the person, each with its own energy, its own supports, and its own opponents. Each new synthesis among the population of differences which is the individual is a fresh alliance, momentarily reflecting the current force of each component. For example, Hal's unwillingness to act was a union of his basic distrust of women generally, his perceptions of a female leader in particular, his imprisoned muscularity and his avoidance of playfulness. Allowing his muscularity its own direction, experiencing the leader-woman in new perspective and using his own playfulness were among the specific changes that realigned his behavior. When old ingredients are developed and new ingredients—such as climbing on his back—added, the composition alters just as it would in a painting or a chemical process. It is this process of developing old, defeated directions and moving into new ones that is the heart of psychotherapy. Through bringing the relevant forces into new contact with each other, one discovers the power of the alienated parts of the self.

An examination of a dream workthrough presented by Perls* will illustrate this view of man as a composition of forces. Without interpretation and without specific attention to resistance, Perls traces the course of the dreamer's various characters and expressions so that each part of the person has a voice in the total development of the dream workthrough. The dreamer's name is Dick and here is the dream he reported:

> (Rapidly) I have a recurring nightmare. I'm asleep, and I hear somebody screaming and I wake up and the cops are beating up some kid. And I want to get up and help him but somebody's standing at the head, and at the foot of my bed, and they're throwing pillows back and forth faster and faster and I can't move my head. I can't get up. And I wake up screaming and in full sweat.

After a few preliminary exchanges, Perls asks Dick to be the policeman and beat up the kid, in response to which Dick plays the policeman excoriating the kid, a role he does not like. Perls then asks him to talk to the policeman. Dick explains the sociologically determined plight of this kid to the policeman, who in response maintains a moralistic view and further tells Dick if the kid is going to hurt people, he's going to get hurt in return. Then Perls invites Dick to play the kid in the conversation. The kid explains the importance of being a member of a gang and being a bigshot through his own violence. He wants to be important. By this time, Dick is be-

---

* Perls, F. S., *Gestalt Therapy Verbatim*. Moab, Utah: Real People Press, 1969.

ginning to sympathize with the policeman's reality orientation and his protection of community interests and the kid is becoming clearer as someone who needs to be cared about and who needs to have a meaningful place in the world. Then Dick senses his own impotence as the kid begins to tell of his need to leave his neighborhood and how he wants help to do it. The policeman gives the kid a hard time and the kid lashes out angrily. Dick supports the kid and begins to feel his own violence, rather than only projecting it onto the policeman or the kid. Then Perls brings Dick further along in developing his own sense of himself. Dick gets into touch with his wish to destroy his own past and to develop meaningful work. The dream workthrough ends with the following culminative exchange which reflects a union of Dick's own self-image, the policeman in himself, the kid that is part of him, his sense of impotence, his need to be a bigshot, and his rationality:

> *Perls*: So close your eyes. Now get in touch with your own violence. How do you experience violence? . . .
>
> *Dick*: (breathlessly) I wanna des-destroy things. I wanna-I wanna break the past. I wanna get rid of all those things that keep me from doing things. I wanna be *free*. I just want to lash out at them.
>
> *P*: So talk to the past. "Past, I want to get rid of you."
>
> *D*: Past, you can't hold me up. A lot of kids have gone through the same thing. There are all kinds of slums in the world. Many people have gone to reform school, been in jail. That doesn't mean that they can't accomplish something. I'm getting my Ph.D. I'm *through* with you. I've gotten *out* of it. I don't have to have you around anymore. You don't have to bug me anymore. I don't have to go back and see what the hell life is like there. I don't have to feel the excitement anymore. I can live where I'm living now. I'm going into the academic world—the real world!
>
> *P*: What does the past answer?

D: Yeah, but you—you know that we're your friends and we understand what you want. Our life is richer. There's more excitement, there's more meaning, there's more to do, more to see. It isn't sterile. You know what you've done. You can't get out of it, you can't leave it.

P: In other words the past experiences the Ph.D. as somewhat sterile? Are you—

D: Ph.D. is—ahh, the Ph.D., what the hell is that?

P: Say this to him.

D: Look. When you have a Ph.D. what have you got? It puts you in the position of being able to do a little bit more in helping to analyze certain problems, and when people are presented with it, they're not going to really do a hell of a lot with it. It's not gonna really make a hell of a lot of difference one way or the other *what* you do.

P: You see, now we enter the existential problem. Now you have got your hang-up, your impasse.

D: I not only want to do something more exciting; I want to do something more meaningful—something *real*. I want to touch it, I want to feel it. I wanna see it grow and develop. I wanna feel that I'm useful. Even in a warm, loving way I wanna feel that I'm useful. I don't want to move the world. . . . This feeling of impotence. All that work.

P: That's a very interesting observation because all killing is based upon impotence. . . . So be the Ph.D. . . .

D: There are three billion people in the world, and maybe ten thousand make decisions. And my job will help those who make decisions to make them wiser. I'm not gonna shake the world, but I'm gonna do a hell of a lot more than the other two billion nine hundred and something million will do. It's gonna be a worthwhile contribution.

P: Do you see how you're getting more and more rational —the opposites coming together now? How do you feel now?

D: I feel I want to be rational.

P: Yah, Yah. I think you did a very good job here.

During the course of this dream workthrough there is no effort to discover what is *behind* the dream. Rather it involves repeated efforts to extend the statements within the dream so that each statement piggybacks on the previous statement until the chain of statements runs its course. Each part of the dream is permitted to speak from *its own* perspective, always affected but never determined by its interaction with the other parts. There is never any question as to who is the *real* me anymore than the small red square in a Mondrian painting is more the painting than the blue rectangle. The prejudicial ownership of identity gives way to whatever emerges from the composition of forces, in this instance, the need to receive and use the Ph.D. degree. What comes through is the sense of a primal reflex toward synthesis whenever the elemental identities come into contact with each other.

The compositional nature of man apparent in the dream workthrough is clearly evident also in gestalt work with personal polarities. There is nothing new about looking at polarities in man. What *is* new is the gestalt perspective that each individual is himself a never-ending sequence of polarities. Whenever an individual recognizes one aspect of himself, the presence of its antithesis, or polar quality, is implicit. There it rests as background, giving dimension to present experience and yet powerful enough to emerge as figure in its own right if it gathers enough force. When this force is supported, integration can develop between whatever polarities emerge in opposition to each other, frozen into a posture of mutual alienation.

The most famous of these gestalt polarities is the topdog/ underdog split,* where the struggle is between master and

---

* Perls, F. S., Four Lectures in Fagan, J. and Shepherd I., Eds., *Gestalt Therapy Now*. Palo Alto, California: Science & Behavior Books, 1970.

slave. The master commands, directs and scolds and the slave controverts with his passivity or stupidity, or ineptness or pretense of trying unsuccessfully to do the master's biddings. The polarities have *infinite* dimensions, however, like how my brother lives and how I live; my kindness and my cruelty; my affection and my cynicism; the raconteur in me and the Sphinx in me; Joe College versus the Dead-end Kid, etc. These have personal flavor; each person grows his own polarities.

The task in resolving the polarity is to aid each part to live to its fullest while at the same time making contact with its polar counterpart. This reduces the chance that one part will stay mired in its own impotence, hanging on to the status quo. Instead, it is energized into making a vital statement of its own needs and wishes, asserting itself as a force which must be considered in a new union of forces. Whether one part is viewed as topdog and the other as underdog is not as important as the valid expressiveness of each part articulating its own specific identity.

Here is an example of a written dialogue between the helpless and angry side of a woman whose long silences in groups had seemed quite normal to her until she came into contact with her anger and the consequent helplessness she felt about coping with this anger. The dialogue shows the original incompatibility between the two sides, then a softening of the barriers so that a new union becomes desirable. She did indeed become a more active participant not only in the group, but also in her professional life where she began to accept greater centrality among her associates.

> *Helpless*: I am really quite helpless. I can't make any real changes in my ways of functioning. I go along keeping quiet about things, letting other people determine the course of action or whatever.
>
> *Anger*: I am getting fed up with your cop-outs! That's all they are. You don't like how things are but you don't do anything to change it.

H: The reason I don't change it is you! If I let a little of you out—you will take over. There will be nothing left of me. You will go on a rampage until you destroy everything! Even now I cry when I think of it—you always make me cry. When I cry I defeat you because then you can't do anything—but I can't do anything either. So it ends up that I'm nothing—only weakness and tears.

A: If you would only trust me I could show you that anger can be useful not just destructive.

H: No!—

A: Then go on being the weakling you are.

H: I don't want that either. It's an impossible dilemma— It's your fault—if you weren't there I could do things. If you hadn't kept me down for so long—if you hadn't denied me, if you hadn't tried to be such a fucking angel so everyone would like you—you wouldn't be in this fix. I know all that—but it doesn't change anything. I can't change.

A: You act like you have to do something—all you really have to do is let me be. Get to know me—relax and let things happen if they will. Maybe if you are not always so much on guard—take the clamps off your jaw, make a direct route from thought to speech.

H: I know what you are saying—It's what I want. I'm thinking of the terrors of anger—and I'm crying again. I see my father standing at the foot of the stairs with a butcher knife in his hand and threatening to kill my aunt—I see him with his pale blue eyes popping and staring and him yelling—and yelling—and yelling—I can't stand it!

A: Stop it—that was him—it's not the whole world.

H: His anger ruined his life for him. He is a bitter and lonely man.

A: Your anger is ruining your life for you because you deny it—is that better?

H: No. I do understand all that—but like I say—it is always the tears that get in the way—

A: Fuck the tears! You can go past them—or with them— or in spite of them—that's no kind of excuse.

H: How can I use your—no—be with me—maybe that's the trouble—I talk like you are some kind of weapon— It shouldn't be like that—I don't want to fight you—or use you—just be part of me.

The final statement in this dialogue reflects a natural and basic movement towards synthesis—a reflex towards integration. Any complex organism will order its forces so as to function with economy, organizing its diverse resources into the smoothest, most graceful and most efficient combination possible at that given moment. To be tender, compulsive, daring, ruthless and affable are a combination of characteristics not likely to be experienced as compatible unless a person can rediscover his range and reorganize these personal characteristics into a new composition. To achieve compatibility where society insists none exists, and where prior experience has failed to find any, requires considerable skill—to say nothing of durability and creativity in maintaining contactful integration among painfully antagonistic characteristics.

At the physical level of reflexive integration, Reich long ago described what he called the orgasm reflex.* Under the effect of a fully potent build-up to orgasm, the individual's movements become smoothly synchronized. We believe that the harmony Reich describes at the occurrence of orgasm is observable in all of the grand functions that call the total organism dramatically into focus. Similar climactic explosions involve the whole musculature also in sneezing, coughing, crying, laughing, vomiting and shitting. Suppose that, in the process of toilet training, a child learns that he can control

---

* Reich, W., *The Function of the Orgasm.* New York: The Noonday Press, 1942.

shitting by tightening up his sphincters and in a Faustian bargain winds up doing this chronically, fending off feared accidents but paying a large price in loss of richness of personal function—a loss he really couldn't have predicted. No more bowel lapses, it's true, but he pays the price by restricted movements of his pelvis or constrictions in his breathing. By way of illustration, try now to tighten the sphincters in your anus very tightly and see what effect this has on your breathing. Now, try talking with your anal sphincters very tight. Not a minor effect, is it?

It is only a small step further to recognize that whatever happens in one part of a person affects his whole nature. Cooperative experiences among component parts of the individual are commonplace: sometimes they interrupt good function; other times they facilitate it. For example, a certain musician has a wooden face, especially immobile when he is performing, and yet his music comes forth expressively, even passionately. It is as if he channeled all the expression into the medium of his playing, diverting it from the rest of his body and focusing it in his arms, his fingers and his violin. Another person studies for an exam while a riveting hammer is blasting underneath his window. He blocks out the noise, diminishing one function while he concentrates on another. Such integrations are necessary. They lead to trouble only when the blockage becomes chronic and the blocked function is not available when it is needed. The musician with the wooden face loses when his responsiveness in non-musical situations is chronically unavailable.

The self-restricting linkage of diverse functions is illustrated by one patient who has discovered that if she runs she will wet her pants. Therefore, she *will* not run, even though it may mean missing a bus or being late to class. Her basic inhibition is in the muscles that control urination. When she runs she cannot control these muscles and so running turns out to be dangerous—a no-no—even though she has no objections to running itself. Other people may block out vigorous laughter because they fear that the laughter will turn into crying. Similarly, many women and some men may burst into tears during the height of sexual passion. Whenever an activity is feared not for itself but for what it may trigger off, the individual suffers a double loss. He has solved the basic problem only by lessening a related function.

Thus, we may see that the individual himself is a group, always recombining and interrelating his members. Kurt Goldstein* described this process of integration when he said:

> All of a person's capacities are always in action in each of his activities. The capacity that is particularly important for the task is in the foreground; the others are in the background. All of these capacities are organized in a way which facilitates the self-realization of the total organism in the particular situation. For each performance there is a definite figure-ground organization of capacities. . . .

Contradictions emerge, of course, in this process of integration, some elements of the struggle being dominated by others, some being obliterated, and some chronically vying for a figural position arising out of the background of one's existence. Originally, the struggle was a valid one in the sense that warring impulses may indeed have been contradictory, each potentially interfering with the other—as wanting to spit may interfere with wanting mother to love you.

No personal need yields gracefully to its antithesis within the individual any more than one country or one individual welcomes the existence of its antithesis. When antitheses collide, the status quo is doomed because each protagonist changes through the effect of one upon the other. Therefore, rather than to risk unwelcome changes, they recoil, but in doing so

---

* Goldstein, K., "The Effect of Brain Damage on the Personality," in Zax, M. and Stricker, G., Eds., *The Study of Abnormal Behavior.* New York: Macmillan, 1964.

they miss the opportunity for a new and dynamic synthesis. For example, a person with strong but antithetical qualities of cruelty and kindness may be irresolute until, by merging these qualities, he becomes a fiery revolutionary, beloved among his own people, tender in a style unknown to the merely cruel person, yet sharply incisive in a style unlikely among merely kind people. Growth depends on the renewal of contact possibilities between diverse aspects of the individual—contact possibilities which have been shut off through erroneous ideas of incompatibility.

The restoration of contact among the various parts of oneself is, of course, not always a bed of roses. Just as the strategy of confrontation in politics carries the potentiality for explosiveness, chaos and alienation, so, too, can the process of confronting conflicting qualities within oneself be abrasive and dangerous. This is particularly true when one quality is firmly entrenched, but only because it is suppressing another quality which is beginning to surge into expression. Sometimes the force required to regain fruitful contact can lead to crazy or extreme behavior where the individual strikes out for a contact which can be palpably felt. The person who must scream his rage to counteract his impotent-submissiveness, the person who becomes sexually profligate to overcome a solidified morality, and the person who sits catatonically silent in a corner rather than get wound up in ambitiousness swallowed whole from his father are all playing risky games, drastically dominating the entrenched forces within themselves. Until this newly aroused energy can reach a synthesis with the original preeminent force, the person behaves arbitrarily—without a sense of wholeness.

In the uneasy alignment that the individual achieved between two opposed qualities in himself, one part of his nature was disarmed of its excitement and activity. In the movement toward integration, this excitement is remobilized and the still powerful energy of the accepted part is not diminished. The individual who is thus engaged may well experience overstimulation and a fear of literally bursting or exploding. He doesn't recognize, because of his inexperience with explosive reactions, that the sense of bursting may move into crying, screaming, dramatic language, strong movement, temper tantrums, orgasms, etc. Up until this moment he felt that his personal boundaries were threatened by expansion of sensations because no suitable release was acceptable. If, under new conditions such as therapy, he is able to yield and allow the explosion to come, he can be as though reborn. If, on the other hand, he cannot tolerate the assimilation of the expansion within himself that this integration requires, he may well be at least temporarily scared away from further growth in this direction. Knowing the difference between these two possibilities is an artful skill, one that requires sensitive tuning in on the part of both patient and therapist.

There is no precise yardstick to identify the limits of an individual's power to assimilate or express feelings which have explosive possibilities, but there *is* a basic safeguard. This is a solid respect for the self-regulation of the individual—not forcing or seducing him into behaviors which he himself has not largely set up.

Even so, the greatest steps forward do not always come from playing it safe. In my own therapy, two of the most powerful moments came when I said, *The hell with it*, in moments of grand sensation—nonverbally willing to risk all. Under the momentum of an overwhelming feeling, a person may choose to give up further choice, as at the height of a roller coaster where, once having made the choice to go, the choice is gone. Once in therapy when I made the choice to yield to whatever would come, I surprisingly found myself in the middle of spasmodic crying, the first time as an adult. The other time I found myself in the midst of convulsive spasms and the deepest shivers. Each time I emerged through the experience reawakened to the wet tenderness of life and a new sense of personal directionalism; not through control but through movement, inexorability, power and presence, the kind of presence that makes the world a unit of one.

4

The Commerce of Resistance

a total stranger one black day
knocked living the hell out of me—

who found forgiveness hard because
my (as it happened) self he was

—but now that fiend and i are such
immortal friends the other's each

E. E. CUMMINGS

Everyone manages his energy so that he makes good contact with his environment or he resists the contact. If he senses that his efforts will succeed—that he is potent and that his environment is capable of nourishing return—he will confront his environment with appetite, confidence and even daring. But if his efforts don't get him what he wants, he is stuck with a whole laundry list of troublesome feelings: anger, confusion, futility, resentment, impotence, disappointment and so on. Then he must divert his energy in a number of ways, all of which reduce possibilities for contactful interaction with his environment.

The specific directions of this diverted interaction will color the person's style of living as he establishes favorites among the channels open to him. There are five major channels of resistant interaction, each of which has a particular expressive style: 1) introjection; 2) projection; 3) retroflection; 4) deflection; and 5) confluence.

The *introjector* invests his energy into passively incorporating what the environment provides. He expends little effort in specifying his requirements or preferences. This depends on him remaining undiscriminating or in an environment which is totally benign. As long as he stays in this stage, when the world behaves inconsistently with his needs he must devote his energy to keeping himself content with taking things as he finds them.

The *projector* disowns aspects of himself, ascribing them to the environment. If the environment is diverse enough he will, of course, be right some of the time. But much of the time he will be making serious mistakes, abdicating his own part in the direction of energy and experiencing himself as powerless to effect a change.

The *retroflector* abandons any attempt to influence his environment by becoming a separate and self-sufficient unit, reinvesting his energy back into an exclusively intrapersonal system and severely restricting the traffic between himself and the environment.

The *deflector* engages with his environment on a hit-and-miss basis. For him, though, it usually becomes a miss-basis, with only a few—and mostly accidental—hits. So, either he doesn't invest enough energy to get a reasonable return or he invests it without focus and it scatters and evaporates. He winds up depleted, getting small return—a bankrupt.

Finally, through *confluence,* the individual goes along

with the trends. This involves very little expenditure of energy in personal choice; he has only to yield to the current of the field and let it carry him along. That may not be where he might want to go, but his associates seem to value this direction and he assumes it must be worthwhile. Besides, it cost him little, so how can he complain?

Let us look more closely at these five channels.

INTROJECTION

Introjection is the generic mode of interaction between the individual and his environment. The child accepts whatever he does not quickly experience as noxious. He may either accept his food in the form in which it is offered or he will spit it up. At first he cannot remake the substance to suit him better, as he will later when he begins to chew. When he can chew, he learns how to restructure what enters into him. Before this, though, he swallows trustingly what nourishment he is provided—and he similarly swallows impressions of the nature of his world.

Since the child must, in the beginning, take things as they come or get rid of them whenever he can, the need to trust his environment is remarkable. If his environment is indeed trustworthy, the material coming in will be nourishing and assimilable, be it food or personal treatment. But food is shoved hurriedly down throats, doctors say the needle won't hurt, and shitting is called dirty and disreputable. The "shoulds" begin early and often have little congruence with what the child senses his needs to be. Eventually a soul is worn down. The child's confidence is depleted by external authorities whose judgments set in, eroding his own clear identity and opening him to adult conquistadors who take over the territory. The surrender is abject at first and forgotten later. So the foreign body rules, keeping the person ill at ease, suspicious of deviations or unexpected arousals, thwarted every time his second-hand value system proves unresponsive to his current needs. The person who has swallowed whole the values of his parents, his school and his society requires life to continue as before. When the world around him changes, he is fair game for anxiety and defensiveness. His manipulation of his own energy operates in support of the introjected standards, and at the same time tries to keep his behavior as fully integrated as possible with his hand-me-down sense of rightness and wrongness. Even when the introjection is successfully accomplished, that is, when it is consistent with the actual world he lives in, he still pays a high price because he has given up his sense of free choice in life.

The fundamental difficulty in undoing introjection is its honorable history as a generic means of learning. The child learns by absorbing what is around him. The boy walks like his father without even imitating him, languages and dialects are taken in, senses of humor are passed on, etc. The child simply experiences many aspects of living in a that's-how-it-is manner and learning is like blood flowing through veins or like breathing. The quality of things just being as they are pulses with a freshness that is hard to duplicate later through the deliberate and discrimination-oriented learning that takes over.

Unfortunately though, learning exclusively through introjection requires an impossibly favorable environment, one which is invariably suited to the individual's needs. When this perfect fit lapses—as it must, of course—the individual must not only select what he does want and is willing to identify with, but he must also resist the pressures and influences which will insist on coming in to him and which he does *not* want. That is where the struggle begins.

At certain ages when the struggle is drastically heightened, as at two and again at adolescence, he begins to resent the incursions from the outside so strongly that he is even willing to sacrifice wisdom in favor of asserting the dominance of his own choice system. He realizes, almost intuitively, that mere wisdom does not at that time have the primacy that he must assign to personal choice-making. I am first and my "welfare" is second, says he. So, we see at two that he says "no" indiscriminately and at adolescence would stubbornly rather flunk out of school than meekly submit to the requirements set by others.

Since he cannot, in the beginning, know the implications of his choices, the introjector takes in his experiences with large doses of faith. For example, a person has no way of knowing, at two, whether he is going to want to walk like his father. He just does. It is only later that he may call this into question and want to swing his hips more or stick his chest out. Considering the primal attractiveness and indispensability of this process, no wonder that one has difficulty giving it up even after other modes of learning appear and make introjection recede in importance. Discriminations between noxious or salutary streamings that enter into the individual become more dependable and take on the flavor of choices, incorporating personal values and style into the choice-making process. Furthermore, the power to restructure what exists increases, impelling the person beyond the mere yes-or-no choice. He becomes able to arrange experience to be personally more suitable, creating what he needs, rather than just choosing yes-or-no.

This move into creative discrimination from the earlier reactive discrimination is dramatically represented by the appearance of chewing. Chewing is the prototypical activity in making the world assimilable to one's needs when it hasn't started out that way.* But the inevitable conflict begins between accepting life as it is or changing it and the conflict lasts as long as one lives.

The primary task in undoing the introjection is to focus

---

* Perls, F. S., *Ego, Hunger and Aggression.* London: George Allen & Unwin Ltd., 1947.

on establishing within the individual a sense of the choices available to him and establishing his power to differentiate between "me" and "thee." There are many ways to do this. One of the simplest is to have him make up pairs of sentences for himself and the therapist beginning first with the pronoun, *I*, and then the pronoun, *you*. Or he could be asked to make up sentences beginning with the words, *I believe that . . .* and then work through how many of those statements represent his own beliefs, culled from his personal experience, and how many of them are stale take-overs from other people in his life. Indeed, any experience that heightens the individual's sense of "me" is a major step in undoing introjection.

For example, an attractive 25-year-old woman was living with a man she loved and who said he loved her. Gloria was upset, however, because Dan was not ready to marry her. She was troubled about the extent of his actual commitment to her and about whether Dan would ever be willing to be married. Gloria dearly wanted to live a married life. Her sense of personal wish was confused, though, because of admonitions by her parents, spoken and unspoken, that a woman should not live with a man before getting married and, indeed, any man who would agree to such an arrangement would not be likely to marry her. Why should he, they would say, since he was already getting what he wanted. Gloria had to go beyond their anti-sexual attitudes and their marriage values and experience her own. When she could accept her own sexuality, appreciation of her real attractiveness to Dan could also expand and give her a sense of choice among men so that if *Dan* should not marry her she would understand that she may have lost him, but *not* all her choices at marriage. In other words, she would not be merely the chosen or not chosen but would feel *herself* a chooser. Though Gloria was unfamiliar with this role, she happened to be plentifully gifted for it since she was attractive, intelligent and energetic. Once accepting her own nature, she could be free of her introjection of parental anti-

sexuality and their estimate of women as only reactively discriminating rather than making free choices on their own.
During therapy she grew in these dimensions first by opening
up her genuine warmth for me and discovering the natural
quality of affection. Then Gloria learned to play with her own
visual attractiveness, trying out her exhibitionism by dressing
dramatically, by feeling how she walked, loosening up her walk
and by looking directly at people as she talked to them. She
felt her own individuality now and wound up marrying Dan.

The introjector minimizes differences between what he is
swallowing whole and what he might truly want if he allowed
himself to make this discrimination. He thereby neutralizes
his own existence by avoiding the aggressiveness required
for destructuring what exists. It is as if anything which exists
is inviolate; he is not to change it; he must take it as it comes.
So he relates all new experience to previous experience, en-
hancing its inviolate quality and insuring that he already
knows what is happening or that he has accepted what is
being said. All life is only a variation on what he has already
experienced, providing him with a buffer against anything
new, but also reducing the freshness which can come from a
sense of immediacy of experience.

Allport* recognized the importance of how people relate
to differences or novelty when he described perceptual styles
in terms of leveling or sharpening. The sharpeners remember
and exaggerate the differences between what they would have
expected and what they are actually experiencing. The distinctions between the familiar and the strange are prickly, like
a porcupine bristling with needles of difference. The levelers,
on the other hand, reduce difference. The outstanding or unique
aspects of experience are diminished. Since the new learning

---

* Allport, G. W. and Postman, L. J., "The Basic Psychology of
Rumor" in Maccoby, E. E., Newcomb, T. M. and Hartley, E. L., Eds.,
Readings in Social Psychology. New York: Holt, Rinehart & Winston,
1958.

doesn't present much novelty, primarily because they have omitted or forgotten the novel details, they don't have to work so hard to retain it.

Powerful impediments to working through the introject, to chewing it literally or figuratively, arise from the triad of impatience, laziness and greed. The intolerance for inevitable difference is actually an intolerance for the aggression required to alter differences before they can be digested and assimilated into the healthy organism. Impatience to gulp something down quickly, laziness at having to work too hard to get it down, or greed to get as much as possible as quickly as possible—all of these tendencies lead to introjecting. For example, these words that you are reading may register convincingly right now or they may require angry rebuttal, prolonged discussion or thought, action in your own work or decisions as to what is not now applicable or assimilable in your everyday life. It is hard to predict how much time you will need for either rejection or assimilation. Most books are read with either the introjector's frame of mind, or with the critic's. They zing quickly into either familiarity or alienation. There are so many books to read and carefulness or attentiveness essential for working through is doled out only sparingly.

The introjector wants to be spoonfed. He is duck soup for the symbol, the oversimplification, the gimmick, the lesson which is easy to reiterate obsessively. The authentically profound and artful concepts which guided Perls and others and which were dramatized by demonstrations and by catchy language, like hot-seat, topdog-underdog, the impasse, mindfucking, etc. have often been glibly swallowed—but not digested—by those for whom imitation and idolatry replaced their own development of a style native to themselves. Drama energized the communication process by clarifying the message and speeding it up. But it is indispensable for personal fullness to discriminate between drama which inspires and clarifies, on the one hand, and cheap language tricks which, if yielded to, make one feel *in* without knowing how one's own development is enhanced.

In therapy, when the introjector's aggression and critique are mobilized, he becomes resonant to his own stored-up bitterness. He has much to be bitter about since he has swallowed what is unsuitable to him and is therefore in the victimized position of all people who have been invaded. A distinction must be made, however, between bitterness and aggression. The former frequently is willing to settle for mere justification of the bitterness while the latter intends to *change* something. These changes may be random, at first, with the individual unaccustomed to knowing his own wishes, knowing only what he *doesn't* want and needs to get rid of. Change for the sake of change, even though directionless and unformed, reawakens the energy in the system and shows that a live organism is reviving. Time enough to worry about directions after the liveliness is restored. This is, of course, a risky philosophy on the order of Frankenstein's monster, because the release of energy which has no direction may move where it hurts. Nevertheless, especially with introjections, energy must be released. This is why the most effective psychotherapy involves risk—as do all rebellions. Rebellion is necessary in the undoing of introjection. So is vomiting, literally or figuratively, because it represents the discharge of the ugly foreign bodies which must be cast out, even though they have come to feel over the years as though they were one's very own. To discover that "givens" are not "givens" at all is an experience which makes real drama of the recovery of self-direction, where a person does not take his existence for granted but is constantly creating it.

PROJECTION

The projector is an individual who cannot accept his feelings and actions because he "shouldn't" feel or act that way.

The "shouldn't," of course, is the basic introject which labels his feeling or action unpalatable. To resolve this dilemma he does *not* recognize his own mischief but instead attaches it to another person, certainly not himself. The result is a classic split between his actual characteristics and what he is aware of about them. Meanwhile, he is exquisitely aware of these characteristics in other people. The suspicion, for example, that another person resents him or is trying to seduce him is a fabrication based on the unaccepted fact that *he* wants to behave this way towards the other person. Whereas the introjector surrenders his sense of identity, the projector gives it away piecemeal.

Restoring to the projector his squandered bits of identity remains the cornerstone of the work-through process. When, for example, an individual bemoans the fact that his father does not want to talk to him, the therapist does not have to buy his perceptions. He may tell the aggrieved son to turn the complaint around, saying instead that *he* does not want to talk to his father. The son may discover that he has indeed played a part in the alienation from father. He may even have started it in the first place by sullenly thwarting father's approaches so extensively that father just gave up talking to him. The therapeutic technology rests on the basic belief that we do create our own lives and that in re-owning our own creations, we become emboldened to change our world. Furthermore, even when no external change is necessary or possible, the sense of personal identity expressed so well in Popeye's "I am what I am!" is in itself a curative experience.

When a projector can fantasize himself as having some of the same qualities he sees in others but has heretofore obliterated from his own self-awareness, this loosens up and expands his too-rigid sense of identity. Take a man, for example, who has obscured the sense of his own cruelty. To experience himself as a cruel person serves to give him a new vigor, perhaps adding dimension to his kindness, perhaps giving him the impetus for changing what only cruel behavior would change.

A graduate student, David, treated cruelly by one of his professors, was both outraged and depleted by the confrontations with this man. In exploring how David would be as a cruel man he discovered that he himself had tried to dominate his professor first. Furthermore, it was a general need of his to dominate a situation so as to retain control of his own independence. Now he was reaping the whirlwind, but knowing he had been the blower as well as the blown made David feel less victimized. Until then he had experienced himself not in a strategic struggle for his own survival but merely as a helpless victim. Once David had himself screamed, ranted and even killed in his own fantasies, the pressure from his projections was removed and all that was left was the proportionate tactical problem which he could more realistically cope with. Coping replaced projective indignation. Projective indignation is a crucially disruptive factor since it results in nursing grudges. This becomes a stale force, chaining the individual to unresolution.

Fortunately, in the above example, David was not so alienated from the monster-in-himself that he could not readily engage in the experiment. This does not always come so easily. When projections form into paranoid self-support, the difficulties mount. At this stage, the projector experiences people as either for him or against him. Any suggestion which faces the individual with re-ownership of his own characteristics is fought so strenuously that it may tie the hands of the therapist. Trust becomes indispensable here because there is only a thin line to walk between re-establishing the patient's self-awareness and appearing to side with the enemy. A person in such a position requires appreciation of his perspective no matter what the verity may be. Any therapist who does not authentically experience this appreciation will be resisted. Re-ownership of the projected material must come from experienced support, or it will not come at all.

One woman was in the throes of debilitative anxiety about her boss. She felt he was out to get her because she was so smart and he couldn't stand a woman with sensitivity, whose wiser approach to their work would only disrupt his dominance and his laziness. I perceived that *her* wish to dominate and *her* laziness in wanting her way without struggle or creativity exaggerated the painful vibrations between them. Any suggestion that she try out this role, however, merely put me on the boss's side, though in fact I deplored this man's behavior only somewhat less than she did. She got over the height of her paranoia only when I was able to bring her into contact with her own nature by asking her to tell me actual stories about her life. Once she became absorbed in real story-telling, directly and with no strategic undercurrents, she felt my support and this took some of the heat off her paranoid adventure.

Projection is not invariably non-contactful. The ability to project is a natural human reaction. To be able to extrapolate what one knows or intuits about oneself as true also of others acknowledges human mutuality. How else would people know what others are talking about? A basic fact of life is that "it takes one to know one." Hence the therapist who is in tune with his own paranoia, his own psychopathy, his own depression, his own catatonia or hebephrenia, is in a good position to respond to another person who may be in the process of self-reduction through an overdose of these toxins. Our own projections do teach us about more than these old-style psychological debilitations. They are usually less categorical, like knowing what it is like to be shy or sexually aroused or stiff or needing to smile or any of the myriad of specific characteristics one may observe in another person. The therapist must reverberate to personhood. He must go beyond the specific configuration which is *his* person and make room for the elements which go into being *any* person.

Each person is the center of gravity of his universe. The fact that yes, Virginia, there is a real world out there, does not diminish one's powers to sense, interpret and manipulate that world so that its ultimate nature is determined by one's own experience. Science notwithstanding, the universe then becomes his own creation just as we have heretofore fantasied that it was God's creation. This fantasy was mustered out of our own humility, giving away our power, or, more cynically, copping out on our own responsibility for the troubles we have created. Perhaps we don't want to believe that we ourselves could cause such self-pain and explain it by the intervention of mysterious god-forces.

Not so; it is our own universe, for better or worse. Man is the axis around which his wheel turns. He is, as T.S. Eliot has said, "At the still point of the turning world."

RETROFLECTION

Retroflection is a hermaphroditic function wherein the individual turns back against himself what he would like *to do to someone else,* or does to himself what he would like *someone else to do to him.* He can be his own target, his own Santa Claus, his own amour, his own whatever-he-wishes. He condenses his psychological universe, substituting manipulation of himself for what he conceives of as futile longings for attentions from others.

Retroflection underlines the central human power of dividing oneself into the observer and the observed, or into the doer and the done to. This ability shows itself in various manifestations. Man talks to himself. Man's sense of humor is evidence of this split because it means he can stand aside and see the incongruity or absurdity of his behavior. Man's sense of shame or embarrassment implies the perspective of self-observation and self-judgment. Man is also self-consciously aware of his own mortality.

There are many artistic accounts of man's split between himself and his observer. Poe's story of William Wilson and Schubert's *Die Doppelgänger*, the ghostly double, both deal with the problem of man running away from a spectral observer who turns out to be himself and from whom, of course, he can never escape. We see this phenomenon also in man's conceptualization of God as the ideal who can always observe his inmost thoughts and workings. The biblical story of Moses trying to flee from the scrutiny of God is an early antecedent of Melanie Klein's* picture of the harsh super-ego that the child constructs which is infinitely more unforgiving than the parental super-ego from which it is derived. The parents only know whether the child writes on the wall or whether he pinches his little brother. The child knows "I wanted to write on the wall," or "I wanted to pinch my little brother," and the *should* system that knows him so well twinges, nudges and tightens. The pain of man's self-judging ability pervades his life.

Suppose the child grows up in a home where the people, although not out-and-out hostile, are insensitive and impervious to his natural manipulations. When he cries, there is no lap for him to fit into. Stroking and caressing are even harder to come by. Soon he learns to soothe and pamper himself, asking for little from anybody else. Later, he gets himself the finest food and prepares it lovingly. He buys himself fine clothes. He treats himself to a smooth-riding car. He provides himself only the most carefully selected surroundings. With all this self-love, he still believes his generic introject, "My parents will not pay any attention to me." What he has not let himself discover is that this is not the same as "nobody will pay attention to me." By uncritically maintaining the introject, "Nobody will pay any attention to me," he is compelled to reply, "so I have to do it for myself."

---

* Brown, J. A. C., *Freud and the Post-Freudians*. Baltimore: Penguin Books, 1961.

He may also choose to retroflect against himself those impulses which would initially have been directed at some other person. These impulses may be either hostile or tender. Tantrums, hitting, screaming or biting were consistently quashed. Again comes the generic introject, "I shouldn't get angry at them," around which the retroflective defense is overlaid. He turns the anger back against himself.

An example of this, in undisguised form, concerns a young man in his early 30's. He had had encephalitis as a child and was left with residual brain damage and arrested development. He loved to talk to people but he couldn't keep the conversation going for long. He would become aware that he was beginning to lose the point foolishly and he would say angrily to himself, "I'm getting silly, I'm getting silly." Shortly after that he would exile himself to the stairs, sitting hunched over, rocking back and forth and pinching himself desperately, repeating, "I'm getting silly, I'm getting silly."

Nevertheless, at its best, retroflective activity can be self-corrective, counteracting the real limitations or hazards inherent in the spontaneous nature of man. In moments of personal surge which would lead to danger, man must *stop himself*, as he would before swimming exuberantly too far from shore. At the highest levels of involvement, the individual's commitment to action may become so strong and uncritical that a counterforce is necessary. For example, a mother presses her clenched fists against her forehead and, in doing so, stops herself before brutally beating her child. Retroflection only becomes characterological when it becomes a chronic standoff between mutually opposed energies within the individual. Then the originally healthful suspension of spontaneous action, temporal and wise, hardens into frozen resignation. The natural rhythm between spontaneity and self-observation loses out and the loss of this rhythm divides man into self-impeding forces.

When a person retroflects repeatedly, he blocks his outlets to the world and remains in the grip of opposed but stagnant forces. For example, if a person chooses to stop himself from crying under the requirements of living with forbidding parents, he does not have to continue this sacrifice beyond the years of his contact with them. The major problem of good living is to keep up-to-date with the possibilities which exist rather than remain stamped on the ass for all time by experiences which were only temporary or which may merely have been errors of perception or intuition. Maybe he only *thought* he had to shut off his cries when he never really *had* to. Furthermore, he may not have to now, irrespective of whether he was right or wrong originally.

Thinking is itself a retroflective process, a subtle way of talking to oneself. Though thinking may have obviously disruptive qualities—interfering with or postponing action—it also is valuable in orienting an individual to those questions in his life whch are too complex to leave to spontaneous resolution. Choosing a career, deciding whether to marry, solving a difficult problem in mathematics, designing a building, all benefit from the mediating influence of thinking. Even in minor decisions, like choosing a movie, one may think to himself: "I don't want to see such-and-such; it's too gory and too depressing for me tonight. What I'd rather see is something that will warm me." Until he had thought of it in this way, the person might not have even known where he wanted to go.

Unfortunately, in retroflection, the split often creates internal abrasion and considerable stress because it remains self-contained and does not move into the required action. Movement towards growth, therefore, would be to redirect energy so that the internal struggle is opened. Instead of operating only within the individual, energy becomes free to move towards a relationship with something outside oneself. The undoing of retroflection consists of the search for the appropriate other.

Nevertheless, though the goal is for the individual to seek contact with otherness, the work-through of the inner struggle must frequently come first. In retroflection, since the impulse to do or be done to in contact with others is severely overshadowed, the interaction within the divided self must be re-energized with awareness. Close attention to the physical behavior of the individual is one way to identify where the battle is taking place. By examining posture, gesture or movement, for example, the struggle that is going on for control of the person's body becomes apparent. Suppose a man tells a woman of a deeply sad event in his life. He observes that, as he talks, she is hunching deeper and deeper into her chair, her arms clasped tightly about herself. He stops because he feels her pulling farther away from him with every word he says, leaving him feeling isolated and alone in his sorrow. *Her* experience, however, is quite different. She is very moved and yet she feels that anything she might do would be an intrusion. Her gesture expresses both her need to hold and her need to hold back. Instead of embracing him, she clasps herself. Her underlying sympathetic impulse has given rise to a muscular counterforce which attempts to keep this impulse under control. Metaphorically, it is as if her arms have become the rope in a tug-of-war between two fairly equal counterforces. Her arms are immobilized in a holding action, going nowhere. All of her energy is devoted to immobilizing the impulse she is afraid of. Another person's battleground may prohibit biting, cutting, insulting or otherwise hostile remarks. His control may be observed in the tension and stiffness of his immobile jaw, on guard against expressing anger. A woman who crosses her legs tightly may be preventing herself from fidgeting provocatively. A woman may pick the back of her scalp raw instead of picking on other people. People expend a tremendous amount of energy in maintaining holding actions like these.

The resistances to releasing the retroflected activity exist at two levels of toxicity. At the milder level, the individual at least does what he needs for himself. A nuzzling person may nuzzle himself, sit cozily, curl himself up into a ball and hold himself warmly. When he can allow himself this much satisfaction, he is somewhat ahead of the game because he is providing some of the warmth and the contact he wanted from another person. But at the second level of retroflection, even this internal attention to his needs is minimal. When he has experienced not only the futility of trying to be close to other people but also himself as untouchable, then even he cannot be good to himself. He has so deeply introjected the original prohibition against touching that he has become his own policeman. He sits stiffly in his chair and when he touches himself —drying himself after a bath—his touch is businesslike. He is on guard against any graceful yielding into contact, even between his own disparate selves. Not only does he not nuzzle up against anybody else, he doesn't nuzzle in this world, not even with himself.

Therefore, in the resolution of the retroflective process, an early stage of release of the musculature or the action system might move the individual toward himself rather than toward others. Movement that breaks the immobilization and restores live energy to the system is movement toward eventual restoration of contact with the outside world even though it may, in the intermediate period, be directed towards one's self. This is all to the good. The person is about as accepting of himself as his introjected or even projected world out there has been. Consequently, the frozen, retroflected person cut off from sexual experience with other persons is usually poor at masturbating, too. In the recovery of his fuller sexuality, he may need first to learn how to masturbate well. When he discovers how to masturbate so that he likes it, he is well on the road to a sexual experience with another person. There are transitions to bridge, of course, but it is easier to teach Spanish to someone who speaks French than to someone who has no foreign language experience. Once the natural flow of energy is reopened, it is more likely to find a rightful direction.

Any new activity which involves muscular energy starts

out self-conscious and awkward. Physical resolution of the retroflected impulse goes through the same stage. When a child is learning to walk, putting one foot in front of another requires deliberate focus. After he learns to do this, he walks spontaneously and without self-consciousness. The same is true of the retroflected impulse. Tight arms, clenched fist, tightened jaw, immovable rib cage or pelvis, heels pounding down onto the floor, grinding one's molars, chronic frowns—all of these muscular expressions of self-control start out in the child as effortful and conscious control. I will not say the bad word, I will not touch the soft and appealing skin of my mother; all of these start out as conscious controls. A child, tempted by wanting to touch the verboten, regards the object and practices saying "no, no, no" to himself as though he were his own parent. Later this gets built in, forgotten, and the resulting tension is taken for granted. Forgotten, indeed, but not hidden because the body has many ways of recording the forgotten message. Knotted stomachs, girded loins, sunken chests, and a whole infinity of dysfunctional character structure result. The hostile individual, with tightened jaw, interrupting his own hurtful, aggressive impulses, wonders why other people can toss off a joke or fling a laughing insult; yet, under similar circumstances, he comes out heavy-handed and punitive. Other people can clap an old friend on the back and say "How are you, you old bastard?" and the friend laughs and responds with an embrace. But when *he* reaches out with arm stiffened, because what starts out as a friendly slap on the back may well wind up a hard impact, he gets a polite handshake in return, or worse, a puzzled look as though he had just landed from Mars.

What is needed to undo retroflection is to return to the self-consciousness that accompanied its inception. The person has, once again, to become aware of how he sits, how he hugs people, how he grits his teeth, etc. Once he knows what's going on inside himself, his energy is mobilized to seek outlet in fantasy or in action. He can face such prospects as whom might he like to sit on, whom might he like to crush in a wrestler's grip or hold in a soft embrace, whom would he like to chew out or whom would he like to bite?

Deflection is a maneuver for turning aside from direct contact with another person. It's a way of taking the heat off the actual contact. The heat is taken off by circumlocution, by excessive language, by laughing off what one says, by not looking at the person one is talking to, by being abstract rather than specific, by not getting the point, by coming up with bad examples or none at all, by politeness instead of directness, by stereotyped language instead of original language, by substituting mild emotions for intense ones, by talking about the past when the present is more relevant, by talking *about* rather than talking *to,* and by shrugging off the importance of what one has just said. All of these deflections make life watered down. Action is off-target; it is weaker and less effective. Contact can be deflected either by the person who initiates the interaction or by the respondent. The initiating deflector frequently feels that he is not getting much out of what he is doing, that his efforts don't bring him the reward he wants. Furthermore, he doesn't know how to account for the loss. The respondent, who deflects another person's effect almost as if he had an invisible shield, often experiences *himself* as unmoved, bored, confused, blank, cynical, unloved, unimportant and out-of-place. When deflected energy can be brought back on target, the sense of contact is greatly heightened.

Though usually self-limiting, deflection can have a useful base. There are situations which are natively too hot to handle and from which people must turn away. Nations, for example, must take the heat off certain issues. The language of diplomacy is famous for removing the sting of expression or the unforgivable insult from exchanges between countries. Many such linguistic conveniences may turn out to be merely phony, but some do authentically try to avoid the dead-ended statement of antagonism which can't be taken back. Many expressions carry stereotyped implications not actually intended. For example, some communications, honest as they may be at the time of arousal, set reactions in the hearer and, though the feelings may be only temporary, these reactions petrify something which in fact was only ephemeral. This is true for individual people as well as nations. If I call you dirty names in the apex of my rage, that does not necessarily characterize my continuing feelings about you. Trust, time, and intimate knowing of one another will bridge such moments, but under circumstances where these are not available, deflecting the rage may be wise and necessary.

Becoming addicted to deflection or using poor discrimination is where the trouble begins. For example, when a parent tells his child the facts of life, but couches them in roundabout language, he is compounding a felony. Parents explaining sexuality to their children is one of life's unavoidable deflections. Technicalities and abstract accuracy only garble further a message which, even when well communicated, is distant indeed from sexual actuality. The kid winds up out of the ballgame, usually not even finding out the score. The same need to water down can permeate any contact which may have troublesome consequences. "I don't really mean *you* but I mean it's the tendency in the world to be rude or to be abrupt or to not give a person as much time as he needs." Thereby the real complaint about being treated rudely is diminished or vaguely diverted from its target.

The deflecting person doesn't reap the harvest from his activity. Things just don't happen. The person may talk and yet feel untouched or misunderstood. His interactions misfire, not accomplishing what he might reasonably expect. Even though an individual may communicate validly or accurately, if he doesn't reach *into* the other person, he won't be fully felt.

For example, Walt, who gave all the information needed when asked a question, never quite answered the question. When I confronted him about this, he became quite furious, a less deflected state than usual. In his fury, Walt announced that he had a right to speak as he wanted to, that if I would only listen to him and appreciate his style, I would know that the question had been answered. His excellence or accuracy, of course, is not enough. Janet preceded Freud but he didn't make the contact Freud made. Similarly, Walt may be correct, but if he doesn't meet people clearly, he will not get the response he needs. I asked Walt to summarize his answer in one word. He did, and when he did, I knew more clearly and pungently what he was talking about than from his previous lengthy gift of information.

Ramona spent a half hour talking about herself, very diagnostically. The casual observer might have assumed she was making contact all the time because she was voluble and at first even interesting. She took the edge off, though, partly by not looking directly at me, partly by using diagnostic stereotypes. Though I could appreciate and was even moved by some of the things she said about herself, listening finally became burdensome. I asked Ramona to make up several statements beginning with the word "you"; she smiled, her eyes lit up and she made the statements. Immediately, there was a new contact between her and me. Ramona's main problem in life, as it turned out, was that she takes the heat off her experiences. She was severely over-stimulated by her father as she was growing up. As she put it, they did everything but fuck together. Now she is still easily over-stimulated by contacts quite assimilable for most of us. While she was speaking diagnostically about herself, she complained about being all knotted up in her stomach and was unable to look at me directly except only occasionally. After making the contact and realizing I was looking at her, she was able to meet me visually. Then, the knotted quality left her, and the period of tension which had been going on for days left, as Ramona put it, as though she had never been tense. She had made the direct contact and had not been burned.

Confluence is a phantom pursued by people who want to reduce difference so as to moderate the upsetting experience of novelty and otherness. It is a palliative measure whereby one settles for surface agreement, a contract not to rock the boat. Good contact, on the other hand, even in the deepest of unions, retains the heightened and profound sense of the other with whom contact is being made.

One of the troubles with confluence is, of course, that it is a flimsy basis for a relationship. Just as no two bodies can occupy the same space at the same time, no two individuals can be of exactly the same mind. If it is so difficult for two individuals to achieve confluence, it is even more futile to strive for familial, organizational or societal confluence.

An individual may choose purposefully to downplay differences in order to remain on the track of a more important objective and to resist irrelevant static. Submerging one's individual style to carry out an assigned role in a team activity like a football formation or singing a madrigal or even a political campaign is a temporary gift of self to the greater unit. This differs from confluence because the individual's sense of self is figural. It remains defined through his personal assent and the clarity of his awareness of himself and his environment. He elects to focus on one element of the group process. Now, if his life is crammed with the requirements for personal submergence, whether he likes it or not, it is obviously going to prove frustrating and unnourishing. Real contact with the demands imposed by such a life could lead to chucking it. This is what happens in many marriages when spouses have finally gotten a bellyful of each other. This was also the case with a young man who finally made the decision to leave a stultifying position in a large hospital after repeated contact with the demands for quiet confluence which were implicit in his job. When he realized that confluence was the price of an unconflictful existence, and that the payments were to be made endlessly, he left to carve out another style of life.

Confluence is a three-legged race arranged between two people who agree not to disagree. It is an inarticulated contract, often with hidden clauses and fine print which perhaps only one partner to the contract knows about. Indeed, someone can be involved in a confluence contract without ever having been consulted or having even "negotiated" its terms. One may buy into such an arrangement through indolence or ignorance and discover that such a contract existed to his surprise only by breaking or disturbing it. Even if vaguely sensed differences may never have erupted into overt argument, there are signs of disturbance in confluent relationships between husband and wife, parent and child, boss and underling, when one of them, knowingly or otherwise, breaches the contract terms. The statement by a wife, "I don't know why he left, we never had a fight in all the years we were married!," or a parent, "But he was such a good child, he never talked back!" to a practiced listener suggest a fragile relationship rather than a sturdy one. Continuity does not depend on uninterrupted harmony but is punctuated occasionally by discord.

Two clues to disturbed confluent relationships are frequent feelings of guilt or resentment. When one of the parties to a confluent contract senses that he has violated the confluence, he feels obliged to apologize or to make restitution for his breach-of-contract. He may not know why, but he feels he has transgressed and believes that atonement, punishment or expiation is in order. He may seek this by asking for or meekly submitting to harsh treatment, scolding, or alienation. He may also try to provide this punitive treatment himself by retroflective behavior wherein he deals cruelly with himself by self-degradation, abasement or feeling worthless and bad. Guilt is one of the paramount signs that confluence has been disrupted.

The other party, who feels that he has been transgressed against, experiences righteous indignation and resentment. He is hurt and offended. He has been betrayed, wronged, and sinned against; he has something coming from the offender. He demands that the transgressor shall at least feel guilty for what he has done and that strenuous efforts at apology and reparation shall be made. He, too, can retroflect in an attempt to provide some of what he desires from the other. This is a necessary effort, since his demands, being unrealistic, are often insatiable. So, he feels sorry for himself and indulges in self-pity and commiseration. What a hard life he leads and what an insensitive and unfeeling brute is this person who has just wounded him so. To make his position even more supportable, he makes himself even more miserable and pitiable, which, of course, only makes him more resentful. On and on, endlessly building up in a spiral of misery and recrimination.

An individual may also try to make confluence contracts with society. Since society does not acknowledge such arrangements, he is doomed to dissatisfaction and resentment. As Stephen Crane put it:

> A man said to the universe:
> "Sir, I exist!"
> "However," replied the universe,
> "The fact has not created in me
> A sense of obligation."

So he embarks on his lopsided agreement with society; he will behave, he will conform and do all the things that he thinks society demands, he will not even think thoughts or pursue ideals or goals save those which society approves of or fosters. And for this, because his confluence is a bargain struck up in order to wrest payment in return for performance, he is to be successful, or well-esteemed, or famous, or free from disease, or untroubled by personal difficulties. There is no intrinsic reward in what he does, since his actions are determined by an unknown other who is eventually supposed to make it all worth his while. He doesn't do things just because he likes to; he is not in contact enough with himself to know *when* he likes what he does. He concentrates mostly on knowing whether others like it. So, when the recompense is not forthcoming in sufficient measure, he becomes aggrieved, resentful or suspicious and firmly convinced that "people are just no damned good!" Or he may instead turn against himself and suspect that if he had only tried harder, or if he had not done such-and-such a thing, he would have made it. He assumes that society agreed to the contract and that he is the one who violated its terms. Tragic it is, when he feels that even his best efforts were not enough to win the nebulous prize he had spent his whole life chasing, as witness Willy Loman in Arthur Miller's *Death of a Salesman.*

The antidotes to confluence are contact, differentiation, and articulation. The individual must begin to experience choices, needs, and feelings which are his own and do not have to coincide with those of other people. He must learn that he can face the terror of separation from these people and still remain alive.

Questions like, "What do you feel now?," "What do you want now?," or "What are you doing now?" can help him focus on his own directions. Dealing with the sensations which result from these questions prevents him from buying in on a standard dream package which may or may not suit his needs. Stating his expectations aloud, first to his therapist, perhaps, and finally to the person from whom these satisfaction are demanded, can be the first steps in sorting out covert attempts at confluent relationships.

Portia tried valiantly to live the kind of life her husband

felt was ideal for a good wife and mother, and yet she was throttled by unhappiness. Sam, on his part, worked at providing her generously with material benefits and was a loving and tolerant husband. Nevertheless, Portia was being strangled by the fiction that she and her husband maintained: affirmation should come only from one's husband and family and if a woman got this, she should be satisfied. One afternoon, in response to my question, "What do you feel now?" Portia replied, "I feel like a blob!" She felt that everything she did was in response to other people's needs: chauffeuring her kids and her husband around, going to Sam's flying class when her husband was out of town and taking notes for him and not acting upset about her trouble with one of the kids. To differ with her husband scared her. She would cry and get headaches. As she became aware that she could not accept her husband's standards as her own, Portia began to feel uncomfortably resentful toward Sam and angry with herself for meekly agreeing to these conditions. Every time she complained to him, she would feel even more guilty, as if she were being unreasonably demanding. Sam felt resentful that his love and the material comforts he provided didn't seem to bring her happiness. He also felt guilty because he suspected, having included this in the contract—that somewhere *he* was to blame for not giving her more. Although there was pain in Portia's reiteration to her husband that she needed more, and pain, too, in his hearing her, the two of them began to work out a new style. She entered graduate school and Sam put off taking a job in another city until she could finish her training. When she becomes free to do things merely—merely!—because they delight her, support from others will become the garnish to an otherwise full portion—graceful and pleasing, but not the main source of nourishment.

By attending to one's own needs and articulating them, one can discover what his personal, unique directions may be, and he can get what he wants. He does not have to strike a bargain with some appeased power; he becomes an independent agent, in touch with where he wants to go and how he might go about getting there under his own steam. Since he sets his own goals, he is not indentured and he is free to change and to move, adapting flexibly to his experience in the present moment and not living up to a contract made long ago.

5
The Contact Boundary

Only the being whose otherness, accepted by my being,
lives and faces me in the whole compression of existence, brings the radiance of eternity to me. Only when
two say to one another with all that they are, "It is
Thou," is the indwelling of the Present Being between
them.

MARTIN BUBER

In the womb we had it made. All we had to do was to swim
in the benevolent environment. The catch was that growth
beyond a certain limit put an end to the tenancy; we had to
get out and, willy nilly, learn to make our own way in a less
solicitous world.

Since our umbilicalectomy, each of us has become separate
beings, seeking union with that which is other than ourselves.
Never again can we return to the original symbiotic paradise;
our sense of union depends paradoxically on a heightened sense

of separateness and it is this paradox which we constantly seek to resolve. The function which synthesizes the need for union and for separation is contact. Through contact, each person has the chance to meet the world outside himself nourishingly. Over and over, he makes the contact, each moment's meeting ending immediately and a new moment of contact following upon the heels of the old. I touch you, I talk to you, I smile at you, I see you, I ask you, I receive you, I know you, I want you; all in their turn support vibrancy in living. I am alone, yet to live I must meet you.

All our lives we juggle the balance between freedom or separateness, on the one hand, and entry or union, on the other. Each of us must have some psychological space within which we are our own masters and into which some may be invited but none must invade. Yet if we insist doggedly on our territorial rights, we run the risk of reducing the exciting contact with the "other" and wasting away. Diminution of contactfulness binds man into loneliness. We see all around us how the reduction of contactfulness can choke man into a condition of personal malaise which festers amid a deadening accumulation of habits, admonitions, and customs.

CONTACT

Contact is not just togetherness or joining. It can only happen between separate beings, always requiring independence and always risking capture in the union. At the moment of union, one's fullest sense of his person is swept along into a new creation. I am no longer only me, but me and thee make we. Although me and thee become we in name only, through this naming we gamble with the dissolution of either me or thee. Unless I am experienced in knowing full contact, when I meet you full-eyed, full-bodied and full-minded, you may become irresistible and engulfing. In contacting you, I wager my independent existence, but only through the contact function can the realization of our identities fully develop.

I have a patient whose mother seduced and fucked and went crazy. My patient, a lovely woman, takes herself too seriously and takes me too seriously, too. She is afraid that if she played with me, she, too, would fuck me and go crazy. I don't think that she would go crazy although she might fuck me. Even that is not likely. Certainly it is not *inevitable*. I told her so, and the timing was right for her to believe me. So, she played with me. She smiled playfully. She walked behind my chair and stroked my bald head. She sat in front of me, not two feet away, and her eyes danced and twinkled and I could see that she met me and knew me. Right then. She loved me, meaning that she dug me with twinkle and excitement. We were as close as fucking, but our lives are not arranged for fucking together. It was twinkly to hear her tell me about her daughter and son and the friends who visited over the weekend. So we knew each other, very simply. She left without demand or deprivation. She had feared capture, feared losing herself in the union where her mother had drowned. Fucking was not really *it*. She knows she can fuck with her husband, but she must play and meet with me and many others because life requires contact at all times and in many forms. Even in fucking she wouldn't lose herself—not if she can learn to dig contact as distinct from togetherness or joining.

Perls, Hefferline and Goodman* describe contact:

> . . . fundamentally, an organism lives in its environment by maintaining its differences and more importantly by assimilating the environment to its differences; and it is at (the) boundary that dangers are rejected, obstacles are overcome and the assimilable is selected and appropriated. Now (that) which is selected and assimilated is always novel; the organism persists by assimilating the novel, by change and growth. For instance, food, as Aristotle used to say, is what is 'unlike' that can become 'like';

---

* Perls, F. S., Hefferline, Ralph and Goodman, Paul, *Gestalt Therapy*. New York: Julian Press Inc., 1951.

49789

and in the process of assimilation the organism is in turn changed. Primarily, contact is the awareness of, and behavior toward, the assimilable novelties; and the rejection of the unassimilable novelty. What is pervasive, always the same, or indifferent, is not an object of contact.

Contact is the lifeblood of growth, the means for changing oneself and one's experience of the world. Change is an inescapable product of contact because appropriating the assimilable or rejecting the unassimilable novelty will inevitably lead to change. Now, if my patient assumes and does not question that she is like her mother, she is not contacting either those ways in which she does, indeed, resemble her mother, or even more importantly, those ways in which she is *not* like her mother. If she is willing to contact novelty in her own sense of self, she is more able to change. Contact is implicitly incompatible with remaining the same. Through contact, though, one does not have to *try* to change; change simply occurs.

Naturally, if change is indigenous to contact, one may well be wary about contact unless one has faith in the resulting change. Futuristic thinking, worrying about consequences, or "rehearsing," as Perls* called it, can scare us and like Medusa's head turn us into immobilized stone figures. Nobody likes trouble, and we all know that eventually consequences will require contact as fully as our present experience does. Take my patient. If she fucks, maybe she will indeed go crazy as did her mother. Who can, for certain, say no? But, in a sense, that's the chance we all take in one form or another. Not very secure, of course, unless we have the faith in ourselves which religionists have often asked us to have in God. Trading faith in God for faith in ourselves seems like a fair trade. No guarantees, but then where has God been lately, either?

Contact is not a quality which we are aware of any more than we are aware of the sense of gravity when walking or

---

* Perls, F. S., *Gestalt Therapy Verbatim.* Moab, Utah: Real People Press, 1969.

standing. As we sit and talk to each other, we would be aware
of what we are saying or seeing or hearing, but it is unlikely
that we would think of ourselves as exercising contactfulness,
Our sensory and motor functions are potentially the functions
through which contact is made, but it is important to remember that, just as the whole is more than merely a sum of its
parts, contact is more than the sum of all the possible functions which might go into it. Seeing or hearing are no guarantee of good contact, it is rather *how* one sees or hears that
determines good contact. Furthermore, contact extends into
interaction with inanimate as well as animate objects; to see
a tree or a sunset or to hear a waterfall or a cave's silence is
contact. Contact can also be made with memories and images,
experiencing them sharply and fully.

What distinguishes contact from togetherness or joining
is that contact occurs at a boundary where a sense of separateness is maintained so that union does not threaten to overwhelm
the person. Perls* underlines the dualistic nature of a contactful interaction:

> Wherever and whenever a boundary comes into existence,
> it is felt both as contact and as isolation.

The boundary at which contact can be made is a permeable,
pulsating locus of energy. As Perls, Hefferline and Goodman**
put it:

> . . . the contact boundary is not so much a part of the
> organism as it is essentially *the organ of a particular rela-
> tion of the organism and the environment.*

The contact boundary is the point at which one experiences
the "me" in relation to that which is not "me" and through

---

* Perls, F. S., *Ego, Hunger and Aggression.* London: George
Allen & Unwin Ltd., 1947.
** Perls, F. S., Hefferline, Ralph and Goodman, Paul. *Gestalt
Therapy.* New York: Julian Press Inc., 1951.

this contact, both are more clearly experienced. Perls* observes:

> . . . the boundaries, the places of contact, constitute the Ego. Only where and when the Self meets the "foreign" does the Ego start functioning, come into existence, determine the boundary between the personal and the impersonal "field."

So, contact involves not only a sense of one's self, but also the sense of whatever impinges at this boundary, whatever looms at the contact boundary and even merges into it. Skill at discriminating the universe into self and not-self transforms this paradox into an exciting, choice-making experience. Customary rules are out, and artful decisions become a necessity. Do I affect a friend or let him swim in his own freedom?

If, through considerations like these, we become punctilious about invading another's psychological space, we leave them and ourselves to stew in our own juice. The contradictory results of insisting on the rights of each individual to do his own thing have left many young people today without a sense of trust in or an awareness of the power of their own creative objections to the forces which will undoubtedly press in on them. If one person's freedom depends *exclusively* on another person *allowing* it, he loses his own sense of the power he must exercise in protecting and defining his own psychological space from natural incursions on it. Envisioning a world where freedom to act is bestowed or guaranteed rather than *achieved* is, regrettably, wishful thinking, utopian and non-contactful. Mastery occurs in actual contact and produces liveliness. Contact, however, inherently involves the risk of loss of identity or separateness. In this lies the adventure and the art of contact.

---

* Perls, F. S., *Ego, Hunger and Aggression.* London: George Allen & Unwin Ltd., 1947.

This view of contact has implications which affect the course of psychotherapy.

First, given that we intend to guide people to a recovery of their contact functions, we are likely to have intense interaction experiences in therapy. We do not avoid them. We may even encourage movement into intense experience when this would be in the line of the person's development. In the example given earlier, the woman's need to begin making the discrimination between "me" and "my mother" led to a contactful experience which, importantly, did not swallow her up.

Furthermore, by making contact central, we have given up the traditional psychoanalytic concept of transference, where many therapy interactions were regarded only as distortions based on living in the past, having no current validity of their own. If the patient sees his therapist as disinterested or as an ogre, we have a whole range of alternatives open to us. We may explore how to deal with a disinterested person or with an ogre. We may investigate what the patient sees that produces this impression. We may try to find out where the disinterest lies: is the therapist actually disinterested or is the patient projecting his own disinterest in what he is doing at that moment? Sometimes his view may turn out to be distorted, but even then there is no certainty that the distortion is based on transference from a previous relationship. Sometimes he may see what is really there, that he is indeed boring, or that his therapist is a bit of an ogre, in which case he is learning something he needs to know. In any case, it is up to the patient to discover the reality of the situation through his own action rather than through the therapist's oracular interpretations about how he is really responding to some historical else.

Witness the experience of a lovely young woman, 20 years old, in the center of a group telling about already having been a drug addict and prostitute and, four years earlier, having had a child who had been given up for adoption. Now she was on a new track in life, helping young addicts and going through college herself. In a peak poignant moment, she turned to one of the men in the group and asked him to hold her. He nodded, and after some hesitation, she went over to him and he held her. At this point she let go and cried. After her crying subsided, she looked up, alarmed about what the other women in the group might feel about her being held and being the center of focus in the room. I said that perhaps she could teach the other women something about how to be held. She was obviously at home being held and showed a fluid grace and welcoming quality which wouldn't hurt anyone to learn. For a while, then, she felt calm, remaining in the man's arms but still tuned in to the reactions of the women in the group, who were actually very moved emotionally and were unjudging. She then asked one of the more attractive and guiding women whether she would hold her. The drama was of such force that it was almost inevitable that the woman would indeed want to hold her. She walked over to where the girl was seated and took her into her arms. At this point the final letting go came, and the girl cried more deeply than before. When she was done, her tension had left, she felt unselfconscious and altogether at one with the group.

Here we see a resolution through experience rather than interpretation. Instead of analyzing her feelings about being the center of attention or how women might object to her sexuality or her shame about drug addiction and prostitution, resolution came through actual contacts with people in the room. She told her story *to them*. She moved toward being held. She was held. She relaxed her resistance to contact by allowing herself to be held while she cried, instead of insisting that she could take care of herself since nobody else might want to. Instead of interpreting her anxiety about the women in the room, her contact with them was fostered. Through the contact, release and reunion came.

What value is there in this experience if the insight is not articulated to serve as a guide for further contact? The answer lies in the more self-determined and pervasive sensibilities we hope for the individual to develop. Piaget once remarked that every time we teach a child "the right answer," we prevent him from learning and inventing many new right answers for himself. Action bears the seeds of internal knowing, a knowing that encompasses the stretching of one's boundaries and the awareness which is thus assimilated. Each time the girl above can ask other women for something she needs, or can be comforted by a woman, or has other new experiences with women, her own world will expand in directions which we cannot now identify or predict. Making this experience into an insight is like tying up all the loose ends; tidy perhaps, but leaving no vital connections into new experience.

It may be tempting for the therapist—who, after all, has his own needs for completion and finishing-off—to say the girl needs mothering or has homosexual qualities or wants to show up other women or any of the many explanatory boxes one might want to put her into, but it is presumptuous to imagine that one can capture a sense of her tragic/hopeful life-flow all in one linguistic stroke. We do better to put our faith into each moment of contactfulness, staying attuned to each moment's action and using this momentum to guide us.

A special aspect of contactfulness comes from the possibility of being in contact with oneself. This does not contradict our statement that contact is the meeting function between ourselves and that which is not ourselves. This kind of internal contact can occur, however, because of the human ability to split oneself into the observer and the observed. This split may be employed in the service of growth, a possibility inherent in much self-examination. The athlete, for example, can direct his attention inward so as to get his experience in order before making an athletic move. A speaker may become aware of a distracting mannerism and attend to it. On the other hand, the split may be interruptive, reflexively turning one inward instead of allowing the more pertinent outward focus. The hypochondriac obsessively in touch with his body regards it as an object, however, not as himself.

The special process which permits the individual to make contact with himself can remain oriented solely towards his own self-contained growth or it can serve as a springboard supporting the development of contactful function with another person. Polanyi* describes the way one person can know another through a process he calls "indwelling":

> . . . when we reach the point at which one man knows another man, the knower (so) fully dwells in that which he knows . . . (that) . . . we arrive at the contemplation of a human being as a responsible person, and we apply to him the same standards as we accept for ourselves, our knowledge of him has definitely lost the character of an observation and has become an encounter instead.

The implication here is that sensing the operation of another person's thoughts or feelings is possible to the extent that we have contacted our own operations and can cast ourselves out of this personal concern into the sense of how another person might do the same thing. When a father teaches his son to ride a bike or tie a tie, he goes back to his own motions to develop his sense of what his son might do. In good teaching, the process bounces back and forth between the teacher and pupil. There are times in therapy when the same rhythm is going on.

I-BOUNDARIES

We have emphasized that contact is a dynamic relationship occurring only at the boundaries of two compellingly attractive but clearly differentiated figures of interest. The differentiation can distinguish between one organism and another, or an organism and some inanimate object in its environment, or an

* Polanyi, M., *The Study of Man.* Chicago: The University of Chicago Press, 1959.

organism and some novel quality of itself. Whatever the two differentiated entities may be, they each possess a sense of boundedness, or they could not become figural and contactable. As Von Bertalanffy* has said:

> Any system which can be investigated in its own right must have boundaries, either spatial or dynamic.

The boundaries of the human being, the I-boundaries, are determined by the whole range of his experiences in life and by his built-in capacities for assimilating new or intensified experience.

A person's I-boundary is the boundary of what for him is permissible contactfulness. It is composed of a whole *range* of contact boundaries and defines those actions, ideas, people, values, settings, images, memories, and so on in which he is willing and comparatively free to engage fully with both the world outside himself and the reverberations within himself that this engagement may awaken. It includes also the sense of what risks he is willing to take, where the opportunities for personal enhancement are great but where the consequences may bring on new personal requirements which he may or may not be up to. Some people are exquisitely sensitive in knowing about risks because they seem to live always at what is called the growing edge of their lives. For most people, the need to be able to predict the results of their actions prevents them from easily reaching beyond the existing forms of behavior where the greatest opportunities are present. If they were to venture into unfamiliar territory, while they might gain an increased sense of excitement and power, they might lose their easy understanding and feel unprepared and alien. If confusion is unpermissible, they may chose to be less venturesome; you don't get something for nothing.

---

*Von Bertalanffy, L., *General System Theory*. New York: G. Braziller, 1968.

Within the I-boundary contact may be made with ease and grace and it results in a comfortable sense of gratification and growth. When a skilled mechanic listens to the sound of a malfunctioning motor he moves in on the cause of the trouble and takes care of it. At the I-boundary contact becomes more risky and the likelihood of gratification is less certain. This auto mechanic approaching the motor on an iron lung is at the edge of his knowledge and feels excited and venturesome. Outside the I-boundary, without great extension, contact is well-nigh impossible. This same mechanic may regard making a lacy valentine for his girlfriend as something alien and unthinkable.

Were an individual subjected to great heat, he would soon lose contact by fainting and he might eventually die if his limits for assimilating heat were seriously trespassed. So also in matters psychological. Where the individual is confronted by severe humiliation or other grievous trespasses which exceed the limits of his permissible experience, he may counter the threatened break-in by losing contact. This may run the gamut from loss of consciousness when deeply shocked, as in hearing of a tragic loss, to blocking out the impact of unpermissible experience through more subtle, imperceptible means, like lapses of memory for unpleasant events, as in more chronic resistances.

The selectivity for contact determined by the individual's I-boundary will govern the style of his life, including his choice of friends, work, geography, fantasy, lovemaking, and all the other experiences which are psychologically relevant to his existence. The way a person either blocks out or permits awareness and action at the contact-boundary is his way of maintaining his sense of his own bounded limits. This has primacy in his life beyond any concerns with pleasure or with the future or with practical aspects of what may or may not be good for him, like Henry Clay who would rather have been right than be President.

Although the I-boundary is not rigidly fixed, even in the most inflexible of people, individuals do show great variability in the expansivity or contractibility of their I-boundary. Some people seem to make great changes in their I-boundaries during their lives, and we are likely to think of those with the greatest changes as those who have *grown* the most. This can range all the way from the fortuitous happening, over which they have little control but to which they seem to respond energetically and skillfully, to those changes which their own efforts have produced.

Our society is growth-oriented; we admire those who can pull off the expansive move from one I-boundary to another. We are all familiar with the Horatio Alger story of the poor boy whose early life was limited to small actions within his own neighborhood and who grew to travel the world and influence great people. This is a paper hero. What we find more often, in actual fact, is that within the same individual there will be both the mobilization to grow in some areas and the resistances to growth in others so that parts of the I-boundary have lagged behind. This produces the phenomenon of the industrial executive who never fully believes in his own power and who in his own heart remains the upstart from the wrong side of the tracks. He goes through the motions of power but always feels out of place and limited in engaging contactfully in his work or his life. Because of this contact lag, he gets only reduced liveliness out of what could be an adventurous life or work. The same holds true for the father who still experiences himself as a little boy, or the wife whose sense of herself remains that of a virgin.

When boundaries are rigidly set, the individual's fear of expansion of the I-boundary might be that he will explode because there is too much sensation or excitement for him to contain; he feels in danger of overload. His fear of the contraction of the I-boundary, on the other hand, is fear of feeling empty, deflated or puny in the face of overwhelming pressure from

the outside. In either case, what the individual fears is the rending of the accustomed I-boundary. He may feel that his very
existence is at stake in severe ruptures of the I-boundary, and
the threat of such rending arouses the emergency function of
the individual. The emergency function includes both great
arousal of excitement and its antithesis, the suppression of this
excitement, which is experienced as anxiety. The paradox arises
because the threat to the individual's I-boundary arouses
emergency reactions which are intended to preserve the boundary, but which may themselves be beyond the boundary.
For example, a person who is fired from his job, or passed
over for an expected promotion, experiences a contraction of
his I-boundary; he is cut off from the opportunities he needs
and feels reduced or diminished in scope. Now, if he experiences this as a perilous rupture of his I-boundary, he may be
aroused to defend himself by whatever means he can, perhaps
by striking back at the individual whose low opinion of him
initiated the experience. But if forceful or aggressive striking
back is outside the limits of his boundary, he is left stuck with
the emergency feelings which have been aroused and yet unable
to assimilate them into the contactfulness which might lead to
purposeful action. The anxiety which results from the need to
suppress the excitement is experienced as disruptive and
might result in the inability to concentrate, inefficiency and
vagueness, or even more serious consequences such as psychosis
or suicide.

On the other hand, sometimes life is a quick-change artist,
sweeping an individual up in a rush of events that call forth
a swoosh of delight at the changing boundary. The memory is
clear of a young crippled boy who had spent his life at first
in a wheel chair, then on crutches, and who had finally been
fitted with his first pair of leg braces. He was intoxicated with
his new mobility. Imagine; he was able to move around the
room, standing, and with his hands free to touch anything he

wanted. He would not sit down, so excited was he with his increased freedom!

The gestalt experiment (see Chapter 9) is used to expand the range of the individual, showing him how he can extend his habitual sense of boundary where emergency and excitement exist. A safe emergency is created, one which fosters the development of self-support for new experiences. Actions which were previously alien and resisted can become acceptable expressions and lead to new possibilities.

One man in a weekend workshop had permitted himself to cry unboundedly about a personal sadness. He reported that he literally felt expanded physically, gesturing to a place about two inches beyond himself as where he felt his skin to be. This is a dramatic example of the sense of expansion that a new behavior can produce. He accepted great risk in lowering his barriers to crying. The risk was that he would be left with a continuing not-me experience, unintegrated and isolated, instead of a growing sense of being able to permit new intensities of experience in his life. For this reason, the weekend workshop needs to be expanded into a program which combines a longer period of time to work with the participants individually and within a group, where goals can be developed and a sense of sequential evolution through time can be respected.

As if one's own I-boundaries were not complex enough in contacting novelty in the environment, or unfamiliar or unknown qualities in oneself, when the subtleties of making contact with another person who is juggling a comparable set of needs and resistances are added to this, the complications become awesome. It is rather like asking two people who are trying to pass each other on a tightrope, both of them carrying a long balance-pole, to make meaningful contact with each other. Yet the wonder is, of course, that we somehow manage to do it much of the time.

I want to say hello to Peter. Peter turns away. His reaction implies to me that saying hello might be experienced by him as an invasion. Now, if I wanted to get to him strongly enough I might take the chance of trespassing and being unwelcome. Who knows, he might be glad if I did. On the other hand, he might find me even more noxious and try to get further away. So I have to get to Peter at the right moment and in the right mood for him and for me to make the kind of contact with him that I may have intended. It is a ratio between the ease with which Peter makes himself approachable and the amount of effort I am ready to invest to overcome some difficulties in approaching him. But even if he insists on remaining aloof, I can still make contact with him in his turning away. I can observe and take in some aspect or gesture with which he does this. I can be aware of how uncharacteristic this may be for him to do. I may note some slant of his shoulder or an expression on his face which may bring me very much in contact with Peter, even though this contact is on different terms from my original intention. Given his mood, this may end my contact with him unless I improvise some new contactful action. For example, if in response to his rebuff I scream at him, I continue the flow of contact and create a different sense of contactfulness in him, too.

This ratio between the constantly shifting I-boundaries of different people leaves the development of contact altogether unpredictable. Each person has to become an expert at assessing the possibilities as his wishes and needs unfold with those of others. Some scenes and some people are more fertile ground for making contact. With other people or in other times, the prospects are barren and the pickings are slim.

Artists seem to be especially tuned in to this process in selecting places and people where contact is possible and nourishing. They try to find a milieu that allows or may even evoke the contact which becomes the lifeblood of their creative energies. This is not always a kindly atmosphere: Zola was roused by the moral oppression of 19th century France, Goya by the ironic nature of life in Spain, Gauguin by the idyllic rhythm of the South Seas, and so on. These were not all pleasant subjects, to be sure, but nevertheless something in them was open to the scrutiny of the artist; for him and for none other did the contact result in precisely his perspective.

If I become sensitive enough to good contact, I, too, will go where I can get it. It might be with people who knew me when I was a child, my family perhaps, who talk my language and really know about my life, or this might be the last place to find anything but stereotypy. Perhaps I could find it with lively, swingy young people, or with sage old men, or blond, non-intellectual people. Maybe contact for me would be in speaking to large audiences, or in telling stories to good friends and in listening to theirs, or silently hearing music together, or alone, or cooking good food, or playing a rough game of paddleball. There may be some few people for whom circumstances play little or no part in determining the quality of their contactfulness. For most of us, though, continuing good contact is a process of ebb and flow, a sensitive ratio of energy between the contactor and the contacted.

For this reason emphasis is placed on the power of the individual to create his own life, and this *includes* the power to recognize the suitability of his environment. This means that he has choice of people, activities, geography, architecture, and the like. No one's power for making contact can be entirely independent of his choice of environments or his creation of new environments. Prison uprisings, student strikes and cries for reform in mental hospitals force us to recognize the importance that the environment plays in shaping the behavior of the people who are bottled up in these institutions, usually through little choice of their own, which only amplifies the problem. We are just beginning to spell out "The relationship between the physical environment—particularly the man-made environment—and human experience and behavior. . . ."* We have to work harder to make contact with a dry tasteless piece of bread in a dusty, crowded factory lunchroom than with a fragrant crusty hunk of homemade bread in a friend's kitchen.

So, too, a sour and stereotyped person will neither arouse nor support good contact as a sparkly, open person might. There are some people who encourage others to explore their newness and to interact with them, and both of them grow thereby. There are others who remain closed off, allowing only minimal contact at the I-boundaries, maintaining separateness and permitting no growth. What more people need is to become experts, artists if you will, at sensing and creating environments where movement outside their present I-boundaries can be supported or in leaving or altering those environments where this seems impossible.

Experience of the I-boundary can be described from several vantage points. These are: body-boundaries; value-boundaries; familiarity-boundaries; expressive-boundaries, and exposure-boundaries.

BODY-BOUNDARIES

People play favorites with their bodies. The awareness of sensation of some parts or functions of their bodies is restricted or placed off-limits and remains outside their sense of themselves. Now, since that which is outside the I-boundary is well-nigh impossible to contact, the result is that these people remain out of contact with important parts of themselves.

One man in a workshop complained of being impotent. In working together, it became apparent that he experienced very little sensation below the neck. His head was his center and it was clear that if he could only screw with his head, he wouldn't be in trouble. Even his rage was limited to his head, where he would redden deeply. As he got angrier, he growled

---

* Proshansky, H. M., Ittelson, W. H., and Rivlin, L. G., Eds., *Environmental Psychology*. New York: Holt, Rinehart & Winston, 1970.

and screamed like a man possessed, but even so he could at first only feel the effects down to his chest. After considerable focusing on his body, with some attention to his pelvic movements, his legs began to tremble. He became frightened when he began to feel the imminence of pelvic sensation and wouldn't let this develop any further. Nevertheless, the result of the trembling sensation in his legs was an unfamiliar radiance and sense of peacefulness throughout his body. Though not completing his work, he did extend his range of body sensations, changing his previous body-boundary.

Beatrice was having trouble making contact with the rest of the people in her group. She started sentences only to let them dwindle off, and her group was left guessing about what she was trying to say. They didn't want to hurt her, but they couldn't feel very strongly one way or another about her because she seemed so insubstantial to them. In one of the earlier sessions, while exploring body sensation, Beatrice had noted with surprise that she experienced no sensation of the back of her head. She had no sensation of anything but the front of her, the facade. She was aware of her face and of feelings in her chest, but experienced no sensation along the back of her body.

I asked Beatrice to sit on the floor opposite Todd and to talk to him. I told her to really push against him every time she said something to him. It soon became apparent, though, that every time she shoved him she interrupted the full force of her shove somewhere between her shoulder and her elbow. I askd them both to stand up and continue talking and shoving. Beatrice pushed against Todd again, but this time only with her fingertips. I then taught her how to use her whole body. Then she used the heels of her hands and pushed harder. I asked her to look at Todd as she pushed and to make sure that she pushed against him hard enough to cause some kind of movement in him. Finally she began to put her whole body, not just the front of it, into the contact. She dug her heels

more firmly into the floor, put her head down and used her
back, thighs and rear end. At this point she started holding
back with her pelvis and I asked her to put her pelvis into the
action against him. After a few minutes of a very athletic
exchange she became aware, as had we all, that she was experiencing the *back* of her for the first time. At that point her
face became dramatically different. Gone was her previous
characteristic expression of the frozen, trusting smile. In its
place was the face of a woman without a preset expression
and who might become either cheerful or sad. The facade was
gone and the group could feel a new substantiality, the substantiality of a person who could "get behind" something she
would say.

VALUE-BOUNDARIES

One patient, a 16-year-old boy, believes that being interested is crucial to man's existence in general, and to his own
in particular. Now his school, on the other hand, requires him
to do things which are not interesting. He is unwilling to un-
dermine or betray his values by doing this uninteresting work,
so he is barely getting by in school with a pretty good chance
that he might flunk out. His value-boundary seemed rigidly
established, perhaps necessarily so because of the pressures
around him to give up his own standards. But the problem
becomes one where he is limited because he allows no room
to make contact with him unless one is functioning within *his*
I-boundary.

The fact is, though, that other values co-exist with the
priority he places on being interested. He likes auto mechanics
even though he doesn't feel that he could remain interested
for many years in the work an auto mechanic does. He would
like, he thinks, to be an aeronautical engineer or possibly an
architect. Clearly, in order to satisfy these preferences he

would have to plow through some material which would be less than interesting to get to what really interests him. But he has freaked out of learning because his rigid adherence to his value system has deprived him of making the discriminations necessary to get what he needs.

So, he must learn to stretch his value-boundaries to include perhaps self-determination, perhaps preparing the ground for doing exciting work, and other values which, when included within his value-boundary, would open the way for creative resolution of what now seem to be incompatible values. He could start by really doing at least those things that interest him rather than settling for a blanket cop-out. He could, for example, take a course in auto mechanics, which he did. He could go to the library, a therapy assignment, and leaf through books—each only as long as he wanted to—which he did. He could talk to some of the students in school who would be interested in talking about things he liked to talk about, which he did. He started going with a girl, basically friendly to his position, who was seriously interested in her own school work. All of these influences loosened his value-system and opened possibilities for expanding his world. Previously incompatible values vied for position and required the development of a self-determined program where, although he still had to cope with the existing system, he did not merely resign himself to it. He did not have to give up his esteem for living interestingly, but he was no longer stuck with the boredom of mere recalcitrance. The expansion of his value-boundary provided new support for action and offered some alternatives to his stereotyped existence. With a *range* of values available to him, he could develop the energy to match his own ingenuity and enterprise against the counterposed energy of "the system." This doesn't mean he approves of it, but he has learned how to get from it what he needs to live his life in a more flexible way.

FAMILIARITY-BOUNDARIES

One family had been going to Vermont every summer for 15 years before discovering that the mother had *never* wanted to go, the children have not wanted to go for the past five years, and only the father still considered it unthinkable that they should go anywhere else. The father was not an autocratic bully; it was just that the familiar had such momentum going for it that it would have taken more energy to interrupt the pattern than any member of the family had been able to muster. Each knew of his own resistance, but the sweep of the familiar pulled them into its orbit.

Shakespeare knew only too well how we cling to what we know rather than venture into the unfamiliar:

> ... Who would these fardels bear
> To grunt and sweat under a weary life,
> But that the dread of something after death—
> The undiscover'd country, from whose bourne
> No traveller returns—puzzles the will,
> And makes us rather bear those ills we have
> Than fly to others that we know not of?

Not only death but change itself calls forth terror and makes some people restrict themselves to functioning in limiting but familiar settings. For these people, change of job, of significant people in their lives or of their relationships with them, as when children grow up or parents get older, are exceedingly difficult transitions. I-am-what-I-am gets hardened into I-am-what-I-have-always-been-and-what-I-always-will-be.

It is not only fear of the unknown that sets our familiarity-boundaries for us. Opportunity lets us experience only a small portion of the possible in our lives; limits of either geography or time restrict contact with the new or unfamiliar. These boundaries are inevitable and are only partly removed through travel, reading, and meeting other people with different modes of living. But the boundary that we set as the line of demarcation between ourselves and the unfamiliar which we *refuse* to contact even though the opportunity may exist, is a limit we have placed on ourselves.

One man was talking in a group about the impending break-up of his marriage and his considerable turmoil and anxiety about it. He wanted to maintain the marriage at almost any cost because he hoped that his wife would once again want to be married to him, although it was doubtful that she ever would. As he talked, his main concerns turned out to be centered around his image of himself, his image of marriage, and his image of his work. He is a minister and his image of a minister is that he does not get divorced. He also believes, possibly rightly, that his congregation and his church feel that a minister should not be divorced. Now although images are a convenient synopsis of a person's nature, they are vulnerable to distortions and oversimplifications that may rob him of much individual freedom to act. So, the troubled minister's question was, "If I am not a husband or father or minister, what am I?" and he answered himself, "I am therefore nothing!" For him there was either the familiar or there was Nothing; and Nothing was disaster.

Disaster does not come so easily, though, for those people who are willing to move through the transition from what looks like the catastrophic dissolution of the familiar into the inchoate. One's future welfare often travels in disguise and its blessings are frequently recognized only after extensive turmoil, when finally one may say my divorce or quitting my father's business or even, alas, my heart attack was the best thing that ever happened to me. One of the difficulties in moving out of the familiar is the temptation to close off the full drama of change before its own attractions have a chance to ripen. The sense of being bereft of all that is familiar is a vacuum which threatens to suck up everything within its reach. What is hard to appreciate, when terror shapes a catastrophic gap, is that this blankness can be a fertile void. The fertile void is the existential metaphor for giving up the familiar supports of the present and trusting the momentum of life to produce new opportunities and vistas. The acrobat who swings from one trapeze to the next knows just when he must let go. He gauges his release exquisitely and for a moment he has nothing for him but his own momentum. Our hearts follow his arc and we love him for risking the unsupported moment.

EXPRESSIVE-BOUNDARIES

Taboos against expressive behavior begin early. Don't touch, don't fidget, don't cry, don't masturbate, don't pee; and so the boundaries are delineated. What began in childhood is continued as we grow up, only even more subtly than the original don'ts. We become more inclusive, even finding new situations where the early prohibitions can apply. The simple little childhood scenes which were involved in the boundary-setting no longer exist, but only the details change. For example, prohibition against masturbation—touching oneself lovingly—winds up as a boundary which excludes touching anybody lovingly. Consequently, when the child grows up his love-making as a man is conservative and limited. As a father, he touches his children only when he has to and when a friend is crying he keeps his distance. In fact, even if he is the person crying, his resistance to touching may prevent him from getting the support that the closeness of another person could give him. As loving as he may be, touching is excluded for him as a means of expressing his affection.

The setting of expressive limits is clear in the story of a young woman of 21. Jennifer is a model for teen-age fashions. She started modeling when she was in her early teens. She is still very young-looking and of slight build. She has hung on to her teen-ageness as long as she could, not even knowing how fully she has succeeded. In addition to modeling, though, Jennifer wanted also to be a singer. Here, however, she was not as successful. Her voice had a light, "white" tonal quality and it lacked the body and maturity that a woman's voice would have; at 21 she was still singing like a teen-ager. Her inhibition against mature expression, because it got in the way of her modeling career, was inadvertently wrecking her chances as a singer.

A minister was planning to give a sermon on the black-white disturbances in Selma, Alabama, where police dogs had been called out against black demonstrators. I asked him to practice giving the sermon to me, and no wonder he was worried—it was a bore! I asked him to do it again, only this time to tell it as though he were one of the Alabama policemen. In this role he told the story differently. His voice was louder and more resonant, more confident. He used anecdotes, his face flushed, and he used his fists. Then I asked him to tell his story once more, but this time to express his own position while using the style and delivery of the policeman. This time he gave a fine sermon, which reached me and later his congregation. During this process of working-through he remembered that as a child he had always admired the bullies in his school. True, they had repeatedly attacked him about being a sissy and had taken advantage of his physical limitations. But they always seemed secure and energetic, so they were the good guys. He had adopted the moral position of the victim; right, righteous, with justice on his side, but with no vigor and doomed to failure. Bully equalled vitality, but he was no bully, so vitality equalled not him. Expansion of his expressive-boundary compelled him to know that *he*, although not a bully, could equal vitality and that he could give back to the bully as much as he had been accustomed to receiving.

It is frightening to push out the boundaries that we set for ourselves. The threat is that we would lose our identity, and in a sense this is true, since we inevitably lose the identity that we once had. Our evolving identity is what we need to discover. The self is not a structure, it is a process. In the act of dismantling old expressive-boundaries it is possible to move on to an expanded sense of self. Jennifer was ready for the mature voice. She is ready to become more than the teen-age expressive-boundaries allow. The minister is more than merely righteous in the service of a lost cause; he can be forceful and aggressive, once he accepts this as within his scope.

EXPOSURE-BOUNDARIES

There is considerable inter-relationship among the various forms of I-boundaries. What may begin as an unwillingness to express oneself can become so habitual that even when the expressive taboo disappears, the familiarity-boundary takes over and continues the taboo.

The exposure-boundary also shares common ground with all the other boundaries. Here, however, the specific reluctance is to being observed or recognized. An individual may know what he values and may have no objection to taking his stand. He may express it and even take the action appropriate to it, but he insists on doing this privately or anonymously. He may criticize anonymously or be generous in an anonymous fashion. He is unwilling to accept the notice of others beyond the boundaries he sets up. Other people may not want to be identified as cruel, seductive, critical, manipulative, sentimental, demanding, naive, aggressive, inexperienced, ad infinitum. Exposure is dangerous, whether it be exposure to the elements or exposure to the scorn or demands of others.

One woman was asked about her experience in a weekend workshop by another member of her weekly therapy group. Irene spoke brightly of the new exercises they had tried and some of the innovative activities they had been involved in and the results she had observed. It sounded great, a 100% delight. As she went on, however, people remarked that her response was more than they had expected, gift-wrapped, and presented with a flourish. Irene admitted then that the weekend had, in fact, not been without difficulty for her. She had tripped and cut a large gash in her forehead which had required stitches and she had been in considerable discomfort over the weekend. Finally she began to cry and was able to recognize how resistant she was to exposing her suffering. She dreads pity; she likes to be thought of as bright and gay. This time, however, Irene was able to receive the sympathy and understanding of the rest of the group without feeling threatened or diminished.

Psychotherapy has made a big deal of guaranteeing freedom from exposure to anyone except the therapist or other members of the group. Confidentiality is accorded as a guarantee against premature exposure of oneself. The individual is assured that he will not be exposed in any *but* the contracted situation. Many private therapy groups spend some time discussing their wishes about confidentiality. No one can guarantee that people in a group, inexperienced in maintaining confidentiality, can be altogether reliable in their sense of what is confidential material and what is not. Nevertheless, they usually arrive at some understanding that what goes on in the group will at least not be capriciously talked about elsewhere and there is often the promise not to mention names or to talk to anyone but spouses about it. Sometimes the issue of confidentiality can lead to laughable situations as when one group member told another that she had seen her at a concert, but had not known whether to come up and say hello because it might be a give-away that they were both members of the same psychotherapy group!

Many people need these assurances or at least want them. The need to work out one's problems at one's own pace and in an arena of one's own choosing must be respected. It is clear, though, that when an individual can come to accept himself in all his various manifestations, his concern about public exposure is reduced. When he himself is not embarrassed or ashamed of being in therapy, he is less likely to care who else knows about it. Acceptability which is obtained by covering up one's actual characteristics is a tenuous kind of acceptability at best.

Some people are questioning the wisdom of confidentiality. Carl Whitaker* has spoken of the importance of returning people in therapy to the communal engagement. He has described community therapy where neighbors as well as family have been invited to share in the therapy sessions. Mowrer** has long advocated the communal confession. Primitive tribes carry out their forms of psychotherapy and exploration of dreams and fantasies with whole families and members of the community present.***

Another element related to the development of the exposure-boundary is the way in which exhibitionism enters into personal growth. The semanticists**** have described various kinds of expression: blocked, inhibited, exhibitionistic, and spontaneous. The blocked and inhibited stages are non-expressive. In the former the person does not even know what he wants to express and in the latter he knows but won't express it. The third, exhibitionistic, stage is reached when the person does express what he wants to, although he has not integrated or assimilated the expression fully into his system. The spontaneous stage comes when the individual expresses what he wants with full engagement and the expression is compatible and assimilated with his wants.

It is during the third stage, the exhibitionistic, where awkwardness and even phoniness of expression may occur. This is frequently a necessary and unavoidable stage because a person

---

* Whitaker, Carl, in a speech given at the Gestalt Institute of Cleveland, 1968.

** Mowrer, O. H., *The Crisis in Psychiatry & Religion*. Princeton, New Jersey: Van Nostrand, 1961.

*** Latner, J., Unpublished Ph.D. Dissertation, California School of Prof. Psychology. San Francisco, 1972.

**** Korzybski, Alfred, *Science and Sanity*. Lancaster, Pa.: International Non-Aristotelian Library, 1933.

who is learning new expressions cannot wait until he has fully assimilated them before trying them out. If he insists, because of compulsive integrity or the need to avoid being clumsy, he might wait a long time before the ideal integration comes. Indeed, it might never come because one does not simply and uniformly move into grace from a blocked or inhibited position.

Nevertheless, exhibiting oneself as angry or loving or sad is not the same as fully *being* angry, loving or sad. Usually, exposure consists not only of the *willingness* finally to take a certain action, but also exposure of the historic *reluctance* to do so. So the first steps cannot be the pure and authentic acts of someone who knows well and endorses what he is doing. Consequently, there is a difference between the excesses and awkwardness of the exhibitionistic phase and the grace and credibility of the spontaneous. Connoisseurs of behavior can tell the difference, just as connoisseurs of wine can make their distinctions. Many a new development has gotten stuck here, nipped in the bud and not permitted the workthrough into spontaneity.

The therapy process, with its stimulation of new behaviors, is vulnerable to exhibitionism and with its emphasis on authenticity it is also critical of it.

This dilemma is as unavoidable as it is regrettable. New and previously unassimilated behaviors do become attractive and possible. A timid person pressed by others to reach out and hug someone may indeed be breaking into a new willingness to experience intimacy. At the same time, though, he may only be playing a new game, partly brash, partly shy, partly intimidated, feeling ludicrous and temporarily suspending his personal integrity. Some willingness to accept the inauthentic and awkward moments is indispensable to growth. Sometimes this is one of the greatest gifts other group members can offer to someone who is making the beginning steps in the direction he wants to follow.

We must, however, be aware of these moments as only a part of the process of expanding one's I-boundaries and not the completed development. Clearing one's throat before speaking may be necessary, but it is not a substitute for speaking.

6

The Contact Functions

Wine comes in at the mouth
And love comes in at the eye;
That's all we shall know for truth
Before we grow old and die.
I lift the glass to my mouth,
I look at you, and I sigh.

W. B. YEATS

Contact is vitalizing. Michelangelo knew this when in the Sistine Chapel he painted Adam about to be charged into life. Adam waits languidly for God's contact to touch him into lively existence. One can feel the drama of God's approach as His extended forefinger reaches for Adam. In symbolizing the divine power, Michelangelo has succeeded in portraying how primary and potent is the touching contact between one being and another.

Our language acknowledges that touch is prototypical of

contact. We get "in touch" with someone; we hear or see something so moving that we are "touched" by it; when we have affected someone enough for him to lend us some money, we have "put the touch on him." For us, contact has almost come to *mean* touch.

Intuitively we are close to the truth. Contactful experiences, even though they may center around one of the other four senses, still involve being touched. Seeing, for example, is being touched by light waves. You have only to imagine looking directly at the bright sun to sense how impactful this can be —imagine looking directly at another person having such an impact! Hearing is being touched, along the basilar membrane, by sound waves; smelling and tasting are being touched by chemicals, either gaseous or in solution.

Because of the preeminence of contiguity in contact, it is tempting to give highest priority to touch itself, thereby devaluing that contact which can be made through space. Hitting, stroking, holding, patting, etc., are among the most obvious ways of reaching people quickly and powerfully. Nevertheless, the opportunities for reaching people through space, as by talking, seeing and hearing, are certainly more abundantly available than touching, even in ideal interpersonal situations. The discovery that a well-placed word can be as touching as a physical stroke expands the luster of everyday communications. But these are subtle influences, requiring that the person tune in more attentively to his own sensations. In order for the non-contiguous contact modes to have the same impactfulness as touch, the individual has to provide resonance. It is this capacity to resound to one's experience that enables one individual to respond contactfully and another to deaden what looks like events of comparable intensity or poignancy.

Added to these basic five contact modes are two more: talking and moving. These seven processes are the contact functions. It is through these functions that contact may be achieved, and it is through the corruption of these functions that contact may be blocked or avoided. It is important, though, to remember that while we may describe seven different contact functions, once contact is made it is the same for all; a charge of excitement exists within the individual which culminates in a sense of full engagement with whatever is interesting at that moment. He may sometimes experience having made "contact." Most of the time such focus is irrelevant and the free flow of contactfulness is experienced simply as a richness in living. Contactfulness may not necessarily lead to happiness—many contacts are indeed unhappy ones—but it is an essential component of one's humanity. Just the dread of unhappiness is often enough to make an individual curtail his contactfulness in order to preserve his "happiness." The trouble is that this is another one of those Faustian bargains, paid for finally by the damnation of ineffectuality and ennui.

All the contact functions are vulnerable to diminished impact, either through personal distancing such as inertia or disinterest, or because of inescapable technical developments. Foods are often wrapped or packaged so that one cannot see them but can only buy a picture of a peach or a tomato or, worse yet, the words telling what is inside. If one *can* see, foods are still either in glass or in cellophane; it is healthier not to touch. Lemons come in packages of six, dried fruit huddle together under their plastic bag, and even fish rest odoriferously demure under their clear wrappings. In factories gauges are indispensable for making quick judgments under dangerous or expensive conditions. Air conditioning makes one wish to be dressed more warmly in the heat of summer. Even on highways a good sense of direction is useless when travel is determined by road signs and one is often directed, like Columbus, to turn east in order to proceed west; a cloverleaf is the shortest distance between two points. On the telephone one's orientation for contact includes only the power to listen and the pungency of talk.

No sense in crying over spilt milk, we must develop new

facilities for contact. Contact is not prejudicial to any age. It is a contemporaneous function with each age carving out its own styles. The pervasive effect of "progress" is that it sweeps people into styles of behavior which are partly the consequences of the new technologies. Georges Simenon* observed that Dostoevsky and Tolstoy, were they writing today, might write much shorter novels. They would not need to describe in such detail something that their readers may have just seen on television. This is an oversimplification but surely we need not seek simply to continue the old ways. The new ways can still permit good contact if we can move into the directions that they open up.

For example, the washing machine replaced what was surely a more intimate relationship with the rough-ribbed washboard which a woman could really feel as she scrubbed her clothes. Most women who have made this transition from their washboards, however, feel they are much better occupied somewhere else, doing things they prefer doing. But for a woman who has not known this particular evolution, the modern washing machine may present a new snare. She must transcend its deadingly impersonal effect. When you play with a machine it may make a machine out of you. Can she transfer the vigor her predecessor used at the washboard to her current activities, or does she bring to those activities the same efficient insensitivity it takes her to get her wash done? Riding freeways is part of the same package. Granted that it creates a great high-speed blur of distance, yet it makes visiting easier, more effortless, less exhausting than in the horse-and-buggy days. Furthermore, and this is crucial, the opportunity for contact on the superhighway may be as exciting as the slow buggyride through the sparsely travelled countryside. Some of the grandest beauties of our age are the highways as they cut through mountains and hills, carving out a form of landscape filled with

---

*Simenon interview in *New York Times* Book Review Section, p. 4, Oct. 24, 1971.

color, texture, movement, proportion and shape which are different from before. The scale changes, but native contact remains always an enlivening prospect. Surely the view of clouds from an airplane is a majestic experience even though the passenger is encapsulated in his seat. The washboard could be depersonalizing in its own way too. In the eye of the beholder. . . .

LOOKING

Try this: look at this book you are reading, at this very page. See the relation of print to the whiteness of the page. See how the margins frame the darker section of print. Notice the texture of the paper and the shape of the letters. Try to see the rows of letters as horizontal lines rather than words to be understood. See how the shadow of the light by which you have been reading falls across the page, cutting a diagonal, perhaps, across the insistent horizontal of the print. Turn the page so that these are now vertical lines and not so tempting for you to read.

Now, if these words have caught you at the right moment and if you can permit yourself the time to make this shift in focus, you will have a brief visual treat which is not much in itself but which could clue you in to the power inherent in the raw visual experience. This power is lovingly described by Joyce Cary:*

> I remember one of my children, as a baby of about fourteen months, sitting in its pram watching a newspaper on the grass close by. There was a breeze along the ground and the newspaper was moving. Sometimes the top page swelled up and fluttered; sometimes two or three pages were moved and seemed to struggle together; sometimes the whole paper rose up on one side and flapped awkwardly for a few feet before tumbling down again. The child did not know that this object was a newspaper moved

* Cary, Joyce, *Art and Reality*. New York: Doubleday, 1961.

by the wind. It was watching with intense absorbed curiosity a creature entirely new to its experience, and through the child's eyes I had a pure intuition of the newspaper as object, as an individual thing at a specific moment.

Naturally, such visual contactfulness is not always in high priority as of course it would not be if you are reading this book for content. Seeing, in that case, becomes an intermediate form of contact which facilitates the contact with the ideas or concepts which we are concerned to understand. Only the rare person, or one blessed with enough leisure, can respond unstintingly to the whole range of contactful opportunities which may exist at any moment. Mostly, we construct levels of priorities for ourselves according to situation and motive. But any time we elect to shift priorities we can experience an exciting sense of choice and we become effervescent people open to change from one possible mode of contact to another. Right now, having looked at the page as an experience of its own rather than as a conveyor of information, you may experience a flavor in reading which was lacking before you included the visual quality of the page into your reading.

We can discern here two types of looking, and this dichotomy applies also to the other contact functions. One of these is evidential contact, where looking provides us with orientation for events or actions which reach beyond the act of looking itself. The other is contact-for-its-own-sake.

When evidential contact predominates, life becomes very practical. I see the typewriter *so that* I can type, I look at my friend as I talk to him *because* I must know whether he is still there or still interested. This evidential function is obviously crucial to existence. A blind man is handicapped not only because he will not know the enlivenment of visual experiences, but also because it becomes very hard to do many things unaided or without visual feedback.

Many of us, although we are well enough equipped for

evidential contact, are nevertheless contact-blind in that seeing, *qua seeing*, is of low importance to us. This reduces excitement in life and probably may even reduce the evidential contact as well. All functions need to exist for their own sake in addition to serving merely practical purposes. So those who delight in seeing are likely to be more alert and sensitive when it comes to seeing evidentially also.

Seeing is not, however, always an unalloyed delight. Sometimes the feelings which accompany or result from seeing may be unmanageable. As the following example shows, there are dangerous choices to be made when a person's ability to assimilate what he may see is borderline and he is running the risk of psychological overload.

Sid, a 47-year-old man, suffered from chronic anxiety almost crippling in intensity. He was rarely free of it, although he nevertheless managed to carry on his work. He engaged in very active ruminations which usually served to rob him of basic experiences of contact and were partly an attempt to distract himself from the pain of his raw anxiety. For a long time in his therapy he was unable to look at me except sideways, almost as though he merely wanted briefly to confirm that I was still there. Gradually, I tried to bring Sid into visual contact with me through simple questions about what he saw when he looked at me, through exercising his powers of looking at objects in the room, and through homework assignments directing him to look at people and objects when he was away from the therapy scene. One day he was able to look at me while talking to me, and his eyes lit up! For the first time it became very evident that he was talking to *me* and furthermore that he *wanted* to be talking to me. At this point Sid recalled an old experience. In his early college days he would get crushes on his teachers very readily, and he had become especially enamoured of one in particular. Whatever the excitement meant, be it homosexual or hero-worship, he was filled with more of it than he could handle. One day Sid went up to this man after class to ask him a question. He saw the man's face clearly and the joy of this sight started to flood him; Sid had to cut off the experience not through decision but reflexively. He described how, at the moment of reflexive interruption, the "gestalt" of the man's face broke up. He could then see only the man's mouth, his eyes, his nose, all as separate entities rather than as parts of a configuration. He became panicky and tongue-tied and began to ruminate, trying futilely to discover the meaning of the face and the implications of the fact that the face was unified at one moment and fell apart the very next. His ruminations took over and he could not recover the basic experience that had started the panic. He had to leave. He went back later to see this professor, who had only a few minutes to spend with him and abruptly sent Sid off to a psychiatrist. Shortly after this he broke down and had to leave school, returning after a year to complete his education. For the first time since then, his experience of me reminded him of his earlier experience, but this time, although he again lighted up in liveliness, he was able to assimilate the intensity of his inner sensations and instead of feeling the threat he felt pleasure and friendship.

Plainly, the assimilation of visual experience is hardly something to be taken for granted. Though most people do not encounter such dramatic effects as this man did, wariness about visual experience is pervasive in our culture. A simple example is the overloading that comes from fright; we have probably all had the experience of closing our eyes or averting our gaze during a particularly scary episode in a horror movie. We bind up a lot of energy into deflections like these as ways of taking the edge off much personal contact.

Looking away is, of course, only one way to deflect visual contact. Staring is the polar blockage, going to the opposite extreme and enabling the individual to block contact through rigidifying the ocular musculature. Staring gives the impression of a person engaged in intense contact, but actually it is deadened contact, as when the arm grows numb after holding onto something tightly for a long time, or the foot falls asleep after being in the same position for a while. The difference between the direct, open-eyed look of the child who gazes intently and with fascination and the stare is that the child *sees* and the starer is only hanging on to seeing. The starer is poised to see but never really accomplishes it. His eyes are unmoved and unresponsive; effervescence is missing and all sense of vibrancy and attraction of the visual object is drained. The person being stared at feels pressed against the wall and feels the need to escape. Staring is the visual equivalent of saying the same words over and over again until they become gibberish and lose their impact.

The basic resolution for staring is, naturally, to recover the willingness to see and to feel the effects of looking. Learning to see the therapist is an aid in this process. The patient must be able, and so must the therapist, to probe the range of visual possibilities that is his therapist. He must be willing to see the kind eyes, the cruel jaw, the grace, the avaricious mouth, the playful gesture, the puzzled expression, the disdainful sneer. Whatever exists, he must learn it is his right to see. And from this he learns that to open his eyes is to count as a unit of one, also—to be seen as well. The eyes that are tightened against crying, for example, and which prevent anyone seeing into them or seeing what might even be behind them, these eyes can finally weep and the tightened muscles can yield to seeing and being seen again. Or the timid eyes, emboldened at last to see what is forbidden, become aroused to look at a whole kaleidoscope of stimulating sights.

Although the basics of seeing are imbedded in the total personal system of the individual, there are some fairly simple therapeutic techniques which may help to recover the willingness to see. One exercise is to open the eyes wide and then close them tightly alternately for ten or fifteen times. The eyes will become loosened by this process and give the individual a sense of how differently his eyes *might* feel to him and how differently he *might* see. This could be enough to activate him to discover his own looking appetite or to become less frightened when the arousal to see occurs next time.

Looking from side to side, without moving one's head is another useful exercise. Often contact-blindness takes the form of tunnel vision, where one sees only what is directly ahead, much as the blinders on the side of a horse's head permit him to move undistractedly forward. Looking at objects in the therapist's office may bring on considerable surprise; frequently, the patient will see virtually nothing in the office *but* the therapist. Looking around seems irrelevant to some people who are like efficiency experts wasting no energy on anything but the immediately defined target. Such "waste" is indispensable, though. There is no way to fix one's attention solely on the "relevant" without sacrificing the sense of context which completes the scene. In fact, certain experiments* have suggested that movement and flux are natural eye activities in good perception. The relationship of the figure—the therapist, his posture, his expression, his clothes—to his surroundings—the chair he is sitting in, how his office is decorated, the lighting which reveals or obscures him from view—is a lubricating influence on the subsequent interactions with him. Context gives dimension and resonance to experience, expanding into what went before and what may follow the present scene. Rigid adherence to figure dries out the interaction because it is a force acting merely strategically and against its own nature. Nature is generous, nay, prodigal and the accompanying "inefficiency or waste" is a by-product of spontaneity. For a sense of freshness in living this generosity may be more efficient in the long run than the efficiency which weeds out the inevitable oscillations in the relevant/irrelevant cycle.

---

* Marshall, W. H. and Talbot, S. A., Recent evidence for neural mechanisms in vision leading to a general theory of sensory acuity. In *Biological Symposia*, VII:117-64; 1942.

LISTENING

"How can you sit there listening to people all day?" some-one asks the therapist. "Who listens?" he explains.

This exchange reveals the sentiment, commonly held, that listening as an act of its own, unrelated to other forms of ex-perience, becomes a bore and an intolerable effort even when you are paid to do it. Listening can, however, be a very active, open process. Someone who is actually listening is avidly re-ceiving the sounds that enter into him—at a concert, for example. This is a lovely process which is all too frequently bypassed as second rate compared with the more obviously active behavior of talking or making other sounds.

The implication is that the action is held in abeyance while listening, that one is ceding the floor or the podium only until his turn comes to take the active role. This is inevitable partly because of the reciprocal nature of talking and listening. One cannot continue to listen to another person if one is talk-ing also. The pattern is something like this: my friend has something to say which he hasn't yet completed but my quick reactivity has already zeroed in on something that stimulates me to respond. Now, I have the choice of responding right then or holding the response in abeyance until he has finished what he wanted to say. If I interrupt him, I risk his displeasure as well as getting only an incomplete version of what he was telling me. Interruptions would become chaotic, and chaos is not one of the favorite conditions in a society where time-binds cause us to lose faith in the resolution of chaos. So, people are brought up not to interrupt, learning to listen to each other mostly by trying to keep both parts of themselves going—the listener and the interrupter. People usually settle for giving the appearance of listening while in reality they are just biding their time, waiting for a chance to speak.

Consequently, given its second-class citizenship, listening is not held in great esteem except for condescending lip service to the piety that certain people are "good listeners." This is not unlike the praise given to the woman who, though not very knowledgeable or skillful in worldly matters or in her own creativity, is described as a good homemaker or mother. Not that these are not estimable virtues; it is nice that somebody does this or where would the home be. But many women will testify that this is just another example of the at-least syndrome, where damning with faint praise is only a thin cover-up for disrespect. Naturally, listening is not enough if it is used only for orientation to the position of another person rather than as part of the total charge of excitement, composing its rhythmic engagement with action. But, as orientation it is basic to consequent action.

The difficulties in beating out the rhythm between listening and talking become evident in any conversation where the viewpoint of at least one of the participants is pre-established or where his requirements from the conversation are predetermined. Hidden agenda like this will always interfere with full listening. A person not only exercises selectivity over what he will or will not say but also over what he will or will not hear. Thus, the individual who expects criticism may specialize in hearing that and very little else. Another may hear only what he can accept as favorable and criticism slides by him unheard. To the degree that these predetermined selections interfere with direct distening, the individual's contactfulness is of course limited.

Each individual constructs his listening skills with established specialties, whether these are listening for support, for criticism, for information, for condescension, for simple facts, for complexities he will not understand, for tone of voice with no attention to the actual message, and so on. No matter what you may say to Jack, he will oversimplify it and lose any sense of detail, and no matter what you say to Marie it will be heard as if couched in qualifications and special contingencies. Some people hear only statements when questions have been asked, so that it becomes impossible to ask a question since it is inevitably received as a demand or an accusation. Some people assume that when someone *asks* them what they are doing he is trying to *tell* them something about their behavior instead of trying to find out. One member of a group once commented that since he uses questions to put other people on the defensive, he suspects that when people ask questions of him, this must be what they too are trying to do. When mother screams, "Why did you knock down your baby brother?" she is not looking for information as much as retribution. When a husband says to his wife as she drives, "I think you'd better pull over to the right side of the road in order to make that turn," what she may hear is, "You damn fool, you've got to make a right turn soon and you're not even ready!"

Because of these disparities, one way of restoring attention and focus to the listening process is to ask the patient to listen to something other than the words that are being spoken. What does he hear in the voice of the other person? Is it breathy and soft, or does it come on hard and aggressive? The same with the tone and the inflection: flat, metallic, monotonous, or excited and contagious? People are often surprised that when they stop listening to the words and attend to some other feature, they pick up entirely new or different messages instead of the old familiar communications.

Another method to insure that the person is listening is to have him repeat what he just heard before responding to it. The other person has to agree that this was what he meant before the next step in the conversation is made. Although these techniques can be used in individual therapy, they appear to be even more valuable in working with couples or with groups, where one may be dealing not only with one person's resistance to listening but also with another person's need to remain unheard and obscure. The therapist, when working with one patient, usually tries to make himself as clear and audible as possible in order to minimize distortion. Even here, of course, there still remain chances to mis-hear something. Those who have seen Perls demonstrate remember clearly that he expected to be heard whenever he spoke; he took failure to hear him as deliberate resistance and would refuse to repeat anything when asked. Exasperating, perhaps, but the effect on the person he was working with was electrifying; he became mobilized to hear every word from then on.

The selectivity described in the listening process may be a source of creativity. For example, some therapists may work beautifully with the sexual implications of what they hear, others can detect the finest nuances of hostility, still others can resonate to the overtones of the creative frustrations in what the patient may be saying. It is not that they read these in, but rather that they hear these themes with sensitivity where another therapist may hear some other theme. This may account for the difference some therapists experience in being able to work well with some patients and not so well with others.

Such listening is no longer a literal listening. It becomes almost an orchestration of listening, *grounded* in the literal but responding to nuances of voice as well as to sequences of words and contexts of meaning. A person who is whining often does so in so subtle a way that only a finely tuned listener can identify it, although all listeners may be subliminally affected. I hear a person in trouble; I don't want to hear; I don't want to care. He will be a millstone around my neck. I hear another person in trouble; I well up; my eyes open; my neck swells; he expresses tragedy which awes me. He knows he is heard.

I once worked with strung-out young people in a coffee house. When I was first introduced to a group sitting around a table, we had been talking for only a short while when somebody wondered out loud whether they could trust me. I asked why not. He said that I might be a policeman. How am I like a policeman, I wanted to know. He said, "You listen, and only policemen listen," a remarkable commentary on the community the young man experienced around him! The fact is, of course, that his observation had merit. Some people may be very engaging and animated, but not much tuned in to listening to each other. Conversations are often stereotyped with certain words ticking off certain responses with no contact with the subtleties of each particular statement. People are often overconcerned with the rightness of their own views without making much effort to relate their views to the opinions of others.

The contactful listener is alert to what is being said, but he also digs sound enough in its own right so that he hears more than just the words. He listens to whatever means something to him and he is affected by what he hears. When the listener hears, he knows he is in good contact and when the talker knows he is being heard, his contact is also enlivened.

TOUCHING

The most obvious way to make contact is through touching. Although the taboos against looking and listening are unmistakable—don't stare, don't eavesdrop—the taboos against touching are even more loud and clear; when children touch something they are not supposed to, they may get their hands slapped or come away feeling they have besmirched what they touched. So they quickly learn they are not to touch valuable objects, not to touch their genitals, and to be careful where and indeed whether they touch other people for fear they might touch them in an inviolate place. So carefulness becomes normal. Shaking hands is okay, but even there the etiquette becomes blurry between men and women. To touch each other anywhere else is rare and carefully structured, resulting in disguised and deflected gestures.*

---

* Morris, Desmond, *Intimate Behavior*. New York: Random House, 1971.

Though the taboos are loosening, people had become so distanced from touching, alas, that the current recovery of the willingness to touch displays the self-conscious exhibitionism that usually goes with performing an unfamiliar function. Touching is getting a bad name because much of it is staged under conditions where it emerges as artifice instead of ripe culmination. People may feel constrained to touch someone whom they are either not yet ready to touch or whom they would rather not touch at all. This compulsion often leads to atrocious timing, like the man in a group who wanted to hug me shortly after the group had begun. Hugging this man was the last thing on my mind at that point in our acquaintance.

The new climate of touching demands practice and patience. Years of experience are needed before our culture can develop the grace and sensitivity that would make touching an authentic part of its existence, as it was with the Etruscans whose ancient paintings show a culture where touching was as natural as walking. During this evolutionary process we who esteem good contact must work towards becoming connoisseurs of touching *as contact,* rather than touching as an initiation rite of membership in the new order.

In groups, especially, the restoration of touching is a means of completing important unfinished business. The immediacy of touch breaks through the intellectual layers into palpable personal recognitions. For example, in one group a lively but sexually naive woman told about her tomboy background and observed that she had never had the sense of really being close to a man. I asked her to touch several of the men in the room. At first she was reluctant, although she was obviously not thrown by the suggestion. Gingerly, she touched one man's hair, and she began to lose her self-consciousness, slapping the next man on the shoulder and stroking another's cheek. She began to be tuned in, at first incredulously, to the fact that she was actually making contact with the men, and that each was receptive to her touch and respectful of her exploration. She grew more and more captivated by her new discovery. When she reached me she crawled into my lap. Soon she became filled with a realization of loss. She began to cry as she told us the story of her relationship to her father who had always held her off from direct contact with him. He had died only about a year before, just as she was beginning to feel that she might get closer to him. Her sadness about the interruption caused by his death was still profound, but instead of the depression to which loss and renunciation had previously led, she now felt radiant at her sense of the restoration of possibilities with other people.

In another group, Julia complained about the fact that Tony, one of the younger men, could not accept or respond to her wish to behave playfully with him and be accepted as a pal of his in the way that he allowed some of the younger members of the group. She was unwilling to settle for the stereotype of the middle-aged, middle-class professional woman. I asked them to talk to each other and to reach out and touch each other lightly and playfully as they did. It became clear that Tony needed, in his repertoire of touching playfully, the freedom to touch vigorously, aggressively and with the energy that was an important part of his style of being playful. Julia, on the other hand, needed to set some realistic limits because of arthritis. What both of them came to recognize was that there were, in fact, some ways in which he had to respond to her carefully. However, some of Tony's cautiousness about her had spilled over into his viewing Julia as "touchy" in general. This interaction taught them that while Julia might not be able to take rough physical treatment, she was not too fragile to hear and understand some of his need to express himself bluntly and vigorously.

These examples of touching are not exceptional in a setting where touching is valued as a central contact function. Through touch we have begun to rediscover the impactfulness one person can have upon another. Once some of the taboos against touching are relaxed, we may not only touch but we may also engage in a whole range of experiences which must be prohibited lest they *result* in the tabooed action—touch. Wariness about the possible consequences of our behavior is often as crippling as the prohibition of the forbidden behavior itself because it may cut off contact long before the dreaded danger point is reached. Thus, the avoidance of touch would not be nearly such a sweat if it didn't also prevent us from getting out from behind our desks, telling intimate stories about ourselves, standing close to other people, speaking warmly or colorfully, and many of the other actions where we might come to touch another person.

The fact is that touching is not the *inevitable* result of warm engagement, but if one is overwhelmingly afraid of it the catastrophic expectations will exert their deadening effect anyway. The gap between what one *ultimately* wants to refuse and what one actually refuses is the neurotic gap; it is the essence of wastefulness in life. It is not our intent to keep people from saying "no" but rather to bring them into touch with their *existential* no. The existential no says "no" to that which one feels "no" about, neither sooner nor later than this "no" emerges. When one *says* no to touch and *means* no to touch, that is not a neurotic problem, although it may certainly bring on abrasions in personal relations. But when one is afraid to stand close to another person although he wants to, because it might lead to touching, he is creating a gap between what he *is* and what he *could* be. The greater the gap, the fewer the possibilities that one will experience the actualization of himself in action. The result? The various forms of malaise described by texts on abnormal psychology and the sense of personal dysrhythmia bemoaned by the existential psychologists, novelists and movie makers for the past half century.

The bind which prevents us from contacting the existential actuality and anchors us in ruminations and ersatz intellectual action requires a two-fold resolution. First, we must learn to identify the existential no, so that we are not frozen into saying "no" prematurely and then remaining, like Tantalus, always nearing our goal but never achieving it, forever dissatisfied and unrealized. Second, we must be able to encompass the implications of our yes's so that we do not wind up committed to something which now or in the future we want out of. Perhaps, when saying yes to something, the initial yes is the beginning of a course of action which will eventually call forth a no, and we need to acknowledge this possibility and bring it into our yes-saying. When we say "yes" to something, we must recognize that even though this may result in a situation where later we will say "no," this does not mean that the original "yes" was stupid or hypocritical or shortsighted.

The simplistic thinkers among us, impatient with mere talk, may be on to the right idea when they advise us to just do our own thing and then take the consequences and stay with them. This means that we would be willing to suffer considerably, it is true, but the suffering would be existential rather than neurotic, and the experience would be pain but not crud.

"Doing your own thing" is rooted in the development of skill in identifying yes's and no's accurately.

TALKING

As a contact function talking has two dimensions: voice and language.

Voice—Musically, the human voice is often taken as the prototype of expressive tone. An instrumentalist's performance is praised as it approaches human vocal qualities. Critics write of the instrument's eloquence, of its singing tone, and of the phrasing. Actors, of course, use their voices as the core of their expressive powers. One of the most remarkable examples of the human voice for theatrically expressive purposes is the Japanese Kabuki theater where the voice extends from a screech to a roar to a whine to a low growl, through a fantastic range of vocal possibilities.

These possibilities, less dramatic and more easily ignored, exist in all communication. The phrase, "How are you?" may convey, depending on differences in voice, a genuine concern with your health, a warm greeting, polite but perfunctory inquiry, impatience to get on with the real business at hand, marking time with meaningless conversation, etc. Actors may practice by taking a single phrase and saying it from the perspective first of a person who is desperately unhappy, then profoundly angry, and finally passionately in love. It is hardly news that one ought to sound different in anger than in love, although there are many people whose voices remain the same.

Larry was afflicted with an emotionally dulled voice and furthermore he didn't even know it was dull, so I asked him to sing his words to me as though he were in an operetta. The suggestion amused him. The first time he sang his response, his face awoke as though he had just been hatched and his beak was poking forward into the world for the very first time. Larry worked on his voice for a full session until, at last, having sung his words, he was able to speak them with some measure of the liveliness aroused in him by singing. At least now he knew the difference between his lively voice and his expressionless voice and he was able to live off this for a while, expressing himself in more animated and various tones. But, alas, the effects faded and he returned to his monotone. This time, though, Larry was quite frustrated because now he knew the difference and he *wanted* his more spirited voice. He missed expressing what he wanted to get across. This time as he was talking, his head was down and he had the air of a sigh around him. I asked him to take a deep breath and sigh, keeping his head down close to his chest. The sigh turned into a moan. As he continued to moan, Larry's voice became deeper and deeper and he began to sense an integration between his voice and the rest of his body. Now he realized that not only had his voice been monotonous but it had also been disembodied. Nevertheless, even though moaning, he felt a strange peacefulness, a sense of unity within himself, a feeling which transcends specific content. After a few moments, he was able to speak again with the liveliness he had discovered anew. This new liveliness will not remain with him permanently either, but each subsequent time he loses it he is more likely to find means of restoration, at first in therapy, later without it.

Each person is fated to work through certain aspects of his nature over and over again, hopefully reaching new positions each time, with less vulnerability to ill effects and greater resilience in renewing himself and finding his way back again. Therapy is devoted to repeatedly working through recurrent themes in every which way until that theme has finally been played through in its many guises and gets pushed aside by others which make their way into the foreground. Before Larry of the monotonous voice can be at home with vocal liveliness, he may need to growl, scream, cry, talk like a woman or a bully, whisper, pant, speak in a foreign dialect, squeak, rant—ferreting out the unfinished voice which he has kept stuck so long. Some of these sounds may have to come at first from directions which others give him, but ultimately they will come as surprises to him, evolving out of his own expressive needs. As he becomes more aware of his needs which demand expression, he will also require a greater range of expressive power in his voice, like a child who quickly outgrows the narrow limits of the keyboard of the toy piano and wants the greater scope offered by the full-size keyboard. Exercises are only a limbering up process for the unfixed game. To be sure, they are central in gathering the force and the stamina necessary for growth, but they will never replace the actual life experience, any more than calisthenics will ever replace the 50-yard dash.

In addition to its expressive function, the voice also has direction and momentum. Think of the voice as having a target which the individual wants to reach through the medium of sound. For an individual to penetrate another person with his voice is an aggressive act. If he enters harmoniously and with a quality of incisiveness which is assimilable, and if he is welcomed, there will be good engagement. If, on the other hand, the speaker is anti-incisive, he may never reach the target. If he is too incisive, cutting too sharply through the boundaries of the person he is speaking to, the normal resistance to being overrun will set in and influence the contact. Some people's words drop somewhere in between speaker and listener, some go right through the listener, some go around or beyond the listener, and some make just exactly the right contact, feeling fresh and right on.

The situation also makes a difference in the contactfulness of the voice. Some people's voices are most suited to the intimate conversation, not projecting far, but perhaps projecting well enough given the distance required. Listen to any Peggy Lee vocal for a good illustration of this sense of private one-to-one communication. Others operate best in public and large-scale situations and their voices swamp the person-to-person intimacy. William was a magnificent public speaker. He entranced his audiences consistently because every word he said carried through to the least of them and to those who may have been farthest away. However, when he was talking to individuals, even though he remained interesting, he still came across as though he were speaking to a large gathering and his words went over their heads and caromed around them. The consequent effect was that William could not establish the intimacies which his general vibrancy would have merited. He was too much for the individual who soon began to feel dominated and uncontacted, sometimes even invaded, by this man.

Laughter is another telling aspect of voice contact. Does the laughter well up out of the individual or is it pumped out? Does the laughter have resonance or is it metallic? Aban-

doned or controlled? One man produced laughter in response
to any and all situations which had even the mildest suggestion
of humor in them. The decibel level of his laughter was always
at its peak, whether something was uproariously funny or only
a moderate tickler not even calling forth laughter in others.
Smiles and chuckles were not in his repertoire. His laughter
was the demand of a person who seized on the closeness of
humor and tried to wring from this moment the last possible
drop of comradeship. His oppressive need for closeness and
his laziness in producing anything that might rightfully elicit
this from others made him greedy and desperate and his
laughter reflected this.

Another man, Ben, spoke with a chronic whine. He told a
group assembled for a weekend workshop about a traumatic
hearing examination in which he learned that a hearing problem of his was a deteriorative process and that he might wind
up deaf. Surely this is a circumstance where the content alone
would have been expected to arouse compassion. Yet there was
little response. The story itself was upstaged by the inherent
plea in Ben's voice and, rather than get trapped in what they
felt was a bottomless pit, the other people in the group just
tuned him out.

A basic gestalt principle is to accentuate that which exists
rather than merely attempting to change it. Nothing can change
until it is at first accepted; then it can play itself out and be
open to the native movement towards change in life. Carrying
out this principle, I asked Ben to go around the room begging
something from each person there. Though this proved to be
a useful experience for Ben, there are some risks involved in
setting up such an experiment. For example, it might have
been humiliating for him to be brought abruptly into contact
with his pleading nature. While humiliation can occasionally
be helpful to someone who can use the reorientation it involves or who can become mobilized by it, by and large it is
interruptive to growth and can be grossly demeaning to the

person involved. Nevertheless, what a person is ready to explore, he is not likely to feel humiliated by. So it was with Ben, who was motivated to discover how he turned people off and who had enough self-support to be able to reconnoiter the pleader in himself. As he went around the room doing his pleading bit, through the exaggeration and the accented focus he came clearly into touch with his own tone of voice. When he came into full sense of himself as beggar, Ben started to laugh heartily, seeing the humor in his weak-kneed pleas and realizing that he didn't need to beg at all. He was a person of his own and he could talk about his hearing loss equal to equal. People could listen without having to give him the exorbitant hand-out. The compassion which was expressed then traversed the distance between Ben and the group without anyone feeling suckered into it.

Simplistically, speaking can be regarded as modified breathing. Therefore it becomes important to restore breathing to its central role as a pulsing source of support for this contact function. People can speak from either breath support or from musculature. That is, they may speak as though their voice were riding on top of a wave of air or they may make sounds through the force of muscular energy which drives the air through their vocal cords. If one takes an adequate breath and fully uses up this breath in the production of sound, his voice has the buoyancy of a ping-pong ball riding on a jet of air. The vocal cords are not constrained to do the hard work of providing the energy—work which they are not equipped to do anyway—and they are free to vibrate, to resonate, and to shape the energy, as the silver column of a flute does once air is breathed into it. Voices supported like this are vibrant, resonant, and appear to be effortlessly produced. When the vocal apparatus is burdened by doing the work that the breathing system should be doing, the labor is apparent; the voice is harsh, strained, and rasps metallically. People in therapy who discover the supportive function of their breath-

ing are almost inevitably delighted at the changes that occur
in their voice.

Language—Language is potentially one of the most powerful agents for contactfulness. Pithiness, colorfulness, pungency, simplicity, directness, all these and more language
characteristics can determine whether you make it to another
person. Good writers know how to be there with their language
because they depend on no other contact function. Here is
Sartre's preface to Fanon's book, *The Wretched of the Earth*.*
Without wasting words he opens up the traffic between himself
and his reader:

> Europeans, you must open this book and enter into it.
> After a few steps in the darkness you will see strangers
> gathered around a fire; come close, and listen, for they
> are talking of the destiny they will mete out to your trad-
> ing centers and to the hired soldiers who defend them.
> They will see you, perhaps, but they will go on talking to
> themselves without even lowering their voices. This indif-
> ference strikes home; their fathers, shadowy creatures,
> *your* creatures, were but dead souls; you it was who al-
> lowed them glimpses of the light, to you only do they dare
> speak, and you did not bother to reply to such zombies.
> Their sons ignore you; a fire warms them and sheds light
> around them, and you have not lit it. Now, at a respectful
> distance, it is you who will feel furtive; night bound and
> perished with cold. Turn and turn about; in these shadows
> from whence into a dawn will break, it is you who are the
> zombies.

First, Sartre makes it very clear and repeats for emphasis
exactly whom he is addressing; second, he does not pussyfoot
or equivocate; third, he describes specific happenings; and
fourth, he rides right into contact with a force which only
thick walls or thick skins could turn aside. As an illustration
it will serve well to remind us that masters in any form of

---

* Fanon, F., *The Wretched of the Earth*. New York: Grove Press,
1968.

expression are masters because their antennae are homed in for good contact; they don't settle for less.

A person's linguistic habits tell a lot about *him* as well as what he is trying to tell. Some of the most fascinating personality studies are written about Shakespeare, detailing his use of language, the words themselves, and the way he put them together. People everywhere can be looked at with the same sensitivity to the way they use language. Some are stingy with their words, measuring each word out carefully, like dried beans, or penny-nails, or bullets. Others will pour out torrents of words, like water lapping up and then fading away leaving no trace or like a fling of brightly colored trinkets, covering up tawdriness, or delighting us in their sparkle and generosity. Some are verb people, some are noun people, some leave out personal pronouns, some will be poetically free, others will be as accurate as surveyors.

One way of deadening the contact possibilities of language is through circumlocution. A college professor, who needs to communicate as the lifeblood of his work with students, was talking to me after two or three sessions about how he always feels graded and furthermore, how he feels that all interactions in life are graded. I asked him what grade he would give me. His answer, straight from the tape of our session:

> I guess I was talking about the grading of you, and I was going to drop into thoughts about last week when you were telling me about your feelings of my importance and my later thoughts about that during the week were that, in a sense, it was a non-real kind of interchange in that you are sincere in your appraisal unless the problem is in finding a feeling of that kind of thing when you are feeling important from one's environment, from signals in one's environment. So that in terms of grading that particular interchange, although I sort of liked it at the time, and thinking further about it, I felt something . . . that it was akin to teacher-student, father-to-child, something out of contact. It is interesting, and I guess this is

why I'm interested in human contacting stuff, because things that I think about that seem to me to make sense, when I get the chance to talk to somebody about it, it isn't quite as impressive in the voicing of it. In the largest sense, my grading of you is in terms of what I feel I'm getting out of our sessions, and on the one hand I feel that the sessions could be productive in a therapeutic sense despite my immediate reaction to it, provided there is some technique of therapy in a demonstrated success, or, on the other hand, an opportunity for real interchange, so, from the latter point of view the group is perhaps equal, perhaps even more equal, in the fact that there are more people contributing more experiences.

His wanderings got across messages to me concerning his standards, the complications he experiences in grading, his skepticism, and his interest in the whole theoretical structure which, for him, underlay any attempt to grade me. He would have wandered further, but I wanted to get some focus on his actual experience, as well as his attempt to arrive at a grade, so I asked him what he was doing and feeling. He said:

I am trying to form my thoughts in terms of my responses to you, which is a response to what I feel is happening in these sessions and I'm trying to put it as *correctly or as faithfully as I can*, the kind of thoughts I have had. I am trying to address myself to the former of the two parts, and I think that you are probably engaged in some kind of existential therapy which I don't see the structure of, and I think that this is why there is my kind of dissatisfaction or uneasiness with it, and it also occurs to me that I might be falling into a self kind of contradiction trap, in that existential therapy, by definition, doesn't have structure.

At this point I asked him to grade me in one sentence. He said, "Question mark." At this point, we both knew that he had finally said what he meant and there was a glance of recognition and meeting between us that all the wanderings had lacked.

Now, this man's circumlocutions were more severe than the usual but they are not so severe as to be unrecognizable. All people who must be totally right or who must cover all avenues or contingencies which might have any bearing on what they say will be so wrapped up in their own internal process that there won't be any excitement available to maintain an unfinished, but nevertheless *pointed,* contact. When contact is made in continuity, one does not have to be right all at once because rightness emerges and builds on the developmental interaction like kids playing a good game of leap-frog. If this man had simply said, "Question mark," right in the beginning, he would still surely have wanted to include some of the other things he said. He probably would have had the chance to do this; I might have responded by asking, "What do you question?" or I might have said, "Up your ass!" but in any case he would probably have had ample opportunity for getting out what remained unfinished.

Jargon is another linguistic trick which gets people off the hook of having to work to make contact; it can easily become a habit between people who know each other, personally or professionally, and who don't want to take the trouble to create something afresh over and over again. Jargon is like the TV dinner, a ready-made product, which is not so bad if you obliterate your own taste. After all, it looks like the real thing on the lid, so we buy it again, conned by our own indolence or haste.

To say what one wants to say is a magnificent act of creation, easily overlooked because people talk so much. In a sense no word is ever exactly the same to two different people—and often not even to the same person at different times or under different circumstances—because the emergence of a word is an event which culminates a whole lifetime of sensations, memories, wishes, images. So each authentic word would logically have its own unique configuration of meaning. Jargony words lack this very quality and are only minimally contactful since they are not really an individual's personal statement. They misrepresent because they make it easy to be glossed over and fuzzily received.

Those of us who have learned the language of the growth center or the encounter group recognize the symptoms. Part of our uneasy awareness comes from the caricaturists who are zeroing in on the stock phrases of our glibness. Many of us are tired of hearing someone say that he wants to "be himself." This formula communicates very little unless it gets anchored in doing certain specific things he wants to do or experiencing something he might previously have been unwilling to experience. But to "be himself" is all he ever can be, that's what he is, be it dissatisfied or phony or inhibited or whatever, that *is* "himself"! Until he knows that *he is* this unsatisfactory or unsatisfied self, jargony mottoes aren't going to do him any good.

Other jargony statements cloak the simplest acts in the most elevated language. So, in some groups, one does not simply talk to another person, one "relates" to him, or one "shares" with him, or the therapist "intervenes." Interaction between people comes to sound like a series of tactical and strategic moves which have some gloriously defined purpose.

It becomes important, then, to clarify language in any way possible. One technique is to ask the person to *be* that which he is describing. If he says he is a radical, ask him to be the radical and personalize what he is only half-saying. So, he might say, "I am a radical, I throw stones." Or, he might say, "I am a radical, I like to get down to the root of things." Another method is to ask questions like how is he a radical, or where is he a radical, or when is he a radical, which get at the specific circumstances of his radical nature and away from the cover-all label.

There are many other language games which take the heat off the uncertainty of contactfulness. Over-explaining is one—trying to play both sides of the game by making it crystal clear what the listener is to hear and how he is to interpret it. One man who is always telling the *whole* story, whatever he relates, winds up a thorough bore because there is no place to go when he has finished. He does not converse; he delivers monologues which leave everybody wondering why they don't like to be with him.

Repeating oneself is another form of contact neutralization. When the first statement fails to make contact, maybe saying it again will do it next time. It's like the nymphomaniac's dream that the next screw will really do it, or the next banana split for the fatso.

Yes-but is a similar contact neutralizer. Perls used to say that he never heard anything before the "but." "I would love to come over tonight *but* I'm busy" is easier to dig if you reverse the position of the two phrases, or if you leave off what preceded that "but" or if you shorten it and ask the person to say simply, "I can't come" or "I won't come." The rest is just a softening up process and insulates the main theme of the statement. Sometimes it is the other way around, and the softening phrase is the main theme: I would love to come over tonight. Where someone's language always involves the asbestos coating, though, it becomes hard to know what the real message is, even for him. *Yes-but* is a signal to be more than usually alert to discern the essential truth of the statement.

If only is not far removed from *yes-but*. Like the man assuring his wife how likeable she could be *if only* she would get over her shyness, or how creative she could be *if only* she would try. He puts it all in benevolent terms and is then surprised when she feels so pressured by the disguised message conveying his basic wish for her to be different from what she actually is.

Asking questions instead of making statements is another way of keeping on the cool side of contactfulness. It is anti-commitment and deceptive because one is implying, by the question, uncertainty and tentativeness. But the real message comes across because implications are read into the questions anyhow. There are questions which are just not questions at all. Someone who asks a person whether he likes his father may be saying, you don't sound like you like your father or I don't like my father, and trying to make this sound like an innocent request for information. To discriminate between simple curiosity and disguised statements is basic in developing contactfulness in language.

Often language is all there is to make contact with, and even minimal changes make the difference between being on target or splashdown miles away from the contact point. One young college student, very bright and very talkative, bores people even though his ideas are very stimulating. He sprays his words around, like a disinfectant, rather than focusing on the person he is talking to. I tried several ways to help him to reach me. One way was for him to look at me as he spoke. Another was for him to point to me each time he spoke to me. The third was to start each sentence with my name. Through each of these he reached me—not only in my experience of him, but in his own experience of himself-and-me. Each time he experienced reaching me with his words he beamed, and several times he burst into uproarious laughter as though he had discovered the secret of the universe!

MOVING

The contact powers of movement are most clearly revealed in the work of the pantomimist. He shows purely through movement how one opens a package and finds in it either a loathesome or precious object, how one approaches a boss to ask for a raise or a stranger to ask for directions, how one moves in kissing an elderly aunt or kissing one's sweetheart. No dialogue or scenery distracts; the focus is exclusively on his moves. In everyday contact, though, movement frequently fades into the background and exercises only a subtle and often undetected effect. But Reich's attention to the body armoring activities involved in repression and current studies of body language* assert the centrality of movement. Movements may either facilitate contact or they may interrupt or hamper it. In entering a room and walking over to a person one wants to speak to, one person acts under his own power and moves freely and smoothly, another moves like a badly made puppet who is being jerkily propelled across the room to perform a social obligation which is not his idea in the first place.

Focusing on movement reveals either the unimpeded, fluid action of a person who supports the activity in which he is engaged or the clumsy, graceless action which is the compromise between an impulse and its inhibition. Reich** describes this behavior:

> ... it is a substitute function for something else, it serves a defense purpose, it absorbs energy, and it is an attempt to harmonize conflicting forces. . . . The result of the achievement is all out of proportion to the energy expended.

Because of the deflections necessary to the compromise and because of the impaired contact resulting from the substitutive behavior, the individual's satisfaction is diminished and he works hard to get where he is going, as though driving with the brakes on.

In working with movement there are two major steps. One is to call attention to noteworthy aspects of movement as they come into the foreground. The other step is to devise an experiment which provides the opportunity to follow through in directions suggested by his movement or by the words which may have accompanied the movement. For example, Steve,

---

* Fast, Julius, *Body Language*. New York: M. Evans, 1970.
** Reich, W., *Character Analysis*. New York: Orgone Institute Press, 1949.

who moved stiffly, walked across the room with a subtly lurching gait. When this was called to his attention, he recalled that he had been continuously ridiculed as he was growing up because he lurched grossly. To avoid ridicule he deliberately sought to repress the exuberance of his motion while walking. He did succeed in repressing a large part of it through tightening the upper part of his body, which resulted in a dysrhythmia between the upper and lower parts of his body— a basic split and quite commonly found. Steve's body expressed his polarity. The upper part was largely immobilized: pendant arms, tight shoulders, lifeless chest. Below his waist he was tense and his movements seemed studied although his legs felt strong and vibrant. According to Steve, the only time he felt able to walk freely was when he was hiking, his favorite pasttime. When there were people around, however, his walk became self-conscious and controlled. I asked Steve to skip across the room several times. At first he was self-conscious, but gradually he began to enjoy himself and lost his self-consciousness. Then I asked him to flap his arms as he skipped across the room, as though he were flying. When he did this his delight grew and Steve realized for the first time that he was aware of a unity between his upper and lower parts, quite different from the vague uneasiness which he normally experienced. When he walked across the room again more normally, the changes in him were apparent to the group. His arms and shoulders were able to move in conjunction with his torso, and his chest no longer appeared sunken. Steve will obviously fall back into his more characteristic ways because one experience is hardly likely to overcome the habits of a lifetime. Nevertheless, he had been made aware of some of the controls he had imposed long ago and he had had an illustration of how it felt to transcend this split.

It is probably hard to accept that a simple set of movements like skipping and flapping one's arms like a bird could make very much difference. As we have observed, this kind

of experience must be repeated and reworked until assimilated. Even those temporary personal changes which result
when working with an individual's contactfulness generally,
and with movement specifically, can be valuable. Although
movement is figural, it extends out of the realm of mere calisthenics when provided with context, placing it against the
experiential background which gives it meaning. In the foregoing example, meaning included the split in Steve's personality between his exuberance and his caution, his feeling of having blocked contact with other people, the drama of having
followed other intense experiences which had already occurred
in the group and the memory of the suffering he had endured as
a child but which he had not recalled for a long time. These
are only some of the factors which merged to give him inspira-
tion and enabled him to experience in sensation what might
otherwise have remained only rational or speculative. Suddenly
there he was, *whole,* and he is less likely than before to forget
that wholeness is indeed possible for him. If you can show a
person where it's at, he is more likely to find it than if he
blunders along in the old familiar ruts. Although that service
falls short of satisfying psychotherapeutic grandiosities, it is
no small service.

How a person sits also tells much about the contact he is
willing to make. Leaning forward while talking or listening
propels the individual into a different contact than turning
one's head aside or bundling it firmly and irretrievably between one's hunched shoulders. In a couples workshop Paul,
sitting next to his wife on the floor, was complaining that Sheila
was perpetually "on" him. He meant by this that she was often
touching him and cuddling up to him when he didn't want it,
although it was okay with him sometimes when he did want it.
Sitting there next to her, his posture was so symmetrical and
he was balanced so Buddha-like, that it would have been hard
for Sheila to find a place for herself. He was so square and
impenetrable-looking that it seemed that only through pointed

energy would she be able to gather herself around him. Paul was a closed figure, admitting entry only on his terms. His symmetry made it quite clear that he wanted his independence from any of her attempts to encircle him. Sheila made him lopsided and his balanced position guarded against the risk of lopsided fall; it also guarded against the excitement of union with her. Someone in the group began to experiment with trying to knock Paul over. Each time he succeeded, with difficulty, our symmetrical friend would recover his balance with alacrity, like one of those push-over toys which are weighted so they quickly return to an upright position. Soon even Paul began to wonder whether he needed this quick return to the status quo. At this point Sheila was given the direction to try again to crawl all over him and to make an opening for herself, to make sure that if she wanted more contact with her husband she did all she could to get it. It became apparent that it was not only the threat of being taken over which Paul resisted, but that intimacy *per se* was also threatening, and it was this dread which made him adopt a posture where he looked so unreachable. A giggle came anyway and Paul yielded to the warmth of the moment, letting it melt his muscles and letting himself receive his wife tenderly and without fear. From then on even his symmetry seemed softer and more receptive. He needs practice in finding his own boundedness so that he can respond to intimacy without fearing takeover.

The same kind of attention can be directed to smaller details of gesture and movement. A listener who nods attentively affirms and accentuates his feeling of contact with the speaker—or his gesture may be a confluent brush-off. The speaker may move his head slowly from side to side while he says he loves his mother very much, negating his own message. Awe, fear, fascination or surprise may open one's eyes or mouth as if the person is making room to permit the full impact to come in. The individual whose gestures are small and confined to himself is broadcasting a different message from the person who spreads his arms wide with abandon and whose gestures leave his body open and unguarded. The person whose nostrils and corners of his mouth describe a strong downward curve may be saying in his movements, "I will breathe this air and speak to you, but I disapprove both of the air that I breathe and of you, too." A teacher's stance in relation to very young children will affect contact. For this reason many teachers kneel to the child's level frequently, closing the distance through which contact must be made and establishing a sense of parity in their communications. The therapist's sensitivity and creativity can lead him in focusing on the relevant movements which might fill in the gaps which subtract from graceful and contactful movement. There are no clear rules, but there are some guidelines for the direction the therapist's work may follow.

First, the therapist may direct the patient to *experience his movements as they currently exist*. Any focus which highlights what is already happening provides a foundation for change. We seek to restore an acceptance of this flux in spite of the pain of experiencing what one has come not to want and has therefore forgotten. With the return of this acceptance, the dynamics for change reappear and lead the individual into directions which are native for him. Thus if I walk lopsided, say, leaning over to the left, when I can attend to my left-learningness I can also attend to what might flow from it. Suppose when I notice that I lean to the left I also discover a movement of my left arm which, when I carry it out to its complete extension, is a haymaker to the jaw of a fantasied or remembered bully. When I give free rein to the punch and snap of my left arm, my forgotten rage wells up anew at the hateful memory, only this time I'm not afraid and there is no holding back as I swing out. The incompleted stuckness of leaning to the left is unlocked and assertiveness returns to my left side, bringing with it the grace released by the new freedom. Only by deadening and forgetting could I have remained compulsively lopsided.

To illustrate further the centrality of the current experience of movement, Arthur was wary about his sense of distance from me. He wanted to be closer but didn't know on what basis he could lay claim to greater intimacy. The danger of appearing presumptuous immobilized him. I asked Arthur to get up and experiment with what would feel like just the right distance for him. After a few moments of talk between us and some adjustments to discover the right distance, he approached close to me and was suddenly very pleased to be where he was. He made a movement with his hands, one against the other. I asked him to feel this movement and let it become what it would. In a few moments Arthur's hands were slapping hard against each other, one with the fingers formed into a hollow circle as it slapped crisply against the palm of the other hand. It made a ringing, hollow sound. Arthur remembered that when he was a kid the boys in his neighborhood made just such a sound when they felt things were beautiful! He beamed in recall and continued making the sound at me and then at the rest of the people in the room who were watching. Then they all began making the sound. Arthur had affirmed his delight in his contact with me and had spread his sense of delight to the others in the group. The attention to his movement not only affirmed his contact in this moment but also restored to him in all its freshness a childhood experience which had been outside his awareness for many years. It is worth noting that it is common for the completion of unfinished expressions to free old memories to become part of the work-through process. This is similar to the psychoanalytic search for unconscious or repressed material from the past, except that the process is reversed. For us in gestalt therapy, the return from the unconscious *follows* restoration of contact, whereas in psychoanalysis the return of the unconscious is regarded as *preceding* the recovery of present function.

The second orienting principle is to guide the individual's awareness and his actions through the succession of blocks into a *full exercise of the movement* we are focusing on. We saw this happen when the man's childhood hand-game united a whole group. We saw it also with Steve who was asked to skip and to flap his arms as though flying. In this stage, the artistry and interaction of the therapist and the patient are critical. Each one's intuition concerning the next stroke must follow and coordinate with the other's. The "good" patient is not the obedient one but the one whose fantasy life is rich and who dares to let his mind and actions flow. To be sure, the therapist plays an important part in setting up the climate where this quality in the patient can flower, but "good" patients can make most of us "good" therapists.

A third guiding principle is to *look for the sources of support* which are available in the individual's body. For example, in walking and standing it is important to note whether the person is using his legs as a foundation upon which he can rest confidently, using it as a base for posture or movement. Some people's legs seem spindly and promise poor support. Others keep their knees locked as if support comes only from rigidity. Still others have legs which flop about and offer only minimal support. Some people look like they are suspended from above like a side of beef in a butcher shop or a puppet on a string, completely missing the sense of support from below, from themselves.

Each part of the body supports its share of the moving person. The spine supports the neck as it rests on the parts below, the shoulders are in their turn also supported on the upper torso, which rests in turn on the pelvic spinal column—like the old song about "dem bones." But what if the neck is distrustful of the supports underneath? It may assume more of the job of supporting the head than it needs to do. So a stiffening up process is instituted which may interfere with the transmission of sensation from other parts of the body to the head, splitting off the function of the head from the rest of the body. Even though the body builds up enough tension to scream or holler, the message never gets through to the head; it may be revealed in knotting of the stomach or backaches or tightening of the upper arms, but the head is not available for outlet or expression so the action has to seek these substitute outlets. The head, too, divorced from sensory information from the rest of the body, is left to its own devices. Cerebral activity, deprived of its sensory basis, leads to intellectualizing. It should be added that when the neck is stiffened it loses its flexibility and is no longer able to turn freely or fully, leaving the person looking rigidly forward, facing those issues in life which are immediately obvious but missing some of what goes on along the sidelines. The neck is particularly vulnerable because it is a narrow and crammed passageway containing vital parts like the throat, windpipe and larynx and because of its swivel qualities sometimes leading us to fear that it is in fact unequal to its task and, to fear that one might surely lose one's head. So, carefulness with the neck is hardly surprising.

The freeing of each part of the body to carry on the supportive function for which it is responsible—*and no more*—is therefore often of paramount importance. To accomplish this, a recovery of trust in the normal supportive system is necessary. The legs, obviously, are basic. But all through the support system, sensation has to be recovered and the barriers to the growth of feelings have to be explored and extended through exercises which increase awareness.

When a person is sitting or lying down he has to be able to yield some of his own internal support and receive external support from the couch or the floor. Seems simple. But some people sit or lie almost as if they were in levitation some inches above, supporting themselves in mid-air. There is an exercise, devised by Charlotte Selver, where one person raises in turn the arms, legs and head of his partner, who is lying on the floor. For many people it is astonishingly difficult to relinquish their own support and rely on another. They do all the work, raising and lowering their own limbs and head independently of their partners' actions. They are in charge, and that is how they insist on keeping it. The feeling "I must do everything for myself" leaves out whatever needs I may have to be sustained by something outside of myself, be it Mother Earth, or just mother. It is a lonely world and a doomed existence for those who cannot experience sources of support which are trustworthy and nourishing.

Finally, in movement we look for *flexibility of the moving parts*. Elbows, shoulders, wrists, neck, jaw, eyes, knees, ankles, waist and pelvis are all parts of the body which are hinged in some way. With what degree of freedom do these parts move when mobilized? In our society, especially, free movement of the pelvic area is frequently blocked. Now, flexibility of many kinds of movement is heavily dependent on freedom of pelvic action. When the ball-and-socket joints permit the pelvis to move freely in conjunction with the legs, the resulting movement has a sense of flow and unhampered progress which is direct and contactful, with no sense of interference from within. Many men block their pelvic movement because our westernized ideal is that women move down there but real men don't. The obvious contradiction is the male athlete, who works best with the most beautifully free swinging pelvic action. Picture a football player running down the field and skillfully avoiding being tackled, or a golfer following through on a drive, or a baseball player putting himself into smacking a ball as far as he can. Women also block the free movement of their pelvis, not because it is so much outside the feminine stereotype to rotate the pelvis, but because of the sexual implications or stimulation which may arise from such action. For both sexes, a common therapeutic necessity is the restoration of flexible pelvic movement.

The rotation of neck and eyes is second in importance.

Flexibility results from being able to swivel as well as to proceed directly forward. A person with rigid neck and unswerving eyes sees straight ahead, period. Some people enter the therapist's office and only after many sessions do they know that there is anything in the office *but* the therapist, so firmly fixed are they on their own purposes. Everything else, anything else, is irrelevant and is to be disregarded. But relevance is linked to context, and by focusing only on the figure of the therapist they leave scant possibility of establishing the sense of context which is central to figure/ground perception and to contactful experience.

How to overcome this sterility? Some sessions will be devoted to experiments which involve the patient moving his eyes from side to side and swiveling his neck so as to scan the office as fully as possible. He will be directed to continue these exercises outside the office, paying attention to details to the side or rear of his direction whether he is driving, sitting, walking. If driving to a meeting, a person who is compelled just to get there will usually fail to notice trees, people walking down the street, the driver in the car ahead, or perhaps the gas gauge in his own car. Flexibility is imperative to contactfulness because anything staying in sharp and unchanging focus for too long becomes dead, like a foot that goes numb when you sit on it too long. People who don't swivel remain fixed and uncontactful. Recovery of movement in the neck and eyes plays a large part in undoing this fixity.

SMELLING AND TASTING

Tasting and smelling regrettably are relegated to minor importance as contact functions. They have only tangential roles in most of the situations which make up the productive stream of life. They are central concerns primarily in leisure circumstances like tasting a fine wine or gourmet food, or in smelling pine trees or spring rain, or in emergency events where we need to smell something burning or acrid gases or to taste so as to know if something is spoiled or sour. We have become dependent on automatic signals and no longer need to rely on our own senses. A timer tells the housewife when her dinner, cooked in an odor-proof pouch, is done. A gauge tells her whether it is too warm in her house, and her clothes are clean at the end of a four-minute or six-minute wash cycle, period. Though taste and smell have only low priority as contact functions in everyday life, they are all but absent in the therapy setting.

There has been some resurgence in the taste function among gestalt therapists primarily because of Perls' appraisal of the eating process as the prototype of the individual's manipulation and assimilation of what his environment has to offer.* At first the child swallows the easily assimilable offering whole; then he begins to chew in order to alter what his world affords into digestible form.

Adding to Perls' conception is the fact that tasting is an evaluative act judging whether or not food is acceptable. Furthermore, tasting is both a stimulation and a reward for eating. The ability to make fine discriminations in any sense modality is given a high priority in gestalt therapy. Even so, it would seem odd to have our patients bring food into the office so that we could explore the chewing and tasting process. We *have* done this with lively consequences, but only rarely. It is not rare, though, to use metaphor in speaking of a person being blessed with good taste and another being cursed with atrocious taste. This implies that some people show sensitivity about the fitness or unfitness of certain actions or objects and that this sensitivity guides them in discriminating assessments of paintings, performances, and the skills of other people in general. The intuitive implication in this use of the word, taste, as referring to people's evaluative skill, is that the tasting

* Perls, F. S., *Ego, Hunger and Aggression*. London: George Allen & Unwin Ltd., 1947.

function is the generic prototype for evaluating good or bad, appropriate or inappropriate.

We have reached the point where taste has been sacrificed to considerations of convenience and profit. Fewer and fewer people realize the difference between homemade bread or cake and the commercial pap oozing out of mass production formulas, TV dinners—five courses all on one convenient tray!— fruits doctored to look attractive but without flavor, frozen foods, easily stored and marketed but vapid, all are common fare and draw little objection from a population that barely recognizes the difference or, even if it does, hasn't the time to complain or feels vaguely that it is complaining about something trivial and unessential. The gap between farm and mouth has contributed only slightly to this lack of discrimination. Cultural values support the undifferentiation which is epidemic. The trouble is that once one surrenders the simplistic and basic contactfulness available in tasting food it is only a short step to devaluing contactfulness generally. Restoring one's own discriminative ability to taste is a step toward restoration of concern with contact itself; not only for its own sake, which could be enough, but also for the primary recognition of the simple goodness of relating fully to whatever is available in the environment.

Gourmets nurture this sensitivity and plan meals so that each part of the meal not only has its own statement to make but also sets up a context of contrast and harmony with the rest of the food, so that hot foods may be set off by cold ones, strong flavors by uncomplicated flavors, and richness by simplicity. Texture and color are manipulated as well, so that detail and subtlety merge into an experience where response flows from one course to another like a symphony or a dance, only much more ephemeral. Each offering is designed to be noted, *not* disregarded.

Smell is one of the most primitive contact functions, and also probably the most disesteemed. What is one of the most contactful senses for other animals has in man become a victim of derogation and derision. Most people do not, and do not want to, go about sniffing each other. And they do not want to be smelled, either. Any casual observer of the advertising folk lore can chronicle how much time is devoted to urging and— for a small charge—aiding us to cover up, remove, or minimize our own smelliness. We must avoid body odors; we must wash our hair frequently, we use deodorants, we use household sprays, we give our dogs food that will even minimize their breath odor, and God forbid we should have bad breath!

Perfumes are an enhancement of contact, but they never quite lose the quality of being an as-though-personal odor, giving off a stereotyped message. One cartoon showed a baggy, middle-aged woman, giving it one last try, standing at a perfume counter where all the fragrances have names like "Night of Passion," "Surrender" or "Follow Me," and saying timorously to the salesperson, "Don't you have something for a beginner?"

Marcia used to sniff characteristically by way of punctuating some of her statements. I asked Marcia to smell anything in the office that she might be interested in smelling. First she smelled the carpet, then a table, and then me. When she smelled me, she became aware of being too close, became embarrassed, and returned to her chair. While she was aware of the great intimacy of smelling me, she came also to remember an old humiliation where she had experienced great agony. Marcia was nine when she came to the United States from Europe. Her new life was very confusing and she had great difficulty in making friends or in feeling at home. One day several of the children gave her a gift which turned out to be a bar of Lifebuoy soap. In those days, Lifebuoy, body odor, and disgrace were all part of one package. Though Marcia could not at that time grasp the full significance of the gift, she did know that she had been greatly humiliated; that she was strangely and disgracefully different from all the other people around her. As she continued talking, Marcia realized that she spends a lot of her energy trying to ascertain how the world smells and has generally decided that it smells pretty bad. This judgment supports her in her chronic need for superiority over others. One of the hallmarks of her character is her connoisseurship of flaws in others. Transforming Marcia's figurative sniff into an actual sniff turned the tables; she had discovered that the actual sniff brought her into intimacy with me and, to her dismay, she became frightened and retreated. Clearly, it was more exciting when her sniff produced intimacy than when it was merely a stale restatement of an old affront.

7

Contact Episodes

We shall not cease from exploration
And the end of all our exploring
Will be to arrive where we started
And know the place for the first time.

T. S. ELIOT

We have described the boundary at which contact occurs and the functions through which contact is made. These, however, are merely the basic components of the contact experience. Contact episodes are the actual events wherein contact happens; these events endow the therapy with substance and drama. Recurrent concerns and themes weave in and out of these episodes and spin threads which become guidelines to major issues in a person's life.

Anne became furious with me because she believed that I was favoring other patients who, she knew, were having magnificent experiences in their therapy with me—and she wasn't having them! She smashed my clock, scattered my lamps and ashtrays and slugged me in the face. I had to wrestle her down to prevent more damage to the room and to myself. When downed, Anne was white with hysteria, spent and in shock. I stroked and stroked her until her color returned and she could see me again. Then I took her hand and said we would clean up the room together. She was relieved at the chance to join me and undo the effects of her rage. When we had the room back together, she was able to smile, her radiance emerged, and she left. The next day Anne phoned to say that she would replace the clock and that she felt the experience had been worth a million dollars to her. I waived the money and accepted the clock. Such episodes go beyond techniques and the therapist experiences himself as a participant in events.

Of course contact episodes do not all have such intensity. Nor do they all include such emergency or such pain. But all contact episodes do have a sequence of contact moments which build into an identifiable unity. These small units of interaction form the basis for the development of a sense of eventfulness in one's life.

Contact episodes have three major qualities: syntax, representativeness, and recurrence.

SYNTAX

The primary quality of the contact episode is its syntax, by which we mean the orderly and recognizable structuring of one part of the episode to its other parts.

The episode begins with the emergence of a need, either immediately recognizable or forming only gradually from a matrix of blankness, confusion, chaos or aimlessness. Many needs flower and are satisfied without any sense of purpose or awareness. Someone tells a joke and you smile, spontaneously satisfying his need to join you in humor. Frequently, however, the person's needs are not only not so easily satisfied but are also obscure; spontaneous moves towards satisfaction are stymied by personal contradictions. Someone tells a joke, but he looks worried and gets no laugh, nor does he get attention for his worries either. Practice in exploring his own experience is necessary before many of his needs can even come close enough to the surface to be recognized. He might not even know that he is worried or that he looks worried and is thereby affecting your response. Without practice, many people who are asked point-blank what they want would have trouble answering. Some might simply not know, others might ask for more details to get leads about how they *ought* to answer the question, others might know quite well and be unwilling to acknowledge it, still others negate simple wants like needing to move a leg, so they search instead for the grand want, and for some the mere act of wanting is so alien that they won't experience wanting anything.

Soon the need does emerge in therapy and the contact episode goes on to the process of playing out the need, developing its details so that it may move toward completion and satisfaction. Then, as the need becomes clearer it may meet resistance because the fulfillment of need in psychotherapy usually does rise in the face of strong resistance. At that point where the power of the need and the strength of the resistance are approximately equal, the impasse occurs. The impasse can be seen as a fulcrum around which the individual's movement may be blocked or advanced.

In the progress toward the impasse, a theme develops which underscores the content of the drama and gives title and clarity to what is going on. The theme may be one person's place in the affections of another, as described in Anne's drama above, or it might be how a person behaves under pressure, as in the example below. The range of themes is boundless, including how to influence one's boss, how to live with one's villainy, how to speak without endless qualifications, how to undo a writing block, and how to give up one's perfectionism. Each theme has its specific personal character and content, and it plays itself out uniquely within the contact episode. The theme points the way, gathering momentum, moving toward the impasse. Here, in the face of the individual's counterforces, the contact episode reaches a climactic moment, opening up new possibilities to break through previous barriers and to move through formerly impermissible feelings or behaviors to completion. The growing excitement, which is now assimilable instead of threatening, supports a surge which finally leads to illumination. Here the individual arrives at a new orientation towards resolutions and alternatives. Acknowledgment of the new experience is common, although sometimes such acknowledgment—especially in groups—can too easily lead to post-mortems which bury the drama of the completed event. After the acknowledgment—or even without it—the individual is free to move on, often to play out the same theme in new contact episodes but with endless variations which endow each repetition with wider dimension and relevance.

Thus, the syntax of the contact episode moves through eight stages. They are: 1) the emergence of need; 2) the attempt to play out the need; 3) the mobilization of the internal struggle; 4) statement of theme incorporating the need and the resistance; 5) the arrival at the impasse; 6) the climactic experience; 7) the illumination; and 8) the acknowledgment. This cycle may last for only a minute, it may play itself out in a session, a year or even a lifetime. The eight stages may occur in different sequences or sometimes condensed into simultaneity. They are guidelines and not to be taken as a cut and dried order.

Here is an illustration of how a contact episode moves through its phases. It is a summary of a taped individual therapy session where Bernard starts out by describing how difficult it is for him to do anything except when he feels the situation is critical. The result is that he is repeatedly governed by crisis situations and doesn't get the things done that he needs to do because he is inspired only by immediate necessity. His experience is that his life is a frantic one, much feeling of urgency, little sense of support and not nearly enough simple peace.

> *Bernard*: When I'm in a crisis situation, I just feel like I flow . . . I can really move. I can recognize that I'm scared . . . all the kinds of feelings I have, but I never immobilize myself.

He continues:

> (Now) it's like I get on the phone and I *do* it. Like yesterday I got on the phone and I did it yesterday. But for three months before that I was pissing around, and that feels crazy to me.

Here we have the first stage of the contact episode wherein the *need* emerges, preceded by a few personal, conversational, informative exchanges that helped, not strategically but naturally, to lubricate the experience of contact between the two of us. Bernard's particular statement of need includes learning to produce not only when urgency erases a sense of choice, but also when he is a free agent and can operate without pressure. At this point in the contact episode we are ready to go on to the second stage which is to find ways of *playing out the need*. My fantasy was that Bernard needed to be pressed up against a wall before he would produce. My next speculation was that he does not *trust* anyone to be behind him or to support him—so he operates best when his back is against the wall. I felt strongly enough about these speculations to play out the need in metaphor as a means of placing Bernard in a scene where his relationship to the wall behind him could unfold. First, I tried to bring him into awareness of how he experienced the space behind him, assuming that by staying with his experience Bernard could contact the empty space instead of merely filling it with projections about the pressures which confront him. In response he fantasied that the space behind him was concave and that he could hunch himself into it like into a big swinging wicker chair. To him, this felt womb-like and he was embarrassed at the thought that a man his age (early 30's) should want something like that. Then his *internal struggle* (stage 3) began to form, rejecting his unacceptable, usually disruptive, passivity and infantness and, at the same time, courting the crisis where he can stand up (like a man) and deal. Bernard said:

> *Bernard*: Yeah, that's what it feels like, just that absurd. I shouldn't want to do that. (Long pause) Well, the other fantasy I had is, in a crisis I stand up straight and there's no need to do that kind of thing. And I feel . . . together. Straight, together, and able to deal.

Here he restates his need, only this time his polar struggle is evident. One of the opposed forces within him says, "I shouln't want to do that," and is also embarrassed, hesitant, hunches his shoulders and is immobilized. His other side opposes by searching for crisis so that he can feel "Straight, together . . . and able to deal." Bernard has to discover that even that part of himself which he scorns as absurd can have its own fruitful possibilities. His fantasy of womb-like retreat is embarrassing enough to deter him from contact with the space behind him. But he must move beyond this embarrassment. With this in mind, I asked Bernard again to imagine the space and the wall behind him.

> *Bernard*: Feels okay, but not too safe because I'm not sure what's in back of it. And it feels loose, so that something could come through it . . . whew!
>
> *Therapist*: Does it bring anxiety to you?
>
> *B*: Not the fact of it, but the fact that I conceive of it that way brings anxiety to me . . . felt a little anxious.

T: What might come through? See if you imagine that.

B: A fantasy of two hands coming through and landing on my shoulders, pulling me back. But like really disembodied hands just came through or out of the wall. They're very strong hands, very big, kinda gnarled . . . and hairy . . . and they just kinda poise like that (gesturing).

T: How do you feel about them being poised?

B: Scary. What I just thought of was, what I just fantasied was that they started to caress me. They caressed me and then took my head, like I started to feel myself starting to go down like this . . . and they took my head and kinda took me up like this, grabbed me.

The mobilized struggle grows. Resistance takes the form of a projected dangerous contact as embodied in the threatening image of the two hands. This projection builds up a head of steam for the movement of the struggle toward the impasse and the consequent climactic resolution. Anxiety is constricted excitement* so we can expect that the pressure which results from constriction of any kind will here serve as a propulsive force, seeking expression. The dialogue continues:

T: What are they trying to do?

B: They keep trying to keep my head from dropping. And it feels like if they let go I would drop my head.

T: Are you satisfied not to drop your head, or do you want to?

B: It feels like dropping my head would be involuntary, that I wouldn't really want to do it but I'd do it anyhow.

T: In spite of yourself and the hands.

B: It's like if I can't keep my head up then the hands can do it, and if they can't, nothing can help. (Very long pause)

---

* Perls, F. S., Hefferline, Ralph and Goodman, Paul, *Gestalt Therapy*. New York: Julian Press, Inc., 1951.

T: It makes you pause in wonder.

B: I just had a quick flash of a whole bunch of people who tell me to do things or not to do things, and it felt like their hands (this was spoken quite rapidly and in a rush). The words that come to me are "am I really that weak?" Sometimes I feel that way particularly on a day-to-day basis with getting things done.

T: Say more about when you feel that way.

B: When I know I should be doing something, when I should be making out a report or writing my paper, I really go limp on myself. When there's an outside expectation, then I do it, you know, some kind of external thing. Which is crazy because I keep putting myself in the positions where I get that kinda thing . . . the external expectation and then it's like I feel that I don't want to follow through or I can't follow through or I feel both.

Here we have a clear *statement of the theme* (stage 4) of his dilemma. In order to get himself moving Bernard sets up a situation where pressure will be put on him from an outside source. His resentment of the external demand, however, makes him resist—by psychologically sagging—what he himself has brought about. He needs to be able to write his reports and his papers, to do his work without immediate and clear-cut outside pressure to compensate for his vagueness about his own directions. My speculation is that Bernard has to be able to make contact with support-without-demand and to allow excitement to rise in him. This excitement must be available to him even when he is not under the severe pressure which obliterates his sense of free choice. The problem is for him to be able to create from a sense of inner propulsion, within the framework of support and expectation but without feeling driven. We proceed by setting up a dialogue between the polarities:

T: So let your limp self speak to the hands.

B: What do you keep pushing me out for, pulling me out

for? I just want to lie down, why don't you leave me alone?

T: What do the hands say?

B: Shape up! Get yourself together! Cut that shit out! Grow up! Take responsibility. Be a man. Don't be smart.

T: How does your limp self feel now?

B: Will you fuck off, already? Bug off, you know! Leave me alone! I'm tired of you! You're a fool! (Deep sigh and long pause) Just . . . you're not worth it.

T: What do the hands do now?

B: Pull yourself together, for Chrissakes, you're acting like a child! (Much louder and more clip to the words) I don't know what the hell I'm gonna do with you! You're a waste! You're wasting your life, you're wasting your time!

At this point Bernard reaches the *impasse* (stage 5). His sense of limpness has gained enough power to confront his sense of urgent demand and the result is a stand-off; he goes limp when the hands caress him, thus transforming the caress itself into support for his limpness. Finally the supporting hands turn to accusation and demand. This results in his resistance to either support *or* demand.

This impasse could be resolved in many different ways. Basic to all of them would be to set up a safe emergency, through experiment or confrontation, where a reshuffling of the familiar ingredients will impel Bernard to move beyond a stale rehash of old contradictions. At this juncture I chose to move behind him, standing there so he might feel *me* in the empty space and be activated by a sense of real contact rather than by his habitual projections:

T: (Standing behind him) What are you feeling?

B: Ummm, first I wondered what you were gonna do and then I heard a noise and I was wondering what you were doing. So I started to look around and I realized it (the noise) was outside the room. I feel both more relaxed and more pressured to do something. (Very long pause while the therapist stood behind him and gently held his neck.) I feel like I want to curl up and be a baby.

T: Then let yourself.

B: (Whispering) You're kidding. Nah, it really scares me. Ohhh (great sigh) I had a flash of . . . like being a baby is putting my thumb in my mouth and crying, and then I realized that's all that being a baby means to me . . . like that's the whole thing.

T: Well, try putting your thumb into your mouth and see what that's like.

B: (Does it. Short laugh) It feels . . . I really felt the tension going out of my body. Like I felt being relaxed. (Very long pause) Wow! When I put my thumb in my mouth, I felt like I didn't have to cry. My fantasy was that I would do both, but when I did it, it was like putting my thumb in my mouth stopped me from crying . . . not stopped me, I didn't feel any need to cry.

Here is the first breakthrough; Bernard loosens the impasse by discovering that forbidden behavior brings unexpected satisfaction. This frees him to experience support without demand and will prepare him to move into his own climactic experience:

T: What is it like for you to have me back here?

B: It feels *really* good! I feel very warm and supported right now. Somehow I feel not concerned about what I say so much.

T: Well, just let your thoughts come now and see what comes to you.

B: I have a kinda weird connection of words. Almost like when I write a poem, I'm not really sure what's going to come out so I feel uncontrolled. Words, uh . . .

Time is righteous and has
No concept of intimacy.
There is a sweet incantation that says,
Right morning, dark night
(whispers) Right morning, dark night
Somewhere sparrows sing
   Until
The thunder is yet to come.
And never before in a sweet mystery, perhaps
   never again
Can rivers flow from south to north.
For old men dream dreams, sing songs and dance.
Beyond horizons that youth can never touch
Is a fast running stream,
Deep into qualities of darkness and high into
   qualities of blue sky.
Only old—only old chiefs
Who know that sometimes the magic does not work
Know that
Time's the consequence of righteous
Of what, foreign I dream.
This tomorrow is *now* in rivers of blood
Coursing through my body.

The *climactic experience* (stage 6) has happened: with great absorption, even awe, Bernard has produced something from internal urgency rather than from projected demand. He experienced the support of another person without going limp, retaining his own expressive freedom and style. *Illumination* (stage 7) is next:

T: Can you feel the rivers of blood?

B: Yeah. In my neck and in my arms. (Long pause) Right now I feel like a . . . like I could be in the eye of a hurricane, where everything is calm, and that would be okay. You could see everything swirling around outside and I could still move. That's what happens to me. I . . . like the day-to-day thing. It's not that it seems so dull and day-to-day. It seems so chaotic, and then *I* feel chaotic

and somehow or other I can't match the chaos. But when
I feel calm like this, I feel like I can manage the chaos,
like it's okay if things are chaotic. I don't need to control
it, I can just deal with it . . . Now I wish I had pencil and
and paper. If I could see what it was that I said (very
long silence). I just feel totally released right now . . .
peace. Very aware of my senses. The room seems much
lighter. Some things, like that painting and that couch and
the pillows, it feels like I'm really seeing . . . I can really
see the colors, you know, for the first time, they don't
seem dull. Now they seem very colorful. It's nice.

With the *acknowledgment,* "It's nice," (stage 8) Bernard
is free to move on; the contact episode is completed.

REPRESENTATIVENESS

Many people have expressed concern about what, if anything, psychotherapy has to do with a person's life *outside* of
therapy. That controversy is a bottomless pit. Good experiences grow beyond their own brief moments of existence just
as surely as one moment moves into the next. This is our faith.
Individual contact episodes are representatives of styles of
contact which exist outside the therapy experience itself and
they exert an influence beyond the hours in the therapist's
office.

All experience can be viewed as having allegorical power,
that is, the power of condensing events which happen over per-
iods of time into smaller units. The therapy experience is especially well endowed with this power because of its intensity
and because of the avowed intention that the significance of
the experience will stretch out into everyday life. In addition
to this power, however, there are three major avenues which
foster the representativeness of the therapeutic contact. They
are: 1) the teaching of skills which may be used in everyday
life; 2) the arousal function; and 3) the development of a new
sense of self.

Teaching of skills—Usually, skills are taught—as in riding a bicycle—with clear goals in mind and fairly clear knowledge of the intermediate steps involved in learning the end skill. Not so in psychotherapy, where the teaching—although occasionally overtly instructional, such as when teaching someone how to get others off his back—is mostly quite subtle and the skills are often not easy to identify. The skills may include using more pithy language, keeping one's eyes open, letting go while dancing, permitting a rush of sensation to the clitoris, asking forbidden or upsetting questions, phoning a girl for a date or walking away from poisonous environments.

The power of the therapist or group to provide support and encouragement for trying out new behaviors is well known. It occurs even though no specific instructions may have been given. Many patients whose sexual fantasies are heard and accepted and who go on to experiment sexually will never be frightened of sexuality *at the same level* again. Many silent people who explore their loquaciousness in therapy will be more likely to seek new ways to speak outside of therapy. Once loved well, by therapist or group, it is harder to return to or to settle for old levels of isolation or timidity.

A wife harangued her husband because he was gone from home so much. According to him, the way she was complaining right there in my office was what drove him away. I asked her what she could do that would be more interesting. She hemmed and hawed for a while and then allowed as how maybe if she were playful with him it might bring him closer. So she smiled at him, and spoke softly about what she liked about him and reminded him of things they enjoyed doing together. She was inviting and her voice was intimate and warm. He was delighted and she discovered that she had the *skill* to bring him closer and didn't have to rely on complaints. Another patient, a woman who experienced most of the problems in her life as having only two polar points of resolution, had to learn to consider alternatives. Her conservative and puritanical upbringing had taught her to view her experience in crisp contrasts of black or white, good or bad, right or wrong and there was no question as to which she was supposed to choose. In therapy she learned how to consider the other side of herself and found in herself an impish humor and originality that could lead her into finding fresh answers to her own problems like personally selling a whole houseful of furniture because she was bored with it! That is a skill.

Such examples are commonplace. Once a skill is learned, it can be used; or, turned around, once a skill is used, it can be learned. When one learns to swim in a safe pond, he can also swim elsewhere. When a woman learns in therapy that she can charm her husband instead of nagging him or a man learns that he can speak vigorously instead of timidly, they are likely to try these skills out elsewhere.

Many of the skills learned in therapy are by-products of the opening or loosening process. As the individual's behavioral perspective—or "ground"—expands, he becomes more hospitable to new activities and feelings. Once, for example, a person feels his nascent sexuality in the animating and permissive atmosphere of therapy, he is oriented to try new sexual behaviors. The consequent development of his sexual skill is not dependent on direct instruction but grows from his own activities through which he discovers how to do what previously was outside his own boundaries. A skill cannot be learned well until it is tried out. By trying it out, the individual lowers his threshold of risk. In fact the whole therapy scene is aimed at altering risk thresholds through trying out in a relatively safe situation what is prohibitively frightening in the world outside. Once the new skill has been tried out, the question is no longer whether the individual *could* engage in such behavior. Rather, it becomes a question of whether he *chooses* to and, if so, under what circumstances. This is not an all-or-none proposition, however. Therapy deals with the setting of new thresholds for experience rather than with only total alteration of behavior.

Thus, the individual may become less easily embarrassed, discouraged or intimidated, or if he does he may not be as debilitated by these feelings. Furthermore, even if he does become debilitated his recovery from this setback may be better.

The incidental learning of skills, through the natural interactive process and without the intent to teach a specific skill, is, of course, inevitable. But in many instances there *is* a clear intention to teach specific skills, including how to use language, how to walk, how to see, how to breathe, etc. When someone learns through practice to speak pungently, to support his own statements, to move his pelvis, to open his eyes and see his environment, say the truth about himself or what he observes, even plan a college curriculum, etc., he is *learning skills*. The therapist need not be reluctant to *teach* somebody something; teaching him does not inexorably mean putting something on him which is not his own, nor must it mean robbing him of the opportunity to learn something for himself, nor does it ignore the fact that life is more than a specific skill.

Suppose the therapist says to one of his patients, "Try moving your pelvis this way," and he tries it and says, "That feels feminine" and the therapist says, "Yes, feminine, but how do you like it?" and he says "It feels smooth to walk like that" and he winds up walking free and easy and not worrying about his femininity. That is not dirty pool. They would both be severely limited if the patient would have to find that out with no instruction or illumination from the therapist. Indeed, what good would the therapist be to him? Of course, there is a risk in teaching somebody and the risk is that the patient will wind up simply going along with directions. Very little is accomplished without risk, though, and this seems a risk worth taking. It is, in fact, unavoidable no matter how zealously one may guard the sanctity of individual initiative and discovery. The patient will frequently imitate the therapist or try to carry out "implied" instructions anyway. So, if the therapist has a skill to teach somebody, it is not enough piously to hope that some day the individual will catch on by himself. Many skills can be taught directly without undermining the integrity of the learner. If my swimming teacher tells me that I keep swallowing water because I'm kicking too low, I try to kick higher and discover it's smoother. I still have to practice doing it to make it work for me, but I'm grateful I didn't have to find it out by myself. I might never have observed this, or only after a long time, time better spent on the next step of learning. So also, if the therapist tells a person whose voice does not project well to breathe slightly deeper and to speak when he still is supplied with air, he is not being deprived of independent function. Indeed, it could be argued that he is given firmer ground for exercising his individual function by means of this simple instruction.

Arousal—Good therapists, whatever their theoretical homebase, are exciting people. Their talk and their actions are incisive and stimulating. After being with them, one feels renewed and heartened for new developments long after the original contact was made. This arousal is a natural ingredient of the experience of contact. The therapist's talent in making contact is his primary instrument for arousing the other person to use his own energies and to become emboldened to make changes. Arousal, in and of itself leads to—perhaps even spawns—new opportunities for resolution. Furthermore, each resolution in itself has fresh arousal potential.

The therapist is not one to let sleeping dogs lie unless he estimates that their appetites, once roused, may be so voracious as to prove unmanageable. The patient, once he has experienced pungency and snap, and has become a participant in the creation of it, will be less likely to settle for dull and routinized conversation, safe but unsatisfying. He is aroused to recreate elsewhere what he has experienced already in the company of the therapist or the group. He may also begin to experience himself as capable of arousing other people. Not only will he be more able to respond to an arousing situation, but he may even learn how to make it happen when he needs it.

The difficulty in trying to make things happen is, of course, that the circumstances outside of therapy are quite different and the frustrations inevitable. But the arousal starts a new process going, one which commonly results in new values and new behaviors, sometimes bringing about changes in bosses, spouses, and co-workers. The consequent dysrhythmia, anxiety, chaos and conflict are part of a turmoil which may lead us to ask if it is all worthwhile. Bosses or co-workers don't understand or can't be bothered. Spouses are harried and distracted. Nevertheless only through the risks inherent in such arousals will change come. Not that such turmoil is indispensable to change, but the risk of it *is* indispensable!

One of the more arousing experiences in life is to fall in love. This happens not infrequently between patient and therapist or group members. Within this love is the spark of mobilization which extends beyond the therapy relationship itself. A 21-year-old girl, altogether isolated from men, told me of a dream in which she had made love with me, and then averred that she would like to do it with me, really. Her desires, strong and awesome as they were, expressed out of virginal directness, warmed me. Though unwilling to make love to her, I did tell her how deeply attractive I felt her to be. She could see how profoundly her openness had moved me. Men have become a part of her life ever since. Her willingness to arouse and be arousable was as though she had learned the language, where formerly she was a stranger.

Still, all is not love that is arousing. Frustration is another common source of arousal. We have mentioned that Perls described much of his own work as founded in creative frustration. His intention was to frustrate the patient in his move toward any goal which *depended* on Perls' cooperation. Impelled by the mobilization evolving from this frustration, the individual would crack through his own paralysis and become sufficiently aroused to obtain satisfaction through his *own* efforts.

Humor is another arousing element which enters into the contact episode, in therapy as well as out. Playfulness, the joke at the right moment, teasing, laughing at incongruities are all part of joining together with another person, not only when he is troubled but also in the expansiveness which humor inevitably calls forth. Hilarity is common in gestalt groups. Sometimes this is escapist, to be sure, but frequently it is part of the spirit of joining together in stimulating events which open people up. For example, in one group Barbara had been describing how she got swamped by family hassles and was unable to disagree with her husband when so much else was going on. We played out a situation Barbara had described where she was driving a carload of kids— and the family dog— to their ice-skating lessons. Her husband decided to take a stand with one of the youngsters who was always late, or losing something, or in one way or another a bottleneck. We lined up chairs in the form of a station wagon, cast group members as the kids and the dog—put her behind the wheel, and had someone play her husband who decided Barbara had to wait until the tardy kid was available. The scene was hilarious— the dog barked animatedly and the kids argued loudly about who would sit where, until an uproarious family comedy was going on. Riding on the exuberance of the humor, our leading lady discovered that she certainly could holler above all this and let her husband know what she wanted, to take off without the tardy kid.

Touching is arousing. Dramatic stories are arousing. New physical movements are arousing. Recognition is arousing. Good breathing is arousing. Leadership is arousing. A roar is arousing. Revealing a secret is arousing. The catalogue of arousing experiences is limitless.

New Sense of Self—People are notoriously clouded, even distorted, in their view of themselves. They hear their voices on tape, or see movies of themselves, and are incredulous. Carl Rogers* believes an individual constructs a self-image from the information he gets about himself from others. These images can range from garbled to accurate. His sense of self also includes the stereotyped attitudes of his society, family, and friends. So, a man may believe that to be a good father he must be stern, but *he* may be an essentially companionable person. Or he may think that to be manly requires him to be loud-voiced and assertive when he is, in fact, a soft-spoken quiet person. The opportunity to acquire new information or unstereotyped responses as in therapy opens him to new views of his own nature and to new views about the implications of his character.

Even more important for changes in self-image than the reactions which others communicate are a person's own discoveries as they have been awakened by new behaviors or newly learned skills. For example, the individual who finds in a group that he responds compassionately to another's sorrow —where formerly he had viewed himself as merely brusque— is free to act further on this discovery, to hold someone who is crying or to say a warm word. These actions themselves, irrespective of feedback from anyone else, are inherently image-changing. The theory of cognitive dissonance** says that behavior which is at odds with an established attitude demands change. This change usually takes the form of altering the original attitude to conform more with the actual behavior. Accordingly, when a person behaves differently he will also change his attitude about himself.

One man in therapy came through as a very sweet man. Nobody sees him that way, including himself, since he has adopted toughness as part of his role as a success-seeking engi-

---

* Rogers, Carl, A Theory of Personality. In Millon, T., Ed., *Theories of Psychopathology.* Philadelphia: W. B. Saunders, 1967.

** Festinger, L., Cognitive Dissonance. In Coopersmith, S., Ed., *Frontiers of Psychological Research.* San Francisco: W. H. Freeman, 1966.

neer. When I remarked that he looked like a sweet man, his face swelled rosily in surprise and hope and he was moved almost to tears. Clearly, some new information was added to his accustomed sense of self.

Naomi's image of herself was that she was intuitively sensitive but a dud at accurate description. Consequently, one day I asked Naomi to describe a painting in my office. She loved this painting and had frequently responded to its changing and glowing colors. This time, though, she was directed to describe it in straightforward factual terms that would make it immediately recognizable to someone who might see it for the first time in a roomful of paintings. As Naomi did this she became aware of the onerous nature of this task—she was gritting her teeth, tightening her jaw, and biting out the words. She recognized, furthermore, how resentful she felt against the adults in her childhood who had drilled into her that the proper way to respond to things was to edit out the delight and retain only the dry description. But now Naomi discovered something else, that she *could* do it without diminishing her love of the painting. When she had finished, she said with an air of grim accomplishment, "Anybody walking into a room where this was hanging with other paintings would be able to recognize *this* one!"

Ted, a conservative man with a half-million dollars in his bank account, lived frugally on his earnings as a physicist. Not only did he abstain from using his money, he did not even experience it as a real factor in his life. When Ted began to comprehend that the money was indeed there and was a source of leverage for action, he began to experience himself as a forcefully independent and wealthy person. First, he furnished his apartment as he really wanted to and—even more importantly—he became hungry to create a new way of life.

In summary, the teaching of new skills, the power to arouse, and the change in one's sense of self all merge to make the therapy experience a spur to new living away from therapist or group. The transition is laced with booby-traps because the protections and simplifications of therapy are missing in everyday life. The changes cannot be immutably molded in the therapeutic setting, either. The first few times the new learning is translated into action in the unguaranteed non-therapy situation the behavior may not fit the individual's personal style, or it may arouse consequences that could not have been foreseen, or it may be perceived mistakenly and need some amplification or further response. Now, obviously, as the individual gets more confident, he will also become more flexible in his behavior. He will be able to revise or to improvise new variations as the changing scene may require. So what he learns in the therapy setting serves mostly as practice for the inventiveness that living demands. Like learning to paddle a canoe—where until one has had the experience of rowing, he doesn't know how deeply to row, how fast he can go, how to turn the canoe without tipping over—the individual learning new ways of staying afloat in his society doesn't always know the effect his actions will have. With increased experience he grows more sensitive to the requirements of new learning. With continuing support for growth, errors can be assimilated, the need for previous self-destructive and crippling props diminishes, and the opportunities for trying out new methods all join together to consolidate the new experiences and transmute them into fresh reality.

RECURRENCE

If it sounds like a struggle to assimilate new images and behaviors because it's complicated to integrate therapeutic developments into everyday life—*it is*. It should come as no surprise, then, that themes requiring resolution would recur many times. While some themes will reappear again and again during the entire lifetime of a single individual, others may be played out during a specific period, never to repeat themselves.

The impasse, the point at which the need to change meets a force which resists change with equal power, is repeatedly confronted until, bit by bit, the individual pushes out his own I-boundaries to include what had formerly been unassimilable. The recurrence of themes represents the piecemeal exploration of psychologically unclaimed territory.

One patient spent the first months of her therapy requiring that she be treated "like a lady." After she became clear about her ladylikeness and its implications, she never bothered about it again, somewhat like an adult who doesn't want to play with a yo-yo anymore.

Another person was recurrently concerned with his occasional homosexual activity and his fears about what this implied about his validity as a person. This theme was worked through via numerous fantasies, reports of his experiences, dramatizations of relevant scenes, repeated confrontations with the therapist. Then he discovered his own potency with women, exercised it, married, and soon not a further word about homosexuality entered his therapy sessions. He didn't *decide* not to bring it in. It just wasn't interesting anymore. Now he began to explore his anxiety about his professional development and his ability to earn the money he needed more urgently than he had before. His facility in making clear professional statements, his willingness to risk being foolish and his inventiveness became the focal points of his therapeutic efforts. Still his anxiety was an important factor in his life—though not as compelling as before— but it centered around new concerns.

One might therefore wonder, what is the good of resolving homosexual problems only to shoulder the burdens of the heterosexual? The benefit is great because in the very act of changing his problems he is coming loose from the basic neurotic quality of stuckness. Anyone who promises that life can be lived with no problems is peddling the emperor's new clothes. A change of problems so that they reflect current living is not to be scorned. One of the grievous aspects of neurosis is that it is so boring. Attacks of panic and anxiety, it is true, could hardly be called boring. Nevertheless, the unvarying quality of much neurotic existence resists meeting the unfamiliar aspects of a situation and instead insists on reducing it to the same old theme. Furthermore, in the process of moving on to new themes one also discovers how to deal with problems in general, including the tolerance for anxiety, confusion, process, climax, and, especially, the faith that, with contact, the problem will yield to his moves. As themes reappear and are resolved, their resolution appears more dependable.

Finally, even when themes recur over a lifetime, the resolutions may turn into a richly detailed style of life rather than simple and repetitive coping. A person may spend his life designing fashions for women because of powerful needs to make women look better than he natively thinks they do. Or he may become a therapist because of an unfinished need to make mother feel better. Or a musician so as to express the ineffable without having to use words. Surely these needs for action involve, at best, growth in inventiveness even while playing out familiar themes. If the range of innovative resolutions is grand enough, these themes can be fruitful motifs for an entire life span.

OTHER INFLUENCES IN THE CONTACT EPISODE

There are three additional factors which can be both interferences and attractions in the development of contact episodes: loving, hating and madness. They interfere because we are afraid of them when they threaten to reach beyond our accustomed limits of tolerance. They are attractive because of the power of riding into whatever directions our inner forces may surge. They are such grand experiences that, in various guises, they pervade many contact episodes. Thus a person may learn a specific skill relating to loving or being loved, he may experience the arousing energy of loving or being loved, and his sense of self may be materially altered by finding himself either a loving or lovable person.

Loving—The spectrum through which loving extends includes the mild forms of friendliness and acceptance and ranges through seductiveness, radiance, sexual play, devotion and the addictive state of being *in* love. Were it not for the addictive properties of love, much of the risk involved in loving would disappear—both in and out of therapy. In therapy—where love is virtually inevitable—one can learn to distinguish between love and dependency, love and obsession, and perhaps even love and sexuality. The rudiments of the working-through process call for the individual to accept his sensations as his own, spun out of his own personal flow, and to recognize that these feelings may be satisfiable in as many ways as his own ingenuity can devise. When, under the favorable conditions of the therapy relationship, he has transcended his habitual barriers to loving, he has discovered how to experience freely the quality of loving without guile, strategy or stereotype. Once expanding beyond the mere conventions of loving, he becomes more sensitive in getting whatever satisfactions exist in the therapy relationship in spite of its customary limits. Furthermore, when these same feelings emerge elsewhere—as long as they don't get hung up on some pre-designated form of love—the chances of satisfaction are greater. With such freedom to accept experience without stereotyped demands, the addictive properties of love are not so threatening and success is not reduced to a single-minded urge focused on only one person, the romantic all.

For example, love for the therapist may inspire one to want to make love with him. Probably he won't do that, but nevertheless he is still open to the many interactions that make the relationship exciting and meaningful. The patient, although benefitting, still needs someone to make good love with. Once this need for love has surfaced, the patient is mobilized to get what he needs from other relationships as they occur. Isn't this then merely a displacement of the sexual urge from the therapist to someone else—an "instead of" experience, based on a sense of simple rejection? Possibly, but only when the person hangs on to his single-minded ideal and tries to make-do anyway. The antidote to hanging-on is the discovery of polymorphism, the discovery that each experience is valid on its own and not merely a substitute for some other experience. When in good form, a person is not just the prisoner of his sensations. Sensations are merely guides to their own disappearance. Feelings *want* to disappear—they have no stake in their immortality. Feelings tend to go all the way in the directions set into them. Then they are gone, only to be replaced by other feelings equally humble and dispensable. Only sentimentality, based on the inchoate fear of premature interruption, leads to the need to hang on, leads to the sense of inviolability and the need for guarantee where one tries to preserve what is basically impermanent. It is up to us, in therapy, to help in the rediscovery of the relay quality of moment-to-moment or year-to-year living. When one unit of experience is ended, another begins, and it is this *process* which constitutes immortality, not creating an idol out of a single experience.

Still, we do not want to minimize the actual dilemma produced in therapy by intensity of feeling. The sense of urgency can become strong, the way to completion can become littered with difficulties, and the need to hang on in the hopes of a particular predefined criterion of completion can become capturing. It is no easy lesson to learn that love does not mean attachment, especially when love is not requited with the familiar, highly-advertised attentions which have been set into our social codes.

Ruth, for example, was furious and even disillusioned when I did not visit her in the hospital when she was there for minor surgery. She had experienced my warmth often in our work together and believed that my failure to visit her in the hospital made that warmth a sham, a mere technique for curing her. Ruth had to learn that the affectionate responses to her humor, her sadness, her flow of images had indeed been authentic. They simply did not lead to my visiting her in the hospital. Now this may have been a valid basis for her anger and disappointment but it did not negate the warmth I did feel for her and the attractiveness which my warmth had made Ruth appreciate in herself. Her attractiveness, however, was not merely contingent on my confirming it in accordance with her stereotyped requirements. It is hard to recognize that the unconfluent love is valid and can be nourishing. Nevertheless, the confrontation with the actualities of love rather than just the customary proprieties moves patients to appreciate love as it is rather than as it *should* be.

Does this sound like a cold view of love, where one of the partners feels no responsibility to respond to the expectations which some contacts engender? Not so. There are some expectations which are crucial, and rightly so, to the level of certain relationships. But, and this is also crucial, these expectations must not be stereotyped promissory notes exacted from previous social contracts. They are part of the process of mutual discovery and they represent a sensitive statement of where one person stands in relation to another. So, Ruth came to recognize that my affection for her was genuine, but that it was not tied to a hospital visit.

How tempting to have been able to interpret Ruth's behavior as representing merely her own foolish repetition of the unfinished business with her father who paid her little attention. The heat of the actual love relationship can be very strong. Breuer discovered this a long time ago when he had to leave the psychoanalytic direction behind because of it. Freud proved to be more able to stand the heat, but even he had to invent the concept of transference to insulate himself. By invoking the concept of transference, he and his followers were able to depersonalize the contact by saying that it had nothing to do with the therapist personally.

In gestalt therapy we try to focus on the relationship as it is. To re-experience oneself as loving is to recover an aspect of full self-experience which is weak or absent in the everyday lives of many people we see. Love is more than a cause célèbre or a socially acceptable case of monomania. It is not attached irrevocably to one eliciting object, but is a function of the person who loves. So, the more he can learn to love many people in many ways, the greater his chances of satisfaction and fulfillment. In the assurances of therapy or in the group, in the continuity of interaction, in the excitement of meeting with attractive people, in the midst of the depth and intimacy of good contact and even in the face of the vulnerability which the need for love often imposes, the patient has optimal conditions for coming to love another person.

We all know that love can be fun and enriching without the accompanying stereotypy and obligation of such issues as permanence, exclusivity, and passion. Loving one's college professor can mobilize a person to take himself and his education seriously and can introduce him to new directions in reading, thinking, and communication. To talk people out of their loving feelings is shameful. People need to learn, rather, that to love someone does not mean we have to marry them, screw them, send them to college, invite them to parties, be with them always. It might, but not inevitably. Expectations, yes; inevitabilities, no!

Hating—Just as loving is the generic condition for a broad range of actions and sensations, so also hatred subsumes a variety of interactive possibilities, including anger, rejection, exclusion, suspicion, fighting, alienation and many others. Hating is a residual crud forming out of the accumulation of unexpressed feelings, words or actions which are spawned by personal threat. Hatred is as central to the contact episode as loving because it is a force born out of non-contact, which surges towards contactfulness. The special contacts which accompany hatred are so engrossing that if they are not faced in the therapy experience the potential for contact is seriously diminished. It is crucial to recover some of the contactfulness which is being held back. The individual fears the sensations which might arise if he were to release his feelings of hatred and he dreads the possible consequences of such release. To tell off a fantasied mother or boss, to pummel the effigy of the neighborhood bully, to scream in rage at the fates, to say no to one's mate, to insist vigorously on one's rights with therapist or group are all experiences of contact which can result in estrangement and impotence if backed away from.

In all of the many forms which hatred can assume, there is a reservoir of excitement so great that it threatens to engulf the individual in its poisonous tide. No one can afford to take such engulfment lightly. So, pacing and timing of expressions of hatred must be carefully ordered to respect the integrity of the individual. If the individual is to be restored to peace by completion, the organic eruptions arising out of hatred must be experienced as timely and culminative, not forced or contrived. Pillow-hitting can be invalid when the therapist or the group, like a gang of cheerleaders, baits a blocked person into voicing his anger. Such coercion can also be self-applied, as when one group member announced at the beginning of a workshop that he had come there for the express purpose of venting his anger. This intention colored his whole approach to the group. They, on the other hand, proved actually to be a source of great warmth to him. For him to have used the group merely as effigies to stick pins into would have served his purposes poorly. Any anger emanating out of such single-minded preordination could only be obsessively farcical, a trumped-up Punch and Judy show. Unfortunately, there are more than enough genuine opportunities for the natural flow of hostility so that we do not have to manufacture them obsessively. They will arise, they will arise.

One patient in a moment of fury took my favorite ashtray and dashed it to the floor, breaking it into unreconstructible fragments. I reached over and whacked her across the ass. It really stung her, and she was terribly startled because she had a guiding impression of the permissiveness of therapy. No doubt about it, even in its brevity, this was a flipover contact episode. Several lessons were learned in this contact. One was how it felt to fling my ashtray down, another was how it felt for me to slug her, another was the humbling—though fortunately *not* humiliating—restoration to reality, still another was the ensuing reconciliation between us. In total, even though she had behaved obstreperously, the resolution was as important a part of the episode as the pain had been. At an earlier time the woman's hostility would have been passively expressed through silence and an air of inadequacy and confusion. However, her previously arid unapproachability turned into wet anger this time, not yet skillfully expressed, but exciting and receptive to resolution. Plainly, the move into angry contact was a fruitful event.

Other manifestations of the hatred-based contact episode are more subtle. The boring talker, the point-misser, the late arriver, the obfuscator, the person unwilling to give an inch may all be deflecting their hostility so as to remain minimally contactful. The deflection makes them appear off-target and unreachable. They need to sharpen their focus and identify their feeling and its directions. For the person who is retroflecting his hostility, the feeling is a little easier to identify; what he needs is to turn it around and direct it away from himself towards contacting the appropriate target. There is nothing essentially new or startling about the recognition of the importance of hostility in psychotherapy. What is new is the concept of the contact boundary as the locus of restorative therapeutic action and the contact episode as the sequence of life events within which the restorative contact is established.

Madness—Deeply embedded at the human core is a reflex-

ive dread of one's own madness. This dread determines and per-
meates the contacts he is willing to permit. The defense against
madness is exercised most powerfully by those whose very
defenses are labeled "mad" by their society. These are the
people who go to great lengths to establish their sanity: the
hallucinator who insists on the reality of what he sees, the
catatonic tightening his body so stringently against the erup-
tion of his mad excesses of excitement that he cannot even
move out of his chair, and the depressive believing profoundly
in the futility of life so that his own crazy needs will not have
to be acted upon.

To a lesser degree, we are all in the same boat, averting
that contact which might threaten madness. The fear of madness must be respected in the development of the contact
episode—partly as a safety measure serving to retain the unity
of the person and partly because fear of madness engenders
a vigilance which unleashes a powerful anti-contact force.

Remember, what the individual experiences if he comes
too close to the edge of the I-boundary is the risk of disappearing, disintegrating or becoming alien to himself. It is also
as he approaches this edge that he experiences less chance of
successful outcome. This is where he fears loss of self-direction,
where his own actions are unfamiliar and the results are uncertain. To go mad is, of course, to experience the most extreme loss of one's own choice system. In milder form one
gets some of the same feeling when faced with being silly, becoming extremely excited, or behaving against one's better
judgment. These mini-madnesses are common explorations in
the therapy situation. The person who will not speak in gibberish, the person who will not touch, the person who will not
make a speech, the person constantly smiling to block his fear
of depression, the person who is afraid to reveal his mastur-
batory shame are prisoners of their own fear of madness. For
them, madness is the unassimilable excess which threatens when
controls are let down. The loss of personal management is at

stake, sometimes a real hazard though not typically. The fulcrum discrimination to be made is whether the fear is mere anachronism or whether it is tuned in to present chanciness. If one really fears that his silliness will turn into hebephrenic permanence or that if he were to cry, he would cry forever, he would surely be wise to block out silliness and crying. The discovery that these outbursts have their own completions and will yield in time to other important aspects of existence is of crucial support in establishing a sense of personal management in life.

The necessary support for exploring these mini-madnesses may come from several directions. One is the sense that the therapist or someone else is so dependably available in case of emergency that one is willing temporarily to surrender one's customary restrictions—like the Yogi who needs a companion when he goes into the depths of his non-being lest someone cart him off for dead.

Kevin was in the throes of terror upon visualizing, with eidetic clarity, children on a playground being swallowed up by a giant monster appearing from the sky. In a violent rush of sensation and impotence Kevin began screaming as though the monster were right there and then he began crying—like bells chiming in his head. Only gradually, by being held and whispered to, could he finish off the crying and be restored to a new sense of peace by his immediate contact with me. "Where will you be if I need you?" is a serious question. It underlies all relationships where a joint adventure beckons and where one senses intuitively that his own resources may not prove ample once the customary vigilance is surrendered.

Another source of support is the expectation and the assurance that one's movement into the previously unassimilable—unthinkable—experience will be gradual and faithful enough to the individual's needs. He needs to know that his I-boundary will be extended without irreparable risk and he will find retreat avenues available, should he need them. He may not need to retreat a great distance, but he must sense that he could back up as much as he might need. This is the basic premise of the experiment, which we discuss in Chapter 9. Essentially it means that we give respectful attention to resistance and that we change the conditions of the exploration according to the nature of the resistance encountered along the way. Suppose we ask a person to look at whomever he is talking to. Suppose he can't. To grade this experience down in intensity, we could ask him instead to look around the room and describe what he sees. Once he can recover his willingness to see under less threatening circumstances, he is more likely to be able to exercise his vision even when conditions are scary. If he fears that looking too closely at another person will arouse some rash action which he would be powerless to resist, he learns that he can look and, though aroused, not lose his sense of free choice. Gradualism can lead to the least painful growth and the least risky, as well as that most likely to be assimilable.

Yet gradualism does have real limitations. Life is simply not that cooperative and one must be willing to accept the occasional confrontations with explosive possibilities. Everyone develops his own life partly according to his willingness and confidence in managing these explosions. The ratio of recklessness/carefulness will very often be a major factor, then, in determining one's style of work or living. The reckless experience is not merely chaotic or out-of-tune with reality. In fact, some reckless person, such as, say, General Patton, may do his job more daringly and more effectively than a cautious person. The reckless patient will often move more than the careful one, but he has to be willing to transcend error and pain along his sometimes fitful way to resolution and growth. Sometimes what looks like recklessness is really sensitive and skillful functioning with smaller margins for error than people operating with less élan. What is foolhardy risk for one person may be dashing and brilliant for another. In this respect, the relationship between therapist and patient resembles wily performers in general, be they circus acrobats, political strategists, lovers, or hunters of wild game. If they miss their target they may be in bad trouble; but the best of them has a mark of the reckless in their spirit—and they frequently wind up in less trouble than many who are more circumspect.

Another source of support when confronting the possibilities of one's own madness comes from the individual's knowledge that he does not *have* to do what he does not *want* to do. It is important to respect the self-regulatory quality of a person's choice. Sometimes, it is possible to deal with a person's objections to a particular action without even returning to the rejected behavior. Suppose, for example, that we ask a man to imagine his mother sitting in the chair opposite him and to speak to her. He says he doesn't want to do that; he doesn't like make-believe. We ask what his objections are. He replies that when he was a young boy he had three sisters who were always playing make-believe and sucked him into their games. One Halloween they all dressed in costumes and he was talked into wearing a girl's nightgown. His friends saw him and from then on it was a struggle to live down the humiliations they poured on him. When we ask how he feels telling this story, he says there is a resurgence of his hatred for everyone concerned: his sisters, the guys who teased him, and for his mother, too, for allowing this to happen. Now, we have a brand new ball game. We are talking with a person who is authentically aroused rather than someone resisting a phony exercise—or worse, going along with it halfheartedly. Now he is asserting his indignation to us and his recovery of self-support instead of a cringing hidden undercurrent is as relevant as if he had gone along with the original task of talking to his fantasied mother.

All these supports help, but the pre-ordinate support for risking the mad experience is courage to face the demon and faith that one can come out of it with sanity and personal unity extended and intact. The person who laughs hebephrenically discovers his joke on the world—and also that the laughter finishes when its time is done. The person engulfed in rage discovers a partner instead of an enemy. The depressed person can contact his deep sadness, full of lively feeling rather than the benumbed stupor of depression. The person afraid of frenetic movement discovers that when he finally tries it he is not swept into the never-ceasing red shoes phenomenon of the manic but that he becomes fruitfully exhausted. The person trying baby talk does not degenerate into burbling babyhood but can explore the playful lover in himself.

Ad infinitum . . . sanity and unity are more easily come by within the confines of secure but courageous living. When one is stretched to his boundaries, one risks his sanity. When this struggle is avoided, one may be comfortable but stagnant. When this struggle is engaged in and won, the free spirit is nourished.

8

Awareness

> To be aware of our body in terms of the things we know and do, is to feel alive. This awareness is an essential part of our existence as sensuous active persons.
>
> MICHAEL POLANYI

A common objection to gestalt therapy is that it is altogether too self-conscious. It is maintained that people in therapy are *already* overly aware of what they are doing. What they need is to be able to give up this awareness so they can behave less self-consciously, with grace and spontaneity. At first glance this objection makes sense. The gestalt therapist repeatedly and frequently asks such questions as what are you aware of; what are you doing; what are you feeling; or what do you want. For a person to answer these questions he may have to abandon the ongoing flow of communication, turn his attention towards himself, identify what was indeed happening therein, and finally be able to report to another person about processes which might ordinarily remain unobstrusively underground or unattended.

Some people regard this process as valueless at best and, at worst, a disruption of the current activity. They view this introspection as a distraction from the expressive stream of narrative or activity—something like asking a centipede which of his legs he moves first, and then watching him wind up hopelessly entangled while he tries to figure it out. However, there are two factors which these objections fail to take into account.

First, a person is often overly self-conscious because his continuous self-scanning parries the chance that he just *might* do something he would not *want* to become aware of. Like radar, he guards himself against behavior which is not under the scrutiny of his own conscious control. He does not want to do anything he doesn't want to become aware of and he doesn't want to become aware of anything he doesn't want to do. The obsessive who is exquisitely aware of the minutest details of his own behavior and the response he evokes from others—but in the dark, for example, about his own latent homosexuality— uses the excessive attention he devotes to these social rumina- tions in order to keep himself safe from becoming aware of his own personal fears. This *avoidance* of the feared awareness keeps him self-conscious—tightened up, off balance, easily em- barrassed and offended—but safe.

In recovering one's willingness to be aware, it is probably inevitable that the individual will engage in some overly self- conscious behavior for a time. Someone who has been bedridden and prohibited from walking for a long period *is* more deliber- ate and aware of each step he takes on his first day out of bed than he will be later. Only after he returns to healthy function can he forget about his movements and walk naturally, with- out needing to pay close attention. So too, for the individual who is trying to grow psychologically. At first the awarenesses to which he is unaccustomed—and concerning which he may well feel apprehensive—bring on a deliberateness and caution which limit authenticity. As these awarenesses become acceptable and assimilable, he is freer to forget about them and use them merely as a support for more spontaneous and genuine behavior.

A second rebuttal to the objections about awareness is that, although an individual may *not* be immediately aware of process in moments of fullest involvement, this is only because he is outwardly focused, his engagement with a figure of interest is engrossing, and his function is acceptable. If he wanted to become aware of his own performance—if it were to become necessary or desirable in order to do better, say— he could do so easily. The most skillful practitioners in all activities can come into awareness fast when they need to or when they are questioned. Here is Pablo Casals* speaking on the artist's interpretive function. Notice how he is in touch with what goes on when he plays, just like a juggler who knows exactly where each one of his indian clubs is at all times. He uses his awareness to orient and inform him in interpretation and performance:

> One of the things I teach my pupils is to know how and at what moment they can relax the hand and the arm. Even in the course of a rapid passage it is possible to find the right moment to relax. (This may happen within the tenth of a second.) It becomes a fundamental necessity in performance and if one does not take it into account there comes a time when one cannot relax (it is like being unable to breath) and exhaustion sets in. This fatigue of the hand and arm mostly comes from the tension of the muscles produced through emotion and "stage-fright." However, the will of the performer must overcome this obstacle, and to this end the conscious practising of

* Corredor, J. Ma. *Conversations with Casals*. New York: E. P. Dutton, 1958.

relaxation will prove very beneficial to complete control during a concert.

. . . If you pay attention you can notice that when we think we are in a complete state of relaxation, we can generally find some part of the body that could be relaxed even more. And don't you believe it is easy to do unless we have been through long exercises which are exactly what we want, to keep up the suppleness of the arm and the fingers. . . . Only this impulse, coming from the center of the body instead of each extremity, will group the different movements in a unified whole, producing better results and less fatigue.

Like Casals, the awarenesses which concern us in gestalt therapy are also those which help restore the unity of the individual's total and integrated function. Before he can alter his behavior in any way the individual must first encompass the sensations and feelings which go along with it. Recovery of the acceptability of awareness—no matter what it may reveal— is a crucial step on the road to the development of new behavior. The individual learns how to become better aware either through various exercises or through sensitive guidance by the therapist who directs the patient's attention to details of his own behavior which are relevant but ignored.

This focus occurs in psychotherapy when the range of human experience is divided into culminative experiences and ingredient experiences.* The culminative experience is a composite form; it is a total and united event which is of central relevance to the individual. In writing these words, for example, the act of writing is a culmination of a lifetime of experiences which have led to this moment and which form a part of the composite act of writing. Furthermore, each movement of the finger, each breath, each tangential thought, each variation

---

* This concept has some parallels with Polanyi's dichotomy of focal and subsidiary awareness. *The Study of Man.* Chicago: University of Chicago Press, 1959.

in attention, confidence, clarity, join together to form the composite experience, "I am writing."

As elements in a composite whole, however, these are all ingredient experiences. Now, these ingredient experiences usually go unattended, but one could explore and discover their relationship to the culminative event, thereby intensifying the experience. The gourmet does this as he tastes a sauce. Initially he encounters the taste in totality, as an integrated and smooth blend. He then begins to examine the flavor more inquisitively so that he may identify the ingredients making up the sauce. He may recognize certain herbs, a familiar wine, proportions of butter, egg yolk, cream. He shifts back and forth in a creative rhythm between analysis and synthesis, breaking down the composite taste into its components and then re-assembling it.

So also when exploring one's own awareness. He may identify the ingredients of the everyday experiences which form the substance of his life. Polanyi* describes the act of understanding:

> It is a process of *comprehending*: a grasping of disjointed parts into a comprehensive whole.

This is how one comes to understand the world, and himself and his experience in that world. He moves between a synthesized experience and the awareness of the elemental pieces which make up his existence in a dynamic and continually self-renewing cycle.

At its best, awareness is a continuous means for keeping up to date with one's self. It is an ongoing process, readily available at all times, rather than an exclusive or sporadic illumination that can be achieved—like insight—only at special moments or under special conditions. It is always there, like an underground stream, ready to be tapped into when

---

* Polanyi, M., *The Study of Man. Op. cit.*

needed, a refreshing and revitalizing experience. Further-more, focusing on one's awareness keeps one absorbed in the present situation, heightening the impact of the therapy ex-perience, as well as the more common experiences in life. With each succeeding awareness one moves closer to articulating the themes of one's own life and closer also to moving towards the expression of these themes.

A simple example of following awarenesses from moment to moment is this illustration from a therapy session. The session started with Tom's awareness of his tight jaw and moved through several intermediate steps to a loosening up of his speaking mannerisms and then to the recovery of some child-hood memories. Tom, a minister, felt that he could not pro-nounce words as he would like to. His voice had a metallic tone and he turned out his words like a brittle robot. I noticed an odd angle to his jaw and asked him what he felt there. He said he felt tight. So I asked him to exaggerate the movements of his mouth and jaw. He felt very inhibited about this and described his awareness first of embarrassment, then stubborn-ness. He remembered that his parents used to nag him about speaking clearly and he would go out of his way *not* to. At this point he became aware of tightness in his throat. He was speaking with muscular strain, forcing out his voice rather than using the support which his breathing could give him. So, I asked Tom to bring more air into his speech, showing him how to coordinate speaking with breathing by using a little more air and by trying to feel the air as a source of support. His coordination was faulty, though—so faulty as to border on stuttering. When I asked him whether he had ever stuttered, he looked startled, became aware of his coordination troubles, and then remembered what he had until then forgotten—that he *had* stuttered until he was six or seven. He recalled a scene from a day when he had been three or four years old; his mother was phoning from some distant place and was asking him what he wanted. He tried to say, "ice cream," but his mother misunderstood and thought he said, "I scream" and took it to mean that he was going to scream at his brother and she became infuriated with him. He recalled still another scene. His mother was in the bathroom and he heard what at first he thought was her laughter. He was startled when he realized it was not laughter at all; she was crying hysterically. Tom remembered once again the horrible feeling of incongruity. As he recounted the story he also became aware of his own feelings of confusion both in being misunderstood by his mother and by misunderstanding her. Having recovered the old sensations, his speech became more open and his jaw softened too. He felt relieved and renewed.

Although awareness can be as democratic as sunlight, illuminating whatever it falls on, we would like to call attention to four main aspects of human experience where awareness can be focused. They are: awareness of sensations and actions, awareness of feelings, awareness of wants and awareness of values and assessments.

SENSATIONS AND ACTIONS*

Identifying basic sensations is no easy task. If the gap could be closed between basic sensations and more complex behavior, there would probably be fewer instances of incongruent or out-of-touch actions. It is common for an individual to eat, for example, not only because he is hungry but also because it is mealtime, or because he may not be in the right situation to eat later on when he expects he *will* be hungry, or because he likes company rather than eating alone, or because he can get a particular kind of food now and won't be able to get it later or when he is in another place. It is only too plain that the individual's sensations and what he does

---

* Much of the material in this section is taken from Polster, E., Sensory Functioning in Psychotherapy, in Fagen, J. and Shepherd, I., Eds., *Gestalt Therapy Now*. California: Science and Behavior Books, 1970.

about them are often only distantly or obscurely related. So it is not surprising that the resulting muddle only adds to the oft-lamented crisis of identity—how *can* one know who he is without at least minimally knowing what goes on inside? And how can he know what is going on inside when so much of his experience seduces him away from honoring the process? He was told as a child that an inoculation wouldn't hurt—and then it did! Now what does he believe, his own smarting arm or the all-knowing adult who has been right about so many things before? And so, the fact is that people who are lonely sometimes eat, those who are angry make love, and those who are sexually aroused make speeches. In such perversions of the relationship between feeling and doing lies the crux of self-alienation.

Sensation exists in tandem with action or expression; it serves as a springboard for action and is also the means by which one becomes aware of action.

The concept of synaptic experience is one way of illustrating this relationship. The synaptic experience is an experience of union between awareness and expression. The term, synapse, is used as a two-fold metaphor—partly because of the basic meaning of the Greek word from which the term derives and partly because of the analogy to the neurological description of synaptic action. The Greek word originally signified "conjunction" or "union". Correspondingly, in physiology the synapse is the functional conjunction between nerve fibers where, through an electro-chemical energy transmission, an arc is formed which bridges the gap between separate neural fibers and links the sensori-motor system into a smoothly functioning union. The metaphor of the synaptic experience focuses attention on united sensori-motor functions as they are represented in personal experience—as *awareness* (sensory) and *expression* (motor). Though at the moment the primary emphasis is on the individual's sensation, expression *emerges* from this awareness and together they form a united experience.

One can sense this union if one becomes aware, for example, of his breathing while talking or of the flexibility of his body while moving or of his excitement while painting. At times of union between awareness and expression, profound feelings of presence and wholeness of personality, clarity of perception and vibrancy of inner experience are common.

People in the arts know the synaptic experience well. The performer in the lively arts—the musician, the singer, the instrumentalist, the dancer, the actor—all remain acutely aware of their sensations and actions. The placement of the voice, the position of an arm, the expansiveness of a gesture, the kind of walk that accompanies the portrayal of a certain role, all depend on a sensitive tuning in to their own sensations. Then they use this sensitivity as an expressive vehicle to reach into an audience. Again, Casals* observes:

> He goes the wrong way who does not question himself or listen to the "voice" of his artistic nature—provided that he has such a nature, of course. What *does* matter is what we feel, and that is what we have to express.
>
> . . . Willingly or not, the performer is an interpreter and can only render the work through his own self.

The creative artist, the painter, the sculptor, the composer, the playwright, the poet, are all people who dance on the very edge of their own sensations. For them the artistic product is a projection. The artist remains at the same time both deeply aware of his own sensations and beautifully articulate in his expression of these sensed and projected parts of himself. For those of us who are not creative artists but who do reverberate to the insights they provide, this merging of expression and awareness seems magical. It is this union that is the matrix of their creativity. Furthermore, in all human situations where this happens, drama is inevitable.

---

* Corredor, J. Ma., *Conversations with Casals*. New York: E. P. Dutton, 1958.

Various therapies differ in their methods of bringing awareness and expression together, but most do share in attending
to the individual's inner processes—sometimes including sensation—as well as to his expression system. Most therapists
would agree that if a patient were to talk about his feelings of
love when his mother sang him to sleep, his story would have
greater impact both for him and his listener if he were aware of
his present feelings as he is talking. His body might be moist,
warm, flexible, tingly, etc. The emergence of these sensations
increases the restorative powers of the story. Through the resulting unity of sensation and words, his story becomes a more
compelling confirmation of his past love experience.

Exploring sensation is not new to psychology. Old Wilhelm
Wundt viewed sensory experience as the root support from
which all higher consciousness grew. Trouble was, his research
never had the so-called humanistic flavor which would attract
the psychotherapist. However, there are many recent humanistic views which do herald a new recognition of the growth-
inducing power of sensation. Schachtel,* for one, accentuates
the commonality of the infant and the adult in their experience
of primitive, primary and raw sensation. He says:

> If the adult does not make use of his capacity to distin-
> guish . . . the pleasurable feeling of warmth . . . (from)
> perceiving that this is the warmth of air or the warmth
> of water . . . but instead gives himself over to the pure
> sensation itself, then he experiences a fusion of pleasure
> and sensory quality which probably approximates the
> infantile experience . . . The emphasis is not on any object
> but entirely on feeling or sensation.

Many people believe that the child's sensation-tone is the
paradigm for purity of sensory experience. But even though
sensations do become cluttered over the years, early experiences need not *remain* merely infantile. The recovery of earlier

---

* Schachtel, E., *Metamorphosis.* New York: Basic Books, 1959.

existential possibilities is invaluable in the search for fulfillment. The early innocence of sensation has been invalidated
by the social forces which dichotomize the child and the adult
into altogether separate creatures. But the adult is *not* just a
replacement for the child; he is the result of accretions which,
hopefully, need not make the childhood experience irrelevant.
A child-like sense may orient and vitalize people even in the
face of later developmental experiences. As Perls, Hefferline
and Goodman* say, concerning the recovery of past memories:

> . . . the context of the recovered scene is of the utmost
> importance. The childish feelings are important, not as a
> past that must be undone, but as some of the most beauti-
> ful powers of adult life that must be recovered: spon-
> taneity, imagination, directness of awareness and man-
> ipulation.

Extending still further in appreciation of the primacy of
sensation are the reports of experiences after taking LSD. Alan
Watts** has said that, while on LSD, he has spent much time
watching for changes in his perception of such ordinary things
as "sunlight on the floor, the grain in wood, the texture of
linen, or the sound of voices across the street. My own experience," he continues:

> has never been of a distortion of those perceptions as in
> looking at one's self in a concave mirror. It is rather that
> every perception becomes—to use a metaphor—more
> resonant. The chemical seems to provide consciousness
> with a sounding box . . . for all the senses, so that sight,
> touch, taste, smell, and imagination are intensified like
> the voice of someone singing in the bathtub.

---

* Perls, F. S., Hefferline, Ralph and Goodman, Paul, *Gestalt Therapy*. New York: Julian Press Inc., 1951.
** Watts, A., A Psychedelic Experience: Fact or Fantasy, in Solomon, D., Ed., *LSD, The Consciousness Expanding Drug*. New York: Putnam, 1964.

This kind of dynamic awareness is also possible in psycho-therapy, but it requires dedicated attention. Concentration is a major therapeutic technique for the recovery of sensation. Everyone knows that doing well at anything requires concentration, but instructions in concentrating are usually vague, moralistic or general. Nevertheless, concentration *can* be a specific mode that involves giving close regard to the particular object of interest; it must be pointed and single-minded. When concentration is focused on internal sensations, events may occur which are remarkably comparable to events arising out of hypnosis, drugs, sensory deprivation, heroic eruptions and other circumstances that take the individual out of his accustomed frame of reference.

Although not as inevitably potent as some of these other conditions, concentration has two great advantages in heightening experience. First, one may readily return to ordinary events and ordinary communication, and second, the experience feels like something one has had a hand in producing rather than having been blasted into an unusual state which is normally beyond one's powers. Thus one may move in and out of accustomed modes of interaction; talking, role-playing, fantasy, dreamwork, using awareness as a flexible adjunct to therapy, one which is more relevant to everyday consciousness.

In the therapeutic situation itself, awareness of sensations and actions serves three therapeutic purposes. They are: 1) the accentuation of fulfillment; 2) the facilitation of the working-through process; and 3) the recovery of old experiences.

1) Different people find fulfillment in different ways; there are action-oriented people and then there are those who are awareness-oriented. Both can lead rich lives as long as one orientation does not exclude the other. The action-oriented person who has not put up a barrier to awareness of his internal experience will—through his actions—arouse his experience of himself. The swimmer, for example, may discover powerful inner sensations; the business executive who has won

leadership of a new company may become aware of strong currents within himself uncovered by this experience. The individual who is oriented towards awareness may also find that,
as long as he does not arbitrarily exclude action, his awareness
leads him to action; the psychologist may write a book, the
restless person may move to another city, and the sexually
aroused person may have intercourse. It is when the rhythm
between awareness and expression is faulty or disrupted that
psychological troubles result.

To illustrate—Kurt, an action-oriented person and a successful businessman, came into therapy because he was not
experiencing fulfillment in life. Unusually vital and active, he
needed to make every second count and became impatient with
any moment of non-productivity. He could not tolerate an
accumulation of sensation and kept ahead of himself by prematurely discharging sensation and preventing its buildup
either through action or through making plans for action. Consequently he was having great difficulty knowing "who I am."
During the first ten sessions we talked a great deal and made
some introductory explorations into Kurt's inner experiences,
including awareness experiments and breathing exercises. Then,
one day when he had been asked to close his eyes and concentrate on his inner experience, Kurt began to sense a quietness
in himself and to experience a feeling of union with the birds
singing outside the window. Many other sensations followed
but he kept them to himself, as he said later, because to describe them would have meant interrupting himself—a wise
but atypical respect for feeling rather than productivity. At
one point, seeing that his abdomen was not integrated into his
breathing I asked Kurt to use his abdomen more fully, which
he was readily able to do. When he did he began to feel a new
ease of breathing which was accompanied by an easy strength,
quite distinct from the impatient strength with which he was
so familiar. He could really sense the difference between the
two kinds of strength; he described himself as feeling like a

car that had been perfectly tuned—a beautiful blend of action and awareness. As he left he remarked that he was recovering a missing link in his life. He felt as though he had *experienced* time rather than having wasted it.

2) The second purpose, the facilitation of the working-through process, can be illustrated by the story of Lila who had recently become an executive in a toy factory. Her secretary had been in this same department for years and was a disorganized and controlling person. The new executive became aware that this secretary was the root of many previous departmental troubles and confronted her with certain departmental requirements. The secretary had experienced this as a great blow and had suddenly looked—in Lila's words—"like a waif." At this moment, Lila felt as though she was sitting face-to-face with another part of herself. She and her brother had grown up in an impoverished section of New York and had indeed been waifs. However, since she had always nurtured her younger brother, she saw only him as a waif, *not* herself. As the facts emerged, it became clear that Lila had in her lifetime alternately supported waifs and played the waif herself.

As she continued, Lila realized she didn't want to be a waif anymore and recognized that in this confrontation with her secretary she had accepted the opportunity to get rid of the waif in herself and become a woman in her own right. As she spoke of this, a new look came over her face, a mixture of absorption, alert introspection and a yielding to puzzlement. When I asked her what she felt, she said in surprise that she felt a tightness in her breathing and in her legs. She attended to these sensations and, after a few moments of silence, looked surprised again and said she felt a tightness in her vagina. I asked her to concentrate on this sensation, which she did. Again, after a few moments of concentration Lila's face brightened and she said the tightness was leaving. Then she seemed startled and suddenly had a deep sensation which she didn't describe but instead burst into paroxysms of crying, calling out the name of the man she loves and with whom she has had, for the first time, a relationship of mutuality and strength. When she lifted her head she looked beautiful and whole. As we spoke further she realized the importance of her confrontation with the secretary—whom she subsequently fired—and the rediscovery of her attitude about waifs. But she knew that her deepest breakthrough had come with the discovery of the sensation in her vagina. The subsequent awakening of her palpable sense of womanhood instead of waifhood gave substance and primal resolution to problems which might otherwise only have been verbalized.

3) Finally, the third purpose served by the restoration of sensation is the recovery of old events. The unfinished situation moves naturally into completion when resistances are redeployed and when inner stimulation propels one toward completing the heretofore unfinished business. Psychoanalysis— although differing from gestalt therapy in many details of conceptualization and technique—has made the return of the old and forgotten a familiar expectation in psychotherapy. But though many words about the past have been spoken in therapy, they are frequently minus the accompaniment of deep sensations. The next example illustrates how sensations rather than mere words may lead the way to the reawakening of a past event which is still influential.

Joan, whose husband had died about ten years previously, had spoken often about her relationship with him but had never conveyed a sense of the profundity of their experience together. In one session, a series of awarenesses evolved including the experience of her tongue tingling, a burning feeling around her eyes, tenseness in her back and shoulders and then dampness around her eyes. Finally, she caught a deep breath and realized that she felt like crying. There was a sense of tears in her eyes and a sensation in her throat that she could not describe. After a very long pause she felt an itch which she concentrated on at some length. With each new sensation the silence and inner concentration were lengthy, frequently lasting for minutes. Silence—when joined with focused concentration—has the effect of building up the intensity of feeling. Soon Joan began to feel itchy in many places. She found it difficult to stay with these sensations without scratching, but she did. She felt somewhat amused about the surprising spread of her itching sensations, but she also began to feel frustrated and sad again, as though she might cry. She mentioned an irritating experience she had had the previous evening at the home of her parents where she had not been able to show her irritation. Then she felt a lump in her throat and after a period of concentration on this lump, a palpitation appeared in her chest. Her heart started beating quite rapidly and this made her very anxious. She verbalized the *pump, pump, pump* sounds and then became aware of a sharp pain in her upper back. She paused at length to concentrate on the pain in her back, then said under considerable stress, "Now I remember that horrible night that my first husband had a heart attack." Another lengthy pause followed in which Joan appeared under great tension and absorption. Then she said, in a hushed tone, that she was aware of the pain, the anxiety and the whole experience of that night. At this point she gave in to profound heartfelt crying. When she finished, she looked up and said, "I guess I still miss him." Now her vagueness was gone and she could convey the seriousness and wholeness of her relationship with her husband. The clear transformation from conventional superficiality to depth was brought on by the build-up in sensation. Through self-awareness and concentration she let her own sensations lead the way rather than her ideas or explanations.

FEELINGS

While it is true, of course, that the feeling level of personal experience is inextricably related to sensation, feelings do have a quality which goes beyond the range of rudimentary sensation. When a person says he is afraid, he is telling what his feeling is. Subsumed within this feeling-tone, perhaps even supporting it, he may recognize specific sensations such as heart palpitations, sweaty palms, fluttery stomach or shortness of breath. On the other hand, he may feel afraid without these sensory accompaniments; experiencing and knowing his fear clearly and intuitively but without awareness of any of the subsidiary sensations.

Feelings include a personal assessment, an attempt to fit this particular event into the larger scheme of one's experience; sensations can be accepted piecemeal and do not seem to require or elicit this sense of fit. Heart palpitations in and of themselves say very little about a person's total being because they are non-specific; one's heart may beat rapidly under conditions which differ as widely as fear may differ from eager anticipation. So, one may even experience sensation richly without accompanying feelings—a common occurrence among hysterical individuals who have many sensations, most of which do not seem to fit the feeling tone at all.

Furthermore, some eastern philosophies, Yoga for example, have the goal of experiencing all sensations without putting *any* personal evaluation on them. They view physical pain or sadness as experiences in their own right and this freedom from prejudice as to the acceptability of their feelings remains a central factor in the establishment and maintenance of a peaceful life. Thus, a toothache can give one as rich a sense of self as any other experience if one refrains from applying the usual emotional judgments about whether it is okay or not. Hard to do—because of the almost reflexive twinge of personal evaluations—but possible in the hands of dedicated and practiced people. The aim in gestalt therapy, however, is not for people to give up these judgments of their feelings but rather to make room for feelings and to use them as a means of integrating the various details of their lives.

In order to accomplish this we call attention to feelings in much the same way as already described in working with sensations. Description of feeling tone, recognition of incongruities or gaps in experience, focusing on what has been discovered and staying with it until the organic expression emerges, all of these use feelings as openings into the cycle of awareness and expression. Once this cycle has been completed, the individual is uncluttered and ready to move on to new cycles of awareness-expression. It is the perpetually renewing fluidity of this process which constitutes an important quality of good function.

Calling attention frequently to present feelings requires an artfulness of movement back and forth between the individual's awareness, actions and expressions. For example, if a person is telling a story in which he is deeply absorbed, to ask him what he is feeling right then may be received as a distraction which must be resisted. Indeed, very often it could be distracting; the sensitive therapist does not shuttle back and forth between the person's story and his awareness in mechanical and arbitrary ways. Underscoring the substance and drama of the story so that it will be more than mere "aboutism" consists simply in according the story the primacy it merits on its own. Sometimes, however, directed awareness is needed to fill the gaps in experience. The cues for focusing on self-awareness come from the individual himself suggesting where the gaps in his self experience may exist. For example, a look of pain gleams across the person's face and seems ready to fade unremarked, leaving no more trace than a ripple in the water, even though pain is at the core of the person's story. To ask what he feels then, or even to ask whether he feels any pain, or perhaps to say, "For a moment you looked in such pain," could be a wedge into new experience—while if skipped over, the story remains just another story. Sometimes the look of pain may reflect an impact already felt and it will enter into the story with no special focus needed—but sometimes it will disappear unfelt into the person's chronic neutralizations of his life experiences. Only the therapist's artistry can make the discrimination.

Gestalt therapy is especially vulnerable to a distracting use of techniques precisely because of its intention to bring together diverse aspects of the individual's function. The therapist has to resist the temptation to pull tricks out of a bag. He must rely instead on evolutionary growth of his observations and suggestions and their rootedness in the situation as it exists at the moment. If this rhythm is achieved, a new experience is created which will have an organic tempo for the patient. If not, the therapist can become bumbling and presumptuous, doing his thing with no regard for the patient. Few of us are either all grace or all bumble, but our task is to exercise our respect for where the other person is so we can achieve a maximum of grace.

One of the major emphases in gestalt therapy is the accentuation of that which exists and this is also one of the primary means of dealing with feeling. So often we will ask "what are you feeling now?" or make statements such as "stay with that feeling and see where it leads you" or "what does that feeling make you want to do?" because we have faith that in doing so we are following the dynamic lead provided by the patient. If his awareness can surface, it suggests the existing feeling and noses out the direction this feeling moves towards. A person may say tangentially and off-hand, "I feel sad." When the therapist says to him, "Try to feel your sadness fully, get into it as though you *were* your sadness," this person may begin to feel his sadness more poignantly than before and can move in to tell of a loss he has experienced that he is still mourning, or remember an event which made him sad or feel, in some way, the depths of a reactivity which gives him dimension instead of flatness.

One evening in a group, Ralph told of his mixed feelings about the end of his marriage; he was in the process of getting a divorce. But his feelings were divided between trying to assess the limits of his own responsibility for his wife who was able only marginally to take care of herself and his children who could be hurt by the unstable situation. So Ralph's sadness could not exist with the purity necessary for clear expression. He worked with the group, trying to sort out for himself what he was responsible for and what was beyond his scope to deal with. After he had done this, he was silent a long while, and then softly he began to recall aloud the hopefulness and radiance which had filled both him and his wife when they had first been married. As the sense of his expectations which were now no longer available to him returned, very quietly tears came into his eyes and Ralph cried—mourning the blasted hopes. So he expressed his sadness in its wet humanity, not disguised by questions of responsibility and not alienating him from the rest of the group.

The accentuation of feeling impels people to express themselves. But this then requires the setting of a relevant scene, where expression can have its fullest opportunity to move toward completion. The mere expression of feeling can become obsessive and unfruitful if not placed into the right context. It is like the weightlifter whose prowess remains anchored in himself, building bigger and better muscles but never lifting anything worthwhile. People can build systems where statements of feeling are muscle-bound too, recurring without resolution. Within the obsessive system, the person who is resentful or loving or sympathetic, for example, will not *express* these feelings so much as he will repetitively *exercise* them. So it goes, over and over again, finding reasons for them, feeding them, accentuating them and giving them direction.

Therapy must break through the boundaries of this obsessive system. Perhaps the feelings are about the wrong thing or directed against the wrong person or expressed poorly. It becomes the therapeutic task to find the right scene and to develop the force of expression which fits the need, as in the following example. Phyllis was pathologically resentful of her boss, a piddling man whom she responded to as though he had the power of life and death over her. Actually, he was small potatoes in her life and his tendency to obfuscation and to throwing up small roadblocks against her influence in her department could have been only minor irritations. Instead, they inflamed her. Expressing her resentment about him in therapy and in fantasy had little effect. One day I realized that Phyllis was a person who needed a lot of special attention and I asked her whether she was accustomed to getting it. She remembered two men she had been in love with who had really given her "star" treatment. In both cases, though, she wound up abruptly rejected. After the second time she realized she had never permitted herself to get the special treatment she wanted. And so I asked her, in fantasy, to express herself to these two men. In doing so she was able to get out of the complex of rage, loss, grudge and resolve which she had previously been left with and around which she had organized such a substantial chunk of her life. By talking to these men in her fantasy, Phyllis aired her unfinished feelings. Following this deeply moving experience, she grew calm and no longer felt the sharp resentment towards her boss. She was able, finally, to reduce him to a more appropriate level of importance in her life. Phyllis had moved —out of the neurotic system in which she had made her boss the center and into a system which was more organically suited to her feelings. That was the context where completion was possible.

WANTS

Awareness of wants, like awareness of any experience, is an orienting function. It directs, it mobilizes, it channels, it focuses. A want is a blip into the future. People who have no wants—depressed people, for example—have no future. Everything seems worthless or hopeless, so nothing matters enough even to want it. If something does happen, and if the depressed person is not too desensitized, perhaps he may acknowledge the happening, but his own experience leans into nowhere.

A want is a linking function, integrating present experience with the future where its gratification lies and also with the past which it culminates and summarizes. Wants grow from where one has been; making sense out of the sensations and feelings which lead to this moment of wanting. Only by touching into where one is and what one wants right now can one forge the central link in the chain of events and experiences which make up one's life.

It seems axiomatic to say that one needs to know what one wants before he can be gratified, but in fact this is not invariably true. Many satisfactions come about without our ever becoming aware of wanting them. I see you smile and I light up too, but I didn't experience *wanting* you to smile—it just happened. Since many experiences like this do just happen, unplanned and spontaneous, many people come to *depend* on these happenings as their primary means of gratification. The problem is, though, that while these experiences are enriching and inevitable in life's unpredictable benevolence, they are like bonuses—unfortunately, undependable. Much of the gratification available requires us, like a sunflower, to face in the right direction and to move, literally or figuratively, in that direction. Knowing what we want, as the sunflower *knows* it wants sunlight, arouses us to move.

Yet many people are only infrequently aware of their wants. Or they are aware of their wants selectively—or only at inopportune times. In gestalt therapy we often ask, "What do you want?" and this question frequently brings on blank expressions, almost as if the question were in a foreign language, one which the patient had yet to learn. What he needs is practice in recognizing his wants. In the absence of clear wanting the individual either becomes immobilized and gets stuck with a stockpiling of sensations and feelings, or he becomes disorganized and engages in a helter-skelter quest for gratification which may lead to activity—but not gratification.

When a want can be recognized and expressed, the wanter

experiences the sense of being on target and moving towards a sense of completion and release. A man in a group was asked what he wanted and replied he didn't know. So he was directed to make a statement to the woman he had been talking to—a statement beginning with the words, "I want you to . . ." He said, "I want you to go out with me." His face suddenly lightened, he lost his blocked feeling and felt restored to his flow of mind. Another man, a college professor, was feeling overburdened by having to cram each day with what seemed to be overwhelming requirements to write, to read, to teach—until his time felt like it was ready to burst at the seams. After a long recital of all the demands he experienced on his already overcommitted life, I asked him, "What do you want?" A pause . . . and a gesture with his hands showing one hand fitting —but *very loosely* and with space left over—into another . . . and then, "I want some *slop* in my life!" Both of these recognitions are simple enough, but to many people they are not readily accessible. Until these wants can be at least recognized, though, focused action is unlikely.

One of the common ways to remain out of touch with wants is to inflate them, to blow them up into global wants, forever undefinable and out of reach. I want respect, I want to be a success, I want love, I want to be a good husband. More to the point—when someone asks what he wants—is for the person to be able to answer that he wants them to quit asking questions, or he wants to learn how to iceskate, or to speak French, or to make love better. These are wants that have attained a figural status; they are clearly defined and the ingredients necessary for their completion are at least available and identifiable. They can become building blocks to new ways of experiencing one's self. Consequently, the aim becomes to pin down the global wants into specific and understandable terms. When dealing with global wants, for example, the questions then become, "What would you have to do to be a good hus-

band?" or "How would people act toward you if they respected you?"

In couples' therapy, Vivian was complaining that her husband, Stan, didn't treat her respectfully and he answered that
he didn't feel that she treated him sympathetically enough. I
asked them to try to articulate their wants more clearly. In the
ensuing dialogue, it became clear that Vivian's desire for respect meant that Stan would have to ascertain how *she* was
feeling when he first came home, instead of immediately dump-
ing on her his woes of the day. What Stan wanted from Vivian
was to listen to what he had to say without her offering any
suggestions about what he might do. It was precisely this that
made him feel she was belittling him rather than sympathizing.
Now, these were things that they could *do,* whereas asking for
respect or sympathy—particularly when each of them considered that they *were* respectful or sympathetic individuals—was
just too vague an order. With the emergence of a clearly defined
want, their own energy could be pinpointed and effective. To
know specifically what they wanted increased the likelihood
of satisfaction.

VALUES AND ASSESSMENTS

Awareness of values and assessments usually centers around
larger units of experience than sensations, feelings and wants.
It, too, is a unifying activity, including and summarizing much
of the individual's previous living and his reactions to it.

Awareness of assessments and values may be seen as central in the earlier example of Lila, the executive who saw the
waif in her disruptive and controlling secretary. Lila's assessment of her secretary as pitiful was followed by her awareness
that her own values required that waifs are to be taken care of
and supported, *not* fired summarily. Finally, when she took
back the projection of her own waifhood that she had displaced
onto her secretary, it became inescapable that she sort out her
conflicting values so that her actions could be rooted in cur-

rent need rather than atrophied evaluations based on past requirements.

The resolution came through the assertive physical sensations of her own womanliness. The impact of present sensation, powerful and immediate, unblocked the stereotyped appraisals and evaluations which she had been permitting to control her actions and enabled Lila to perceive more clearly the directions in which she wanted to go. Through the synthesis of her own waifhood and womanliness she was able to arrive at new values: 1) that people who seem waiflike do not automatically need protection; and 2) that everyone who needs to be taken care of is not a waif. So then she was free to judge that her secretary, although indeed waiflike, was nevertheless destructive and needed to be fired. She was also free to accept that she could need love from another person without being a waif; that she does not have to be a waif in order to engage fully and warmly with another person who is both strong and giving, like herself.

It is well to remember that when we deal with awareness of values and assessments we are tapping into a whole range of judgments and internal contradictions. The values an individual constructs for himself frequently have to be rebuilt when they contain anachronistic material. So, for Lila to have the value that waifs are to be taken care of meant that she and her brother were not to be disregarded, an act of assertion which she needed at one time desperately to affirm. The conviction that she was the one to do the caring was a judgment of great survival value. This was not a whimsical value, capriciously arrived at; it was a necessity. But perhaps no longer. And so her early appraisal must become figural enough to be reevaluated and the determination made as to whether it is still in fact a necessary and useful value. If so, if it still serves a current need, it will persist; if not, if it is a hangover serving a need which no longer exists, it can be finished off and she is free to move on to other more synchronistic values.

The role of projection in the assessment Lila made of the waifhood of her secretary is also important to describe. She could accept and assimilate the precarious position of her brother, no need to defend herself against that—but she could not accept this as true of herself, that would indeed have been too scary. In addition, in order for her to see herself as the one who *does* the caring for the helpless younger brother—a non-reciprocal relationship that worked only one way—it was essential not to regard herself as much of a waif as he. She, at least, was the stronger, wiser, older, more resourceful, etc. She needed to remain in contact with weakness and vulnerability, *but* she could not tolerate it as applying to herself; weakness existed to be sure, but it was not her characteristic—it was out there in people who were in some way her dependents. Thus she was able to project onto her secretary—who was in the position of an inferior and a dependent—the waifhood that was intolerable for her to accept as part of herself.

In the safe emergency of the therapy situation Lila could permit the mounting excitement aroused first by awareness of the pitiful waif in her secretary and, then, in herself. She was, at last, able to undo the projection; to take back her own dis-owned waifhood. The value that she had to protect waifs could be assimilated with discrimination; those waifs who needed to be cared for were to be distinguished from those waifs who were destructive and required a different response. And finally, Lila arrived at a new resolution which could integrate the soft-ness of her womanliness with a need to nurture and be nurtured from a position of choice and parity between equals—mutual and non-threatening.

9

Experiment

Nothing that survives, that is still alive, can be treated impassively.

BERNARD BERENSON

Although the importance of action in the learning process has been recognized for a long time—from John Dewey through Paul Goodman, John Holt and George Dennison, among others—most people settle for "aboutism" as their customary approach to problem solving. They talk about a problem with others or think about it until they hopefully arrive at a position they believe is worthy of action. Then, assuming the right moment for action hasn't already passed by, they may try it out.

All too frequently, though, such decisions turn out to be "aboutist" blueprints stifling innovation and inductive improvisation. Action based exclusively on past deliberation, without the lubricating influence of current invention, is likely to

233

become mechanical and lifeless. Trial and error seem wasteful and free development of new and chancy directions appears to be downright heresy. Take the all-too-common example of the young student for whom going to medical school was so obligatory that he panicked at considering alternatives, even though his work there was a study in misery. The die had been cast so irrevocably that he could no longer even identify whether the decision had been his own or his parents'. The time wasted, the unfaithfulness to parental or past values, the dread of uncertain directions impaled him to the original commitment. Anchored to the past, he could only ruminate about making changes but was frozen out of action. This kind of decision-making degrades error and individuality both, equating them as undesirable and distracting. In a society with fast and hard standards for results—such as our society has become —the ante has gone up so high for making correct and decisive moves that errors are just too costly and few feel they can afford exploration of ideas or possibilities that might not pay off.

Gestalt therapy tries to restore the connection between aboutism and action. By integrating action into the person's decision-making process, he is pried loose from the stultifying influence of his aboutist ruminations. Decisions are best made when one's action begins to indicate a recognizable direction to which he can say yes. A young man may come to see medicine as the direction for him only after he takes a biology course and likes it, visits a physician friend of the family to find out how germs spread, is turned on by a first-aid course in his life-saving class, and so on. If he makes a decision at this point, it is compelling and personally rooted.

The experiment in gestalt therapy is an attempt to counter the aboutist deadlock by bringing the individual's action system right into the room. Through experiment the individual is mobilized to confront the emergencies of his life by playing out his aborted feelings and actions in relative safety. A safe emergency is thus created where venturesome exploration can be supported. Furthermore, both ends of the safety-to-emergency continuum can be explored, emphasizing first the support and then the risk-taking, whichever seems salient at the time.

One man, for example, tortured by his boss and immobilized by this man's power, imagined the boss sitting opposite him in the therapy setting and wound up screaming to this image that he would like to kill him, kill him, kill him! It had been in him before to scream these words, but the risk of retribution from the ponderous force he was opposing was just too great to gamble with. Even when this risk was minimized—after all, just he and I were in on this fantasy—he was still running the danger of being overwhelmed by his own fury. Becoming flooded with feeling is risky in spite of environmental supports. It is because the supports *are* there that one is willing to take the chance at all.

On the face of it, bringing unfinished business, started elsewhere and relevant elsewhere, into the therapy scene could be an imitation of reality, mere psychological game-playing. The experiment must not become a palliative or a substitute for a valid engagement. Instead, the experience is more comparable to art form. The artist does not merely recreate the scene he sees. He combines the reality "out there" with his inner experience and the synthesis is a discovery, even for himself. So also in the therapeutic experiment. The individual is not trying just to reproduce something which has already happened or which might happen. Instead, he relates to the reality out there by expressing his needs at that moment in time. What he is doing is not rehearsing for a future event or rehashing an old one but experiencing in the present what it is like for him to flow from awareness to experimental action. Once he senses the rhythm of this existential momentum he may well behave differently in the world outside than he had previously. But, equally important, his behavior outside will not be an exact replica of the therapy event.

The experiment is neither rehearsal nor post-mortem. If the man who hollered at his boss were to go on and follow this scene as if it were a script for the future, he would be patently absurd and self-defeating. However, as a preparation for more inventive contact with his boss it could open him to his own self-support and previously immobilized ingenuity.

Our creative experiment differs from art form along at least one important dimension. A comment from Herbert Read* will help to clarify this difference:

> We therefore cannot *know* a self; we can *only* betray ourself, and we do this, as the phrase indicates, fragmentarily and unconsciously. We betray ourselves in our gestures, in the accents of our speech, in our handwriting, and generally, in all those forms or configurations (gestalten) which automatically register the track of the stream of consciousness. All art is in this sense an unconscious self-betrayal, but it is not necessarily an awareness of the self betrayed.

Taking Read's view of artistic expression, we differ in that we do indeed try to bring into awareness that self which has been "betrayed." This is, in fact, one of our main purposes. It is this very availability of awareness which supports the individual, orienting him to his needs and propelling him into actions which express and culminate his natural sense of self.

In a sense, then, we are engaged in a reversal of the artistic pattern. The artist digs into his personal reactivity and produces the finished work of art, which is his statement of where he is at that moment in his existence. The finished work of art is in tangible form which he makes available to others, hoping to move them, orient them, astound them, delight them—in some way to present them with his perspective on their common human experience in a way that is not as ephemeral as existence usually is. In therapy, we cannot hang up or frame our produc-

---

* Read, H. *Icon and Idea.* New York: Schocken Books, 1965.

tions; there is no "finished product." The person who creates does so exclusively for his own purposes and probably would be reluctant to have his creations made public. Where the artist aims at a finished opus which will communicate with others, the patient's art form leads to actions which create in himself an expanded dialogue with his own nature as well as with others.

What happens in the creative experiment is like artistic expression because it, too, has qualities of unusual excitement, discovery and emergency. Even though the working-through process was carried out privately and only the completed result is open to public observation, the artist puts his psychological life on the line through his work. So it is with the patient in therapy who may tremble, agonize, laugh, cry and experience much else within the narrow compass of the therapy environment. He, like the artist, is traversing uncharted areas of experience which have a reality all their own and within which he has no guarantee of successful completion. Once again he confronts the forces that previously steered him into dangerous territory and the return trip becomes as hazardous as he had reflexively feared. The therapist is his mentor and companion, helping to keep in balance the safety and the emergency aspects of the experience, providing suggestion, orientation and support. By following and encouraging the natural development of the individual's incompleted themes through their own directions into completion, the therapist and patient become collaborators in the creation of a drama which is written as the drama unfolds.

There are several forms which the experiment might take. We have divided them into the following five modes: 1) enactment; 2) directed behavior; 3) fantasy; 4) dreams; and 5) homework.

ENACTMENT

One of the early criticisms directed against gestalt therapy was that it was an acting-out therapy. It *is* an acting-out therapy, but not in the pejorative sense implied in the psycho-analytic definition of acting-out. Acting-out has gotten a bad name because traditionally it has come to mean a person carrying out in an unintegrated and irrelevant fashion ideas which have been introduced in therapy or which have been stimulated by it. A therapist might indeed get very edgy when he thinks that something that has transpired in therapy will cause behavior elsewhere which will be either embarrassing or harmful. The patient who would screw his mother after the therapist remarks that Freud called the prohibition of incest the most maiming wound of mankind would have a very un-settling effect on his therapist. Still, the implications of a non-acting-out therapy are that the patient will settle for working through his problems while remaining inactive outside the therapy, will also know when he has arrived at maturity and will *then* have the good sense to behave appropriately.

This attitude is a burlesque. It requires a steadfast un-awareness of current knowledge about the learning process, namely that for its best effect learning *requires* action. Acting-out may have been the only avenue of expression open to the analytic patient since the analytic couch denied him the natural movements into action aroused within the therapeutic process. Rather than ignoring this crucial factor in learning, gestalt therapy fosters the act, looking for timeliness of the action and its fit into the person's life.

Earlier we referred to the four levels of expression de-scribed by the semanticists: blocked, inhibited, exhibitionistic and spontaneous. Blocked and inhibited expressions, you may remember, are those which are not made public, either because the individual's impulses are not recognized or because the expression is held back even though the impulse has been recognized. The exhibitionistic expressions are those which are not well assimilated into the action system of the individual. The spontaneous expressions are those which emerge naturally and fully, well integrated and graceful.

The acting-out person is in the exhibitionistic phase of expression, *showing* us what he is about but not *being* what he is. This is a critical phase. First, because it is often necessary to traverse it in order to arrive at the spontaneous. Secondly, it is critical because one can easily get stuck in it and take it for spontaneous instead of recognizing its trial quality. People who insist on pure spontaneity for their expressive action may well refuse to engage in the exhibitionistic phase. This may mean that they will block out anything that makes them feel awkward or phony in spite of the fact that new behavior may be quite valid even though not yet well integrated. Tolerance for the exhibitionistic phase is often necessary before a person can make deeper changes in his nature. Will a pedantic individual be willing to risk sounding foolish or unwise? If not, he remains what he is—pedantic—but if he can venture into the unfamiliar behaviors he may lubricate his pedanticism into juicy wisdom.

The exhibitionistic phase has at least this to recommend it —in comparison with the blocked or inhibited stages—the person is keeping alive his need to do new things and when he is faithful to this need he is intuitively self-supportive, even though he may be awkward, vulgar, strange, unaccountable. The man who propositions every women he halfway likes is hardly as appealing as the man who knows what he wants and when he wants it. Nevertheless, the fledgling Don Juan, if he is not stuck on his greed and exhibitionism, may eventually discover proportion, timing and what it takes to develop a relationship. Unfortunately, it is very easy to get stuck so it becomes the task of the therapist to recognize the difference between exhibitionistic and spontaneous behavior. Too often, game-playing, bravado, and stereotypy are wrongly touted as integrated new growth.

Enactment, for the gestalt therapist, is the dramatization within the therapy scene of some aspect of the patient's existence. It may start from a statement he makes, or from a gesture. For example, if he makes a small gesture, we may ask him to extend this movement to a fuller dimension. Suppose when he does he finds that the movement feels like a lion sitting on its haunches. We ask how that feels. He says it makes him want to growl. Go ahead and growl. So he does; with this he begins to move around the room, pawing at people. By the time he is done he has frightened some people, amused others, beguiled others and discovered his own held-in excitement. This excitement shows him a new side of himself—the power side, the animal side, the side which moves vigorously into contact—and he begins to realize something of what he has been missing in life. Well timed, and recurring at appropriate moments, such characterizations tap into the individual's action system, opening up new directions.

There are many forms that enactment may take. We are choosing only four examples, though enactment may be used to add pungency and drama to many human experiences.

1) *Enactment of an unfinished situation from the distant past*—This is the experience of Sue, a woman determined not to be afraid. Characteristically she would become frustrated, confused and stubborn, but only rarely afraid. Her voice was like gravel and her neck and shoulders were very tense. Her throat was very constricted so I asked her to stick her finger down her throat to try to elicit her gag reflex. I hoped that this would help loosen Sue's throat and bring her voice into better resonance. Furthermore, this mini-emergency might also give her a sense of the fear which she compulsively blocked. She stuck her finger precipitously into her mouth, and ended up coughing and slightly nauseous but—no fear. She didn't gag, either. I asked her to do it again. The same thing happened; precipitousness, cough, no gag and no fear or emotion. We talked a little about her precipitousness in life. Then I asked her to try it again. This time Sue was able to elicit the gag reflex, although she coughed again and interrupted the full spasm of gag. She remarked that some part of her remained

unreachably impassive. She remembered that she had first experienced this now familiar feeling when her brother—five years older than she—would attack her. She could never succeed in stopping him from sadistically pinning her down and choking her. The more she said "please" or "stop," the harder he fought. She learned that if she became impassive he would be more likely to desist. So what started out as a desperate impassivity, designed to manage her brother, has continued long beyond her brother.

At this point our enactment begins. Instead of talking about her relationship with her brother, I instructed Sue to remain impassive no matter what I might do. She agreed. I walked over, put my hands on her throat, and began choking her. She remained surprisingly flaccid. Finally she tried to stop me, vigorously trying to pull my hands away from her throat. When I did not relent immediately she quickly relapsed into flaccidity again. Then I stopped. She observed that I might have hurt her since she hadn't let me know the effect I was having. I could feel some aggression gurgling up in her. I then suggested that when I approached her again, this time she was to defend herself as vigorously as she could. As I went over towards her with the intention of choking her again, Sue rose before I could reach her. She lurched for my throat and began to grapple with me and soon we had wrestled down to the floor. After a moment, against her full and very powerful resistance, I forced her down on her back and was in the process of pinning her shoulders down against her strong opposition. She was becoming quite flushed and finally exploded the word, "STOP!" So I did. Then we talked. She was deeply affected, not only by the physical exertion, but also by the return to old feelings and by the new ending which revealed to her that I was not her brother and that she might have an effect on what might be a not-so-intransigent world.

The abrasive sound of her voice, her tight neck and shoulders, the absence of fear, her stubbornness and impassivity were all cues—incomplete in themselves—which unfolded as parts of the developmental enactment. Step by step the drama moved to reveal her own nature and the unfinished business from her past.

Perhaps this enactment was risky and unprofessional. It was both. However, the risk was within acceptable limits because I had already worked with Sue extensively and judged that she would not be flooded by the powerful physical contact and that she also trusted me enough so that—even during the experiment—she would know that she would not become alienated from me. The second criticism—that this was unprofessional—is an outdated view of professionalism. The therapist's professional responsibility is to engage and to do whatever it takes to help her recover what she has lost on her way to his office. Just as Sue's early experiences had not been watered-down versions of attack, the engagement between her and her therapist could not be a watered-down contact either.

2) *Enactment of a contemporary unfinished situation*—The distant past is not the only repository of unfinished business. Most of us are faced with unfinished business every day. Much of this unfinished business is assimilable, but some of what remains unfinished is not just sloughed off and it sticks in the craw. Until it can be completed, it ties up a lot of energy. The consequences are lethargy, hostility, self-depreciation and the whole range of personal experiences that therapy focuses on.

One man in a group, Victor, complained resignedly about the intolerability of his wife's interference in his life. She managed to interpose herself between him and anyone he might happen to be talking to. So I asked him to continue talking to the group and appointed one of the women in the group to get physically in the way between him and whomever he might talk to. This she did energetically, playing her part somewhat like a basketball star guarding a high-scoring forward. The fun and liveliness of the scene contrasted sharply with Victor's sedate and sterile account. Soon he, too, swung into action, mobilized to get his communications across to the others in the face of this interfering woman. He talked louder, he became more assertive in language and manner, told her to shut up and get out of the way, stretched around her, elbowed her around so that he could move in front of her and in general would not be dissuaded from getting through. During this scene it became obvious to him that he had given up his previous passivity and he was able to recognize how he had meekly surrendered to his wife, assuming that she was more fascinating than he was and giving up any attempts to interest people in himself. He also realized that aggressiveness could be taken lightly and did not have to result in heavy-handed competitiveness.

Enactment can be fun. This is not to diminish the importance of making the discrimination between fun that is merely evasive and fun that lubricates an event with no loss of illumination to the people involved. There is hardly a group we have worked with which has not had moments of hilarity. In fact, in one instance where humor was clearly missing, we focused on it until it arose. When it did, it proved to be a decisive element in the group members being able to take each other *seriously!* Until the humor appeared, the scene was lifeless. After it did, the trust between people grew as did their interest in each other. Work in the group reached more profound dimensions. Playfully and jokingly, one may explore what—without the gracefulness of laughter—would be either too painful or out of perspective. The joke, clowning around, exaggeration, and caricature are all portraits. They are sketches about a central feature of an individual that he may only dimly perceive. Furthermore, the humor is a creative recognition of the redeeming aspects of what may otherwise be experienced flatly or as merely negative.

The gamelike quality inherent to enactment is also a source of vitality. Nevertheless many people have difficulty with enactment. Most often, their sense of relevance is close-cropped and they have trouble making the shift in mood from their serious, intellectual expectations to what they regard as playing games. Sometimes the timing has to fall neatly within a very small margin of error or these individuals refuse to make the timing fit by even a slight exertion. They will participate only if the conditions are just right. Children, on the other hand, intuitively appetitive, respond with rapt interest in their experiences by moving these experiences into their games. So they play doctor, school, house, cowboys and Indians. . . . The game is not a put-on but the creation of a new reality which has a force of its own and which is more susceptible to their personal involvement. So, too, with the enactment of adult experiences. Mobility of mind and body are restored when one is no longer governed by *real* reality but can invent and meet new conditions. Surprises occur because these are inherent to the game instead of being determined by another person's characteristics, the nature of society, or practical implications. These creations, as Freud observed about the creation of the dream, are like microcosms which bear on real life but are not limited by its complexities.

Great drama has the power to illuminate our lives. When I saw O'Neill's *The Iceman Cometh,* I was aroused into a new sense of unconditional love which influenced my relationships with people for months. The effect faded, to be sure, but it returns even now after 15 years. Drama in therapy has comparable power.

3) *Enactment of a characteristic*—Words are only shorthand expressions of what a person is trying to say. Many of them—especially key words—require elaboration and amplification if they are to be understood in their full, unique meaning. The same is true of the concepts a person may have about either himself or others. So, suppose someone says that he wishes he were a kind person but it is impossible because in his life the winners were canny and manipulative. It is necessary to find out what personal definitions he has constructed for kindness, canniness or manipulativeness—definitions which

come from his own experience of these characteristics. He could give examples of how he has been kind or how he has seen others behave kindly. He might give as an example a time when he refrained from criticizing a fellow worker—one image of kindness.

However, when he enacts his image of kindness it will probably differ importantly from how he verbalizes it. So, too, with canniness or manipulativeness. One man's canniness is another's animal alertness or still another's paranoid vigilance. By taking the word as an absolute, never investigating its personal significance, the word acquires a life of its own. Reifying the word in this way removes it from its practical function as a more-or-less efficient way of referring to a process which remains alive and has continually changing referents. Enactment is one way of keeping alive the words a person uses to characterize himself or someone else. Keeping his language connected to action permits feelings of change and growth; the person is less likely to experience himself as stamped on the ass —indelibly this or that.

Cyrus, a member of a group, was bewailing the fact that his parents were canny people, shrewd and opportunistic. He was repelled by this style. That would not have been so bad, except that he so zealously guarded against the appearance of these characteristics in himself, that he had become a lethargically kind man—likeable but flaccid. I asked Cyrus to give us a lecture on the uses of being shrewd and clever, hoping to get him connected to these characteristics. As he proceeded, he began to lecture us bombastically, with great relish, on how to operate real estate holdings with an eye to profit. Cyrus really knew what it would take and he swung into it, towering above the rest of us from a lofty position standing on the couch. His energy and excitement swelled and he recognized that he was enjoying what he was doing! Not only that—he was even intellectually more fruitful than usual, had a better flow of ideas, used livelier language and had a more forceful delivery. All of this dash had been corked up in him because of his definition of canniness and his unwillingness to be caught dead being that way. Caught dead he had been—but by his own labels.

I might have taken a different tack and asked him instead to go around the room being kind toward each person there in his own way. This would give him an opportunity to experience his own kindliness more clearly and develop it into a livelier, more personal kindness than his usual brand. After all, canniness was not his only verbal stereotype—he had some hackneyed ideas about how to be kind also. The point is that canniness and kindness are not all he needed to investigate; he needed to get unstuck from labels in order to find out who he *himself* was. The basic process is to recover a sense of oneself in action and to recognize one's individuality rather than to perpetuate the idolatrous stereotype.

One of the richest sources of information about a person is the metaphors used to describe him, either by himself or by others. The metaphor is like words, though. Its individual meaning must be probed and enactment is a fertile way to do this. One example concerns Maeta, a young woman who described herself as "being all tied up in knots." So, I asked her to tie herself up in knots and play out her own personal metaphor. This she did, twisting her arms, legs and body around in convoluted fashion, literally tying herself up. I asked her how she felt all tied up this way, and Maeta replied that she felt immobilized, tightly constricted and tense. What did she feel like doing? She felt like getting untied, and I directed her to do this gradually, untwisting one limb at a time and experiencing each of these loosenings separately. As she did this, she was surprised to realize that she was fearful of untying herself! No matter how painful and paralyzing being tied up in knots was, it was at least an identity of sorts, and if she got completely untied, she didn't know who or what she might become!

4) *Enactment of a polarity*—The enactment of a polarity also dramatizes personal characteristics, but in this instance

there are *two* opposed characteristics, like being devilish or angelic, big or little—or two opposed directions like staying or leaving, speaking or being silent. Such splits within the individual may bind him into ambivalence or confusion or may propel him into resolution merely for the sake of getting off the hook of uncertainty. So he settles for what looks like the patent victory of one side of him, with the defeated or suppressed part going underground and sabotaging the apparently winning characteristic through guilt, foot-dragging, playing dumb, depleting energy, joylessness, and other self-defeating maneuvers. The effort devoted to keeping the squelched characteristic servile or silent is a doomed effort—it *will* pop up in inconvenient ways to assert whatever validity it can muster, like all resistance forces which have been compelled to go underground. The struggle is like the farce which often results when a hurried parent tries to get Junior quickly into bed by short-changing him on parts of the bedtime routine: story-telling, singing, tucking him in, and so on. Junior keeps hollering—he knows he hasn't got what he needs—and won't go to sleep. The upshot is that more energy and time are spent in trying to abbreviate the bedtime ritual than it would have taken just to have followed through on the regular procedure.

So also with the polarity. Ignoring parts of oneself results in a stand-off, like the con-man and the little kid who sees through the phoniness of his arrangements and keeps raising troublesome questions. "Go away kid, ya *bother* me" didn't work for W. C. Fields and it doesn't work very well in daily attempts to con oneself, either. The disowned devil will pop up anyway, to the great embarrassment or discomfort of the angel—or he will require so much vigilance against his unwelcome appearance that the individual feels insecure and constantly on guard even in his angelic moments. Worse yet, the withdrawal of the devilish energy makes life less fun or may leave the angelic person less cunning than he needs to be in order to live well.

The basic requirement in working with polarities is to restore contact between the opposed forces. Once contact between these parts is established, each party to the warring struggle can be experienced as a valid participant. They can then become allies in the common search for a good life, rather than uneasy opponents maintaining the split. Almost invariably, when contact is restored, the individual discovers that these distrusted parts had many redeeming features and his life expands when these are recovered.

We are *not* looking, however, merely to make trades where the tables are turned and the angelic person gives up that side of himself and becomes only a devil. This is the Dr. Jekyll and Mr. Hyde spectre and to settle for this kind of coexistence is not union; it is personal dissociation. A temporary flipover might have beneficial effect in the total process. It is sometimes unavoidable that in order to re-experience one's underside, this submerged part of oneself must be permitted full power to break through the customary barriers to expression. Thus, there are times when a sweet person may become temporarily and arbitrarily cruel while playing out this side of himself. In the course of time, the union with his now-disowned sweetness would have to be re-established for him to emerge whole. The faith required that such union will happen is very great—most people cannot easily allow such radical changes to occur. But the faith in organismic self-regulation, implicit in gestalt therapy, is that if each part of the person can be heard, it will not seek to establish a dictatorship but will move into inclusion in a community of characteristics which go to make up the individual. A dictatorship is established in order to achieve something in the face of great pressure, like becoming orderly in the face of great parental demand. The disorderly side must be driven underground. When the individual can *attend* to some aspect of his nature instead of driving it underground, he will not need to resort to repressive measures to stifle unwanted messages. The unity of the person is based on inclusion, on composition, not mere specialization. There is much to be said for the efficiency of the personal dictatorship; convenient, one-minded, decisive. This is an uneasy efficiency and although many people appear able to pull it off successfully, the losses which many others suffer are too great to bear—witness the epidemic ambivalence, the poisonous prejudice and the yearning for simple solutions.

One of the common methods for bringing about a new composition of forces is to play out the dialogue between the polar parts. One woman, Carla, likened herself to a painting in which the background was blue with small red dots scattered on it. The blue, to her, represented her basic mood in life: depressed, formless, serving mostly as background, unwilling to be obliterated but having no shape of its own. The red dots were her moments of happiness, clearly articulated, but small, isolated and nowhere near covering enough territory. I asked Carla to begin a dialogue between the blue ground and the red dots of her painting. The blue background observed that it might be easier to be happy if it had some kind of shape, like the red dots; it wanted to be clearly articulated, too. Carla realized that being more specific would mean that she would have to be as clear about her sadness as she was about her happiness. This she usually resisted, settling for undifferentiated depression instead of clearly focused sadness—she called this being unwilling to complain—but it also kept her from making any specific changes in the unfulfilling parts of her life. The red dots listened, then, as the blue background told of the sadness of the limited relationship with a boyfriend and of her feelings of powerlessness at work. Once these unsatisfying parts of her life could be identified, Carla had taken the first step in making changes.

Another brief dialogue follows between the big and little sides of a woman who often felt she had to put on a bright, competent facade to cover up her uncertainty and need for assurance.

Little: (crying) I feel so little. I feel helpless and weak . . .
I need somebody to take care of me. I don't *want* to be big
and have to take care of somebody else. They always
want me to watch over someone, and I'm too little!

Big: Come on, don't be like that. You don't have to be
like that. I'm big and I can do things. I'm able to get
things going.

Little: I don't *want* to be big . . . I'm little . . . I'm only
3½ and . . . I'm watching my little brother and . . . he falls
off the porch! I'm too little to watch him. I feel so bad!

Therapist: Sounds like a big job for a little girl.

Little: It *was* . . . I shouldn't have been doing it . . . it was
too much to expect. I've always been asked to act big and
do things and I'm little!
(pause)

Now I feel bigger . . . I'm 11 years old and I'm asked to
go to Cape Cod and watch my cousins. And I worry about
who will watch my baby sister . . . there's a river in front
of our house and I'm afraid she'll fall in and nobody will
see her.

Therapist: So it's *you or nobody.*

Big: That's baloney!

Therapist: What's baloney?

Little: Somebody will watch . . . it doesn't *have* to be me!
(crying) I want to be little and have somebody *hold* me.
(curls up into a ball on the couch . . . stretches out her
hand.)

Therapist: What do you want now?

Patient: Oh, I don't know . . . I feel like a baby! It's silly!

Therapist: What you want is silly?
(long pause)

Patient: Could you . . . could you hold me?

So I sat next to her on the couch, took her onto my lap and held
her. She continued to cry, and little by little the tension and

stiffness drained out of her. After about five minutes I asked her just to experience what it was like to be held. After about five mintues more, I asked her what she was aware of.

> *Patient:* I feel more relaxed right now than I have ever been.
>
> *Therapist:* Do you feel *big* or *little* right now?
>
> *Patient:* I don't feel little . . . I don't feel like a baby. But I don't feel big either. I mean, I don't feel like I have to act big and pretend I don't want to be held . . . I . . . *That's* the baloney! I can be big and still want to be held!

Polarities take many forms, like the masks in the Greek theater where each character stood for himself and yet for more than himself. So, polarities can represent the battleground between intellect and emotion, between competence and incompetence, between brightness and stupidity, between dependability and irresponsibility, and between maturity and immaturity. In the enactment of these characteristics the individual can give full voice to what they demand and what they contribute in his life.

DIRECTED BEHAVIOR

Some changes in behavior do not require deep prior workthrough but may, nevertheless, alter how the individual experiences himself and how he experiences and is experienced by others. It is a common admonition that in therapy we do not tell people how to behave. In gestalt therapy sometimes we do— selectively, and for exploratory purposes. Through simple instruction and guidance the patient may do something which uncovers or highlights behavior which may have been blocked out of awareness and, through this, to discover a new slant on previous behavior, familiar relationships and earlier experience.

For example, if a person sounds as if he is whining, but *he* is not in touch with that quality in his voice, he might be asked to whine deliberately and exaggeratedly. The tight-jawed person might be asked to speak like an idiot or a nutcracker or as if he had lockjaw. The soft-spoken person might be asked to speak as if the other people in the room were at a great distance from him; the person who seems to be making speeches might be asked to make one; the person who qualifies everything he says might be asked to cut out any qualifying remarks. Although directed behavior has a little of the flavor of enactment, it differs in that it is more practical, more limited to specific behaviors, and more directly instructional—not as open-ended as enactment. While it is true that its effects may often have dramatic consequences, the intention is not to create a dramatic scene but rather to put new behavior into action during an actual encounter.

Directed behavior is *not* intended to make a person do things he doesn't want to do—or just do things blindly without feeling them. It *is* intended, though, to give him the opportunity for relevant practice in behaviors he may be avoiding. Through his own discoveries in trying out these behaviors, he will uncover aspects of himself which in their turn will generate further self-discovery.

One person in a group was assigned the role of interferer because of his expressed reluctance to speak when he might be interfering with the ongoing event. For a while, his behavior was indeed interruptive, but as he went on with it, what began as interfering behavior changed into real leadership. Naturally, the instructions had not been intended to produce interference generally, but to permit his energies to be released even in the face of feeling like an interloper. If one has to wait until there is nothing going on so as to avoid interfering, he has a long wait ahead of him.

Another young man in a group would speak diffidently, couching his observations carefully and taking great pains not to "impose" his views on anyone else. I asked him to follow every comment or statement he made with the phrase, "and I really mean that!" At first he mumbled the phrase a little, throwing it in halfheartedly, but then he began to enjoy what he was doing; his eyes sparkled and he grinned, and the phrase became louder and clearer each time he said it. The other people in the group responded to him, asking his opinion and relishing with him the vigorous assertion of his belief. From a position at the edge of the group he became central to the evening's action.

Still another example of using directed behavior is one which aimed at mobilizing self-support. Adlai, a physician, felt badgered and rejected whenever his statements were not immediately accepted by his colleagues. When his words were received skeptically, he would stiffen up and isolate himself from further exchange. Adlai was a rather vague man, who had a tendency to say outlandish things as though they were God's truth. For several weeks we worked on his powers for supporting his own statements, because it was as though he expected all the support to come from his colleagues and did little to support himself. In one of our sessions, he told of a patient who was dying of uremic poisoning; he believed the man should be helped to die, since he had so little chance of survival. Adlai felt that he was cowardly or he would have been able to administer a killing dosage of drugs, which he was clearly unable to do. In trying to support his view about the justifiability of killing this man, Adlai went into considerable detail about this man's life and family. The more he talked, the more he became aware that his patient was making strong efforts to remain alive despite the pain and, furthermore, that his family wanted him to remain alive. So, preset judgments about the evil of pain to the contrary, he had been right not to hasten the man's death. Formerly, he would have gotten stuck with feeling cowardly. But when he was able to uncover the supports for his behavior, his act became a warm and responsive experience rather than a brainwash job against possibly justifiable killing.

A young man, Rick, handsome as Adonis, who had lived

a life of adventure, had been impotent for years. He had been a volunteer fighter in Viet Nam, offering himself for the most dangerous missions; he was a deep-sea diver, had explored the wilds and the primitive tribes in Brazil; had played professional Rugby; and chopped down trees for relaxation. It became clear, as he recounted his experiences, that Rick had a large stake in keeping his cool in the face of high danger. His personal courage and grace in trouble were remarkable—but unfortunately he could not make love with a cool penis. One day Rick was talking about his impending graduation from law school and what he might do afterwards. He was considering two alternatives. One was to enter politics and become a crime buster—a good way, in his opinion, to start the political adventure of setting his own metropolitan area on its feet. Although from some mouths this would sound like a grandiose scheme, from him the possibility was romantic, perhaps, but not unlikely at all. Another direction was offered him by a wealthy and prominent friend who wanted to make a place for Rick in international business activities and even as his own aide, eventually, if the prospect of a presidential cabinet post materialized. Rick described both of these choices at considerable length and with exciting detail, but with no vocal intonation, facial coloring, movement or sense of awe that these prospects would have aroused in most people. He was not an arrogant man and I had the sense that he might blush at any moment—but, of course, he didn't. One blush in his penis would, for him, be worth many stories, because it would signal the recovery of the willingness to experience sensation and the consequent recovery of sexual potency, which he did indeed later achieve.

Since directed behavior is an excellent method to use in the attempt to recover sensation I told Rick to tell me these stories again, but this time with passion and excitement, much as an actor might do. I explained to him that, although what I was proposing might at first seem artificial, *I* had missed the excitement in his first telling and suspected that *his* own loss had to be more grievous than mine. So he began retelling his stories, to the accompaniment of a few pokes in his chest from me to arouse his reactivity. By the time we were done, the aggression in his system was apparent; his chin jutted out, his fists were clenched, his breathing had increased and the color rose in his face. He began to look lithe and even younger than his 28 years. His stolidity left and he looked agile and physically powerful, with energy to spare. This sequence of directed behavior had brought him into touch with the power of his bounded energy. Penis later, I thought.

FANTASY

Fantasy is an expansive force in a person's life—it reaches and stretches beyond the immediate people, environment or event which may otherwise contain him. Sometimes these extensions may be puerile or obsessive, as in many daydreams. But sometimes these extensions can gather such great force and poignancy that they achieve a presence which is more compelling than some real life situations.

Thurber's Walter Mitty depicts the grand and futile fantasies of a henpecked husband. But Thurber's creative energy transforms this into a portrait which is grander in terms of liveliness, action and completion than any ordinary daydreamer. Usually, the daydreamer is reluctant to flesh out his daydreams even in fantasy, so he winds up doubly blocked—afraid of events or his own feelings and—even worse—afraid of their shadows! So the ruminative fantasizer replays skeletonized themes, stripped of the aggression, the sexuality, the clever manipulations, etc., all of which are the stuff that makes his innards pulsate. When these fantasies can emerge in the therapy experience, the renewal of energy may be vast, sometimes bordering on the unassimilable and often marking a new course in the individual's sense of self.

Four major purposes which can be served through the use of fantasy are: 1) contact with a resisted event, feeling or personal characteristic; 2) contact with an unavailable person or unfinished situation; 3) exploring the unknown; and 4) exploring new or unfamiliar aspects of oneself.

1) *Contact with a resisted event, feeling or personal characteristic*—In an example used earlier we described the experience of one man, over-reactive to threat, who was asked to give free rein to his visual imagery as he lay on the couch with his eyes closed. He visualized a scene in which children were at play in a schoolyard. As his fantasy continued, a huge alligator appeared out of the sky, superimposing itself over the scene. He began to scream in terror, as though the alligator were right there. Then he paled and shivered, as though in shock. I went over to the couch, held him and soothed him until his sense of security returned. Gradually he began to talk about his father and the rages he used to fly into, directed either at himself or his mother. When he was done, he felt relieved, a feeling he had not experienced for years. Not long after this session he was willing to seek out his father and was able to speak to him, feeling an equality which had heretofore eluded him, not only with his father but with most people he encountered.

It is remarkable that a person can fantasy something and, even without overt action, develop the kind of release that one might normally expect to issue only from such action. Two plausible reasons might account for this. First, although the fantasy is essentially non-action, it may be accompanied by or produce action which can form a dynamic nucleus for the experience. In the above fantasy, although my patient was, of course, not actually playing in a schoolyard, he did scream in alarm when the alligator appeared—which is a grand action in its own right. He was soothed by me—an accompanying action—and he went on to relate relevant experiences with his father—another expressive action. Furthermore, he continued the momentum and wound up actually talking to his father, so the fantasy had the effect of stimulating a real live action with his father.

The second reason for the efficacy of fantasy is that the return and assimilation of feelings is an important development, *irrespective* of whether an actual resolution of a life scene takes place. To experience terror—*and get away with it*—means that one can be less threatened by feelings that one imagines may ensue from actual behavior; terror becomes less than altogether poisonous.

By the same token, if one cries during a fantasy, one may become less likely thereafter to avoid those experiences which may lead to crying. If fantasy leads to a relaxed experience of one's sexuality or one's affection for another person or one's anger at having been mistreated, these emotions, once they have been released and assimilated even in response to a fantasy, become more likely to be available as part of the person's emotional repertoire in everyday situations.

Naturally, the restorative influence of the fantasy experience depends on the circumstances. It is possible that when the dreaded event is returned to—even in fantasy—it may turn out to be fully as devastating as was anticipated and the individual may get so frightened by this experience that he is impeded from further exploration. Consequently, it is very important that sensitive attention to pacing be a factor in the introduction of these experiences and that timing be rooted in the self-regulation of the individual as a primary influence in the development of the fantasy.

In the above example, the patient's experience bordered on interrupting his progress rather than facilitating it. It is not unlikely that, had I not brought him back into contact with me and into a sense of the meaningfulness of this incident, he could have had just one more terrifying experience, confirming anew his wariness in life.

2) *Contact with an unavailable person or unfinished situa-*

tion—In addition to the force generated by intensification of experience through fantasy, fantasy is often the only route back to a generic situation. A parent may be dead, an old flame gone to another city, or a childhood friend no longer important enough for actual contact. Even when a situation is available in terms of time or space, it may still be either too frightening or too impolitic to go to it directly. Fantasy becomes invaluable then because it recreates what is close to reality yet is relatively safe, while going beyond gossip, strategy or ruminative speculation.

In one group, we fortuitously happened on a rare combination of fantasy and reality. One person had been embroiled in a struggle on the first night of our workshop and failed to show up the next morning. This was very upsetting to several people in the group who still had some unfinished business with him. One man in particular was very deeply concerned, so I asked him to close his eyes and visualize the absent man and tell him what he wanted to tell him. He went on at length talking to the visual fantasy with his eyes closed, during which time the absentee walked into the room and sat down silently. The speaker soon opened his eyes, saw that the man he had been addressing was actually there and discovered that he no longer felt upset about him. They were able to start talking from a new perspective as though the original problem had been worked through.

Usually though, the people one has unfinished business with are just not available. They have died, moved away, become alienated, don't belong in one's life anymore, or the time has long since passed to rehash earlier dealings with them. One woman, for example, felt she had been treated badly by her husband's family at the time of their marriage. Many years later she was still resentful about what she felt had been insulting treatment. So, in a fantasy she imagined a large gathering at which all of the family, some 50 or so relatives, were present. She visualized them sitting and—in the style of the early

Russian silent films—beating their breasts, rolling their eyes, and with dramatic gestures saying over and over, "I am *sorry*, I am *sorry!*" Staying with the ludicrousness of the fantasy and what it would take to expunge the old grudge, she was finally able to move past her resentment.

Another young woman, who had lived through a nightmar- ish three months undergoing extensive plastic surgery as the result of an automobile accident which had killed her closest friend, was strangely moved by seeing the obituary of the plastic surgeon who had operated on her. She had begun by commenting that she felt he had been gypped by life since he had died at 58 just when he might have been getting ready to slow down and spend more time with his family. I asked her if she felt *she* had gypped him or, possibly, that he had gypped her? It turned out that she had really wanted something from him that she hadn't got—his unresponsiveness in the face of her pain and fear had left her with an almost reflexive dread of being dependent in any way, and a feeling that she makes too big a deal out of the minor irritations in life. She forbids her- self to talk about her really deep sadness. I asked her to visualize the doctor and to talk to him in her fantasy, saying what she would presently like to tell him. Here is what she said:

> Dr. ————? Do you remember me? It seems like a long time ago to me . . . maybe five or six years ago. My face was all messed up and . . . you put it back together again . . .? I want you to know that the way . . . the way in which you approached me really caused me a lot of fear and it stayed with me, *long* after my face was put back together. And I guess I want you to know because *I* would feel better if I told you about it, and I think that somehow maybe you could hear what I say and apply it with other people that you work with, other patients. All I'm asking is . . . for you to *listen* . . . when I talk or when I ask you a question about what are you going to do to me, and what's going to happen. Then if you can answer those questions for me, then I would know that you're *there*,

that you're not just a mechanical thing, mechanically putting me together. That . . . that *you're* here as a person and *I'm* here as a person, obviously in need of some help, but I'm still a *people*. And so are you. You know, if you had been aware of that, it would have been easier for me to relate to you. And I would have felt a whole lot better. (very softly) And that would be it. (and finally, whispering) I feel like maybe I've finished. I hope so.

Here is one last example of the power of fantasy to complete the experience with something or someone who is no longer present but with whom an intense link remains, vital and compelling. One man, after a series of visualizations of a patchwork quality, a scene here, an image there, finally saw the face of a girl he had known in another country when he was very young. He had loved her, but was too young to have known that that was what he was feeling. He had never told her, and had left because he was returning home from the Army. But now, as he was visualizing her, I asked him to talk to her. He told her about his feelings and, doing this, he entered into a sense of the softness of his nature, which he rarely experienced anymore. When he opened his eyes he observed that he felt as though he were awakening from a dream.

3) *Exploring the unknown*—Unfinished business is not all that fantasy may address itself to. Perhaps even more basic to fantasy is the function of exploring the unknown for orientation in the face of the complexities of life, to prepare for future actions and to sharpen one's sensibilities in general. Herbert Read* has spoken about this quality of the arts:

The vitality (of artistic imagery) thus realized, is selective; it is a concentration of attention on one aspect of the phenomenal world, that aspect which for the moment has predominant biological significance. Far from being a playful activity, an expenditure of surplus energy, as earlier theorists have supposed, art, at the dawn of human

---

* Read, H. *Icon and Idea*. New York: Schocken Books, 1965.

culture, was a key to survival—a sharpening of faculties essential to the struggle for existence . . . it is still the activity by means of which our sensation is kept alert, our imagination kept vivid, our power of reasoning kept keen. The mind sinks into apathy unless its hungry roots are continuously searching the dark sustenance of the unknown, its sensitive foliage continuously stretching towards unimaginable light. The mind's growth is its expanding area of consciousness. That area is made good, realized, and presented in enduring images, by a formative activity that is essentially esthetic.

Such a view sees fantasy as more than a way of catching up with the past, compensating for errors brought about by blocked expression or overwhelming circumstances. It sees in fantasy the generative power to develop a repertoire of alertness and preparation. Spontaneity may be an idol of current humanist culture but it is highly overrated as the sine qua non of good living. Many of the events that count most in an individual's life require a depth of focus which is best not left merely to chance. Spontaneous action which grows out of sensitive exploration of possibilities and alternatives is rooted in knowledge rather than whimsy.

Read* quotes Leo Frobenius describing the respect paid to the value of fantasy preparations by African pygmies. Frobenius had asked the Africans accompanying him in his explorations to kill an antelope because the food supply was low. They said that they could not do it right away—it required preparation—but they could do it by the next day. Frobenius was curious about what these preparations might be, and so, in his own words:

> I left camp before dawn and crept through the bushes to the open place which they had sought out the night before. The pygmies appeared in the twilight, the woman with them. The men crouched on the ground, plucked a small

---

* Read, H. *Icon and Idea*. New York: Schocken Books, 1965.

square free of weeds and smoothed it over with their hands. One of them drew something in the cleared space with his forefinger, while his companions murmured some kind of formula or incantation. Then a waiting silence. The sun rose on the horizon. One of the men, an arrow on his bowstring, took his place beside the square. A few minutes later the rays of the sun fell on the drawing at his feet. In that same second the woman stretched out her arms to the sun, shouting words I did not understand, he shot his arrow and the woman cried out again. Then the three men bounded off through the bush while the woman stood for a few minutes and then went slowly towards our camp. As she disappeared I came forward and, looking down at the smoothed square of sand, saw the drawing of an antelope four hands long. From the antelope's neck protruded the pygmy's arrow.

No more eloquent testimonial is needed to demonstrate the primitive recognition that spontaneity is rooted in personal preparation and that fantasy enters into preparatory activities.

A more modern version of the value of fantasy for the preparatory experience is the custom of Jim Brown, the famous football player. He has said that his week of preparation for Sunday's game included visualizing the details of the coming game as he imagined they might occur. This readied him for clear focus on the game, provided a sense of familiarity with the demands which would confront him and kept him at a high level of alertness and stimulation.

Although fantasy preparations lean into the future, they are not predictions of the future. Therefore it does not suffice merely to imitate the fantasy—one has to swing into discovering his own sources of creativity within the fantasy and to focus these in on the basic requirements of the job ahead. The folly of trusting to spontaneity alone is that it underestimates the dedication needed for authentically respectful contact with the exigencies of living.

Seth felt pessimistic about the chances of an admired colleague getting the promotion that would keep him in their organization. If this man left because he didn't get the promotion, Seth would be placed in an untenable position. So it was important that his boss recognize the need for the other man's promotion. Seth had set up a meeting to bring these two men together—but he felt he didn't know how to talk to them. We played out the conversation: first I played the boss and Seth played himself, then we reversed positions and I played Seth while he played his boss. In both instances the conversation became very animated and clarified several issues, one of which was that the anticipated meeting was not necessarily going to turn into a fight. Furthermore, even beyond the specific tactical possibilities, the fantasy dialogue helped him clear out some of the junk in his head so that he wouldn't get locked into being vindictive or presenting unnecessary ultimatums. When the conversation finally did take place, it went surprisingly smoothly and Seth was able to touch off a harmony that led to the promotion of his friend. Interestingly enough, he said little in the actual conversation that was repetitive of the fantasied conversation. It turned out to be a new conversation, altogether spontaneous, but the spontaneity was based on a free mind and profoundly respectful concentration.

4) *Exploring new aspects of the individual*—Still another purpose of fantasy may be to probe characterological qualities of an individual, whether or not they relate immediately or specifically to other aspects of his life. Take, for example, the man who sees himself as an unvaryingly soft person, not able to muster up enough aggressive force to get what he wants. Suppose he is asked, as I asked one patient, Ned, what he imagined would happen if his aggression were to emerge unbounded. Ned—greatly aroused by our prior exchanges during which I had goaded him—replied that he was afraid he might bowl me over. I asked him to close his eyes and imagine himself as a bowling ball and me as a tenpin. He imagined himself rolling toward me with great force, greater than any force he had ever seen, more like a hurricane than a bowling ball, and

he hit me squarely in the middle, splintering me as I flew through space. He felt excited; his next image was of hitting me in the jaw with his fist and again I flew out into space, no longer visible. At this Ned got frightened and wanted me back. I instructed him to call me back. After some reluctance he did call out loudly and there I was, in his fantasy, intact and regarding him benignly. His mood softened and he just smiled at me in his fantasy and embraced me and then he began to cry warmly, appreciating the tenderness he saw in me even though he had used the full force of his aggression against me. When Ned opened his eyes, he saw me and said hello as though I were a long-lost friend returned.

Valerie had come into her therapy session burdened by the innumerable developments that were the result of her having recently taken a decisive step in her life. There was the conflict of whom to tell, how much she wanted to discuss with some people and not with others, how some people might react to her decision and what styles of interaction she might have to work out with them. As she went on describing these eventualities, she began to respond to them in a familiar fashion—which was to put herself on what we had come to call her "automatic pilot"—closing herself down until she operated at a minimal functional level: tightened posture, restricted breathing and poorly focused, almost fuzzy vision. I asked her to close her eyes and to restore her breathing by visualizing a beach scene where her breath could come in like the waves: slowly, steadily, without pressure, rhythmically. Soon it became clearer how Valerie's pinched shoulders limited her breathing, so I asked her to make room for her breath by extending her arms along the back of the couch on which she was sitting. When she did this, her face became radiant and her breathing did indeed grow deep and rhythmic. She described how the fantasy of the waves coming in had expanded when she moved her arms and that now she visualized a great surf, with strong waves rushing in over a beach strewn with pebbles, covering some of the pebbles, rolling some around and just washing in lightly over others. She showed with her arms the motion of the expansion of the waves and how this fit in with her now-free breathing, expanding when she inhaled and coming together on the exhalation. She opened her eyes, after a few moments, and remarked with deep calm that now she felt she had room and strength to deal with the consequences of her recent decision and that she no longer needed to shut herself down in order to handle troublesome issues.

DREAMS

Dreamwork occupies a special place within the variety of experiments we are describing. Strictly speaking, the dream is the *basis* for the experiment which aims at bringing the dream to life in the therapy experience. Perls invented several techniques for endowing the dream report and workthrough with immediacy.

First, he would instruct the dreamer to recount the dream as if it were happening in the present. The narration would not consist of statements like, "I went into this large room where a group of people had gathered" but rather, "I'm going into a large room and there is a group of people gathering there. . . ." This simple linguistic device immerses the dreamer into his own dream with greater force than telling about the dream.

More importantly, the dreamer is helped to play out parts of his dream as aspects of his own existence—a workthrough of the dream as present event rather than past history and as action rather than as a base for interpretation. The dream becomes a starting point for an altogether new experience.

Perhaps the best known aspect of Perls' dreamwork is his view of the dream as projection. That is, all of the dream components, large or small, human or non-human, are representations of the dreamer. He says:*

---

* Perls, F. S. *Gestalt Therapy Verbatim.* Moab, Utah: Real People Press, 1969.

I believe that every part of the dream is a part of yourself —not just the person, but every item, every mood, anything that comes across. My favorite example is this:

> A patient dreams he is leaving my office and goes to Central Park. And he goes across the bridle path, into the park. So I ask him, "Now play the bridle path." He answers indignantly, "What? and let everybody shit and crap on me?" You see, he really got the identification.

I let the patient play all these parts, because only by really playing can you get the full identification, and the identification is the counteraction to the alienation.

Alienation means "That's not me, that's something else, something strange, something not belonging to me." And often you encounter quite a bit of resistance against playing this alienated part. You don't want to reown, take back, those parts of yourself which you have pushed out of your personality. This is the way you have impoverished yourself . . . If we can bring these things back to life, then we have more material to assimilate. And my whole technique develops more and more *never, never interpret.* Just backfeeding, providing an opportunity for the other person to discover himself.

This view of the dream as projection dominated Perls' later work and many of his demonstrations and theoretical discussions were devoted to showing how the dreamer projects himself into his dream.

However, the dream as projection is only one perspective Valuable as this view is, we want to amplify dreamwork to include also its suitability for exploring the contact possibilities available to the dreamer and its generative power for unfolding interaction between dreamer and therapist, or dreamer and group members, or dreamer and aspects of his own existence which are not merely projected parts of self. Life, as well as dreams, is, after all, more than a projection. If I dream of a bridle path, I may indeed identify with it, projecting a part of myself onto it. But I may also relate to it on its own terms, in

In full theoretical perspective, however, the dream is indeed more than a projection of various aspects of the dreamer; it is a stage whereon contact can be activated so as to depict the present existence of the dreamer. Some of these contacts are fearful, some are distressing, some are delightful, some are confusing, some are poignant, some are practical—they stretch into all the shapes contact is capable of assuming. So we may see that if a dreamer dreams of jumping from a high diving board into a devious swimming pool which empties itself of water as she plunges towards it, there are many directions the dreamwork explores. In this dream, as the dreamer played it out, she talked to the tricky swimming pool, she played the disappearing water, she dove from the board, she became the pool, filled again and shining, and finally became a lone swimmer who slipped out at night to swim in the unoccupied pool. Through these many guises she came also to know more about her own sexuality, ephemeral, untrustworthy and private but also full and gleaming.

A good way to illustrate how projection and contactfulness merge is to present one of Perls' own dream workthroughs and show how he himself worked with contact as well as projection. Here is the dream of Jean.* The dream starts in a New York subway where the dreamer discovers a muddy, slippery, incline going down into the earth. Jean's mother—who is dead—is with her, so Jean makes a toboggan out of a cardboard carton and slides down the chute with her mother behind her.

Perls begins the dream workthrough with a few remarks which both orient and encourage Jean about the purpose of working the dream through: "So, Jean, could you tell again, the dream? Live it through as if it were your own existence, and see whether you can understand more about your life." When Jean expresses her fear at going down, Perls directs her to talk to the chute, bringing her into *contact with the dream*

---

* Perls, F. S. *Geltalt Therapy Verbatim*. Moab, Utah: Real People Press, 1969.

environment rather than treating it only as projection. Then he uses the projective possibilities of the dream by asking her to play the chute, and she soon accepts the projection as her own; she experiences her own slipperiness. To be sure, there is some denial through laughter, but on the whole she does not seem much bothered about being a slippery person. As Jean moves through her dream and discovers the cardboard carton, Perls has her play the carton and she expresses one of her values—she can be useful even though she may appear to be just a leftover. But she begins to examine her value and becomes aware that she just wants to be "sat on and scrunched down." By asking her to repeat this, and tell it to the group, Perls heightens her awareness of self and brings her into *contact with the other people present*. As she speaks, she makes a pounding gesture and Perls asks her whom she is hitting—tapping into her chain of retroflected suppression and anger. When Jean replies that she is hitting herself, Perls moves beyond the retroflection—asking her whom is she hitting *besides* herself— and brings her into *contact with the external target of her anger* —her mother—and makes her aware of her frustrated need to be in charge of her own movement through life: "Mother, I'm scrunching down on (ouch) you! And I am going to take *you* for a ride instead of you telling me to go and taking me wherever you want to. (Yells) *I'm taking you along for a ride with me!*" Perls responds with his own perception of her statement, using the *contact between himself and Jean* as a crucial aspect of the interaction: "I had the impression it was *too much* to be convincing." Here, by feeding in his own perceptions he articulates the unspoken but still influential fear that Jean has of her mother. He asks Jean *to talk to her mother* and she says: "Mom, I'm *still* afraid of you but I'm going to take you for a ride anyway." This is *contact,* rooted in her awareness—no projection here. She is aware of her fear but she wants to move on, a clear example of how focused awareness leads on to action.

As they move on, Perls points out to Jean that she is avoiding moving on her own legs, that she is relying on the support of the cardboard carton and on gravity to carry her. He asks her what is her objection to having legs and Jean recognizes that although it was her mother who didn't permit her to stand on her own two legs she had taken over that action and continued to do it to herself even after her mother's death. Perls asks Jean to speak, not as a child but as a 31-year old woman, to her mother.

Jean: I can stand on my own legs. I can do anything I want to do and I can *know* what I want to do. I *don't need* you. In fact, you're not even here when I *did need* you.

So, why do you hang around?

Perls: Can you say goodbye to her? Can you bury her?

J: Well, I can now, because I'm at the bottom of the slope, and when I come to the bottom, I stand up. I stand up, and I walk around in this beautiful place.

P: Can you say to your mother, "Goodbye, mother, rest in peace."

J: I think I did that in the dream. Bye, mother—bye.

Perls is leading her to complete the unfinished situation with her mother and it is this contact that opens her to crying because it is in contact that real stimulation can occur.

P: Talk, Jean. You're doing great when you talk to your mother.

J: Bye, mom. You couldn't help what you did. You didn't know any better. It wasn't your fault that you had three boys first, and then you got me. You wanted another boy, and you didn't want me and you felt so bad after you found out I was a girl. You just tried to make it up to me —that's all. You didn't have to smother me. I forgive you, mom. Just rest, mama . . . I can go now. Sure, I can go—

P: You're still holding your breath, Jean.

Concern with the dreamer's body is important because holding her breath would neutralize her sensation and interfere with her personal mobility.

> *J:* (pause) "Are you really sure, Jean?" Mama, let me go—
>
> *P:* What would she say?
>
> *J:* "I *can't* let you go."
>
> *P:* Now, *you* say this to your mother.

Here Perls is helping her undo her projection and leading her to identify with the process of holding on rather than assigning that to her mother only.

> *J:* I can't let you go?
>
> *P:* Keep her—you're holding control.
>
> *J:* Mama, I can't let you go. I need you. No. I *don't* need you.
>
> *P:* But, you still miss her, don't you?
>
> *J:* A little. There's somebody there. Well, what if nobody was there? What if it was all empty? And dark? It's all empty and dark—it's beautiful. I'll let you go. I'll let you go, mama. (softly) Please go—

In this workthrough Jean took the initial steps in undoing her projections about her mother. She glimpsed some of her own reluctance to letting go of her mother and discovered that the climactic contact with her mother—saying goodbye—left a gap in her own life, which, at least for the moment, she could experience as awesome but beautiful.

Perls' deft shifting from one emphasis in the dream to another gives depth and dimension to the experience. He deals now with the dream as projection, now with the dreamer's awareness of her own present feelings, with her own body sense and, most powerfully, with the dreamer's contactfulness with her own mother. Underneath all of these developments is the unarticulated sense of Jean's contact with Perls which supported and energized the emergent flow of the dream workthrough.

These shifts in emphasis underscore one of the great developments of the gestalt method—the flexibility with which the therapist can choose the focus which seems right for himself, for the patient and for that particular moment in time. The range of possibilities open to the gestalt therapist depends always on a sensitive response to the present interaction—it is not a stereotyped use of awareness or body-work or linguistic gimmickry. Some people with a great range of behaviors and perspectives may be able to move easily into the experiment, while others are immobilized by their sense of contrived experience or by their embarrassment at enacting an accentuation of their own existence. We do not want to press people into some pre-designed mold but rather to establish the best way for each unique individual to work. A person who cannot develop a visual fantasy may be able to develop a contactful relationship with the therapist. Another, who doesn't work well with dreams, may be able energetically to talk to a person he visualizes sitting across the room. There is enough range in technique and perspective to encompass diversity in personal style or preference. Through using this range, the gestalt therapist can move fluidly among the different aspects of the therapy experience.

So far we have discussed the dream as a self-contained means of exploring one's own nature; only the dream and what the dreamer himself does with it have been the focus in the dream workthrough. But the dream can also be used as a starting point for discoveries about present relationships with other group members or the therapist or with a recognition of an existential position which bears exploration using the dream only as a point of departure.

Take, for example, a man who dreams of a large frog who

is always watching him, ready to jump. This prospect makes the dreamer edgy and distracts him from the rest of the dream events which he can hardly remember. The leader may elect to underscore the dreamer's discomfort at being scrutinized by asking him to describe his experience of the group as he tells them his dream. The dreamer replies that they look very alert and attentive. The leader asks what he would like to tell the group and the dreamer says to them, "I wish you wouldn't pay such close attention to me." What is the dreamer's objection to such close attention, the leader wants to know. The dreamer is afraid they might see something in him he doesn't want them to see. So, the dreamer may be asked to imagine what each person sees as they watch him—or he may be asked to check out with them what they do see. Either way can begin an interactive process, highlighting the dreamer's sense of being watched and his fears of being jumped on. The nature of the ensuing engagements is unpredictable. The dreamer may single out a particular bug-eyed individual and make contact with him in whatever way he wants until he achieves some resolution of felt threat. He may reverse roles, scrutinizing each member of the group in turn, exploring his own projected voyeurism or confronting his own unwillingness to see something threatening in the other person. Or the dreamer may discover that he has some unfinished business with the group about a time when he thought they jumped on him. Whatever directions the dream experience took it would maintain a natural relevance for his relationship with other people and for his awareness of himself and his position vis-à-vis his world. Working through to resolution could leave him less vulnerable to the threat of being either watched or jumped on and freer to watch and be watched with less distortion or blotting out. The dream workthrough in one sense may thus never actually return to the dream itself but rather responds to its existential message about the person's life in the same way one could respond to his remarks, or his movements, or his stories—as another one of his expressions which illuminates his experience.

Joseph Zinker* has developed an extension of dreamwork which also goes beyond the dream itself. He uses the dreamwork as theater, where people in the group play out the various parts of the dream. This offers the group members a range of opportunities for enacting a facet of the dream which may relate not only to the dreamer, but also to their own lives. The dreamer can cast people to play parts of the dream or they can volunteer; he can direct them as to how he wants them to develop the dream or he can give them free rein and get tuned in to how others may experience the qualities he was depicting in his dream. Zinker points out how valuable this approach is in incorporating group participation as opposed to the observational role to which they are usually relegated.

Here is an example of an actual group enactment of a dream described by Zinker. The dream includes the statement "I see my mother approaching and I feel strangely uncomfortable in my chest." Two people in the group volunteer to play parts of this dream. One chooses to play the crippled boy, a son whom he pictures as suffering from emphysema. A middle-aged woman volunteers to play the part of a domineering mother. Both people show evidence they are personally involved with this kind of characterization. A segment of the exchange goes like this:

Boy: All my life I have needed you to take care of me but now I'm beginning to feel your suffocation . . . I mean my suffocation. I feel that you are choking me to death.

Mother: When you were very young, you were sickly and I have tried to protect you from unnecessary discomfort . . .

Boy: (interrupting) Yes, and by the time I was seven, I

---

* Zinker, Joseph. Dreamwork as Theatre. *Voices*, Vol. 1, No. 2, Summer, 1971.

was afraid to go to school by myself and I would vomit when I got there.

Therapist: John, how do you feel in your stomach right now?

Boy: All right, but I still feel like she is choking me.

Therapist: (to mother) Myra, put your hands on his neck and squeeze a bit . . . let him get in touch with the suffocation.

Mother: (follows directions) I only want to take care of you.

Boy: (tearing her hands away and coughing) Then get off my back! Let me live! (He looks as though he has suddenly taken his first full breath this evening.)

Member of the group: She doesn't hear you.

Boy: (hollering very loudly) Get off my back, let me breathe, let me live my own life! (panting deeply)

Another group member: I want to play alter ego for Myra. (to boy) If I let you be, let you go, will you hate me all my life?

Mother: (completing statement) If I could only feel that you will love me when you leave, it wouldn't be so difficult.

Boy: I need you to help me leave and I will always love you but differently . . . as a man, a strong man, not a cripple.

(The pair embraces spontaneously and Myra cries because she realizes that she will have to talk with her son who flunked out of college and came home six months ago.)

Though only a few people participated directly in this segment of dreamwork, the possibilities for total group involvement are clear. Dreams can have many characters, particularly when inanimate objects—equally valid statements about the dreamer as the animate ones—are included. In one of my groups, Bud, a young graduate student on the verge of dropping out of school, reported a dream in which he was trying to get into a tall building. As Bud approached the building, a sinister figure in a cape tried to dissuade him from entering; but he didn't yield to this trickery, moving past the cloaked man, up the stairs and into the building where he took an elevator to the top floor to try to tell someone about what he had encountered at the entrance. But there was no one to respond to his complaint. I asked him to cast the group as parts of his dream, and to instruct them as to the basic elements of their roles but allowing them to improvise as they went along. One man played the dreamer, focusing only on his desire to get into the building; that was all he knew and all he wanted to know. Doggedly he resisted the temptations and persuasions of the caped man, who was played by another group member as a wily, lively and conniving character. Another group member played the stairs in measured precision where movement either up or down could take place—the stairs didn't care. And so on: the elevator, patient and resigned, moving in preordained patterns, and the top floor, superior and secure in its position but totally unresponsive to Bud's dismay. As the group developed the dream I asked Bud to speak to each of the dream-characters and when he did he recognized a piece of himself in each. There was his stubborn determination to get through graduate school, to arrive at the top of his profession, where he felt he could really be powerful enough to do the kind of work he deeply wanted to do, but which he suspected might not be all that relevant to his real goals. There was also his wish to quit, tricky and ominous. There, too, was his dismay at the mechanical and conforming nature of his role as graduate student, moving according to other people's measures and directions, not his own. Nevertheless, at the conclusion of his dialogues with the dream-parts Bud realized that he didn't want to quit graduate school and that he could stand behind his decision to continue with integrity.

Though this specific drama is interesting on its own, it also accentuates the flexibility and theoretical validity of going beyond the purely projective facets of the dream into confrontation with an active world. Here, where people and things behave in unpredictable ways and often go off in surprising directions of their own, the dreamer goes beyond his own fantasies about the nature of people and the world-out-there.

HOMEWORK

A few hours a week are hardly enough time for growth. A few weekend workshops a year, although certainly capable of powerful mobilization, are hardly enough for growth. Something has to continue to reach beyond the guided therapeutic tour to assure a potent level of impactfulness.

The fact is that it is only through one's actual life experiences that many of the new possibilities uncovered in therapy can take on a feeling of reality. A new marriage, a new job, a new baby, a new sexual relationship may all be worth many therapy sessions. When the wrong choices are made, though, one may suffer painful consequences. It seems a drastic solution, though, to wipe out the troublesome possibilities by also wiping out the major growth possibilities, too. This cautious approach is not immune to hazard, either, replacing risky action with sterile, obsessive yearning after growth.

The aim is to educate the patient to a sense of his own readiness. Furthermore, even if a course of action turns out to be a mistake, a mistake—identified, understood and clearly perceived—is often more likely to be a part of growth than waiting for the exactly right moment and right choice which one tries to divine from the therapeutic perspective rather than day-to-day action.

Although the danger in making big decisions has resulted in bracketing-off the therapy experience from everyday life, there remains a whole range of less momentous possibilities for action. Thus, while what we call homework may not always involve the crucial confrontations inherent in larger decisions, nevertheless, by using homework, therapeutic involvement can be broadened beyond what the patient may otherwise be able to afford—in either time or money. Instead of having one or two sessions a week, the individual could have as many as he wanted, exploring his own actions and awarenesses under the guiding influence of the therapist even though not actually in his presence. Imagine the impact therapy could have if one devoted as much time to practicing what was learned during the therapy session at home as is customary with piano lessons or golf lessons or typing lessons or yoga!

A piddling example may illustrate how this can be done. One very lazy man—who might be called passive-aggressive or even borderline psychotic—proposed his own homework assignment of making five business calls a day. This seemed well within his ability and a lot more than he had been doing until then. When he started doing this he discovered some of his resistances at first hand. For one thing, he found he did not have a clear conception of what he was offering the people he called. So, we worked at clarifying what was only very general and vague in his thinking. For another thing, he dreaded ending conversations and while he could always linger—too long—with people face-to-face, saying goodbye was even more difficult on the telephone. The whole issue of taking leave and his felt isolation from others were worked through in therapy, spiced by actual identifiable experiences. He came to be willing to make these phone calls and developed a fuller sense of himself as participant and shaper of his own business life.

An obvious objection to this kind of homework is that it may parallel the oppressive demands of an environment in which the individual has already been burned. It could be argued that for the therapist to join the parade might only be reinforcing a new "adjustment" system—once again breaking faith with the individual's organic needs. However, this possibility is minimized when the homework is established with a person whose own *choice* is kept central and where this choice is rooted in live concerns, palpable and really going on. There reaches a time in the patient's development where—like learning to dive off the high board—preparatory experiences and abstract theory about high diving are not enough. There are some things one simply has to go ahead and do. The fantasy that ideal growth evolves effortlessly and unattended is a lovely fantasy. Would it were so. Perhaps it is for some lucky few. If one needs a divorce, for example, no amount of therapy can substitute for taking this step. Shakespeare refers to thoughts which "in their currents turn awry and lose the name of action." Perlsian poetry calls this "mind-fucking."

Homework, like other forms of experiment, must be dovetailed into the particular conflict area of the patient. It is behavior which is cantilevered into the patient's future—based within the experience of therapy but probing into an area requiring new behaviors. The specific tasks are limitless. One person may be asked to brag to somebody, even if only a momentary statement, every day. Another is asked to date girls younger than he is. Another is asked to relate his day's experience to his wife. Another with obsessional fantasies at bedtime is asked to write out her fantasies. Another is asked to write whatever comes to his mind about his dissertation a half hour a day, no matter how useless the material might turn out to be. Another is asked to find out from his father how much money, exactly, his wealthy father had transferred to him. Another is asked to decorate his apartment lavishly. Another is asked to chew his food until it becomes liquid. Another is asked to write out successions of statements beginning with "I wish" and "I like." On and on and on go the possibilities, always related to the person's emerging direction and always putting him into situations where he must confront aspects of himself which are blocking his movement or his awareness.

Here is an example of a homework assignment that played an important part in one person's expansion. He was plagued with bodily anxiety, particularly in his anus, scrotum, penis, and stomach. Pains and other distresses kept him always off balance and he was a frequent visitor to doctors, trying to get relief from his symptoms. He was a graduate student, was deeply worried about whether he would ever get his Ph.D. degree and was extremely shy with people generally, but most painfully with women. Later, he did get his degree and he did establish a powerfully satisfying sexual relationship. He developed a confidence and faith in his future about which he had only experienced pessimism before. His bodily troubles lessened in degree and they occurred only infrequently. Naturally, his homework was only a small part of his therapy and it is impossible to assess the degree of its contribution to his growth, but it was as important as any other single unit of our extensive work. In his sessions he saw the split between what he called "my body" and "me." I asked him to write out a dialogue between the two parts. Notice in the dialogue that he gives identity to each part of himself. Then, as the dialogue proceeds, his "me" takes on some of the vigor of his "body" and he moves toward integration between the two parts of himself so that they may come to live together. Here is the homework dialogue:

Me: So when does it begin?

Body: When does what begin?

Me: You know—the ailment, the physical symptoms, the business.

Body: Soon—soon—last year it began around November —there's time yet—when you really get involved in this study for this test bit—then I'll start—you'll suffer good!

M: But why—do you do this? I'm good—I treat you well. I'm like a Jewish mother to you—I worry—run to those goddam doctors, who I despise, at the slightest malady. Why do you make me suffer so! It's getting worse each year—I can't take it more than last year!

B: I do it because—you've got to suffer perhaps. I'll never tell you really why—you've got to suffer, that's part of it—

but also—and more important—is that you are a *stupidass cripple* and you ain't never gonna get that fuckin' degree! Why now after all this time—do you think you can carry something out—be successful! You stupid asshole! You don't know anything! Nothing! You'll always be in a cloud trying to figure things out—trying to figure me out!

M: Yes, I've had trouble—I've fucked around a lot but this time I *really* want to finish—to get my Ph.D. I *like* sociology! And I *want* to teach—besides—this is the last bit for me—all the chips are on this one! I'm feeling okay now—how about it—I'll try and be less distraught this year—to self-inflict less pressure. How about it? Can you lay off—? I'm kinda optimistic now—because one forgets the power of your rage—and the helplessness to cope with it.

B: Can't say—we'll see—

M: Okay! Fuck you! I'll match you! I'll ignore you—I'll play it through—I'm going to get this damn degree! I'll suffer if I have to!

B: You stupid ass! You know damn well how versatile I can get—I'll have you running to that charming health service every fuckin' day—you'll see!

M: Okay—I know you can do it—and in the last analysis, I always give in because I get scared. Look—let's get together—we do so nicely in other things. Athletics and movement, and I feel as one with you in my physical movements—we go! We flow! It's nice. Cannot we congeal on this ailment stuff? To move together? What does it take? You're right! I can't make it all alone! You have me by the balls (and you even have affected me there too) —so come on! Let us air it out. Is it possible—or not?

B: Don't know. To tell you the truth, I don't understand all that goes into it either, I'm piqued—goaded to stick it in you. Let's see—this is tough. My compulsion is to block you from reaching any self-satisfying success.

M: That I sense—as if I'm not supposed to get it or reach anything. But—I *have* had success—at camp, athletics, in school, in certain interpersonal areas. So why not this? *I can do it!* If you'll lay off!

B: Those other things were minor—short term stuff—not real commitments!

M: Okay—I'm committing—or I'm not committing! What's so permanent about a Ph.D. and teaching vis-à-vis the nothingness and limits of life?

B: Look—okay—let us try—we'll become one. You're trying. I still have some inertia though, some residue nonsense that has to be let out—some that has to be let out—some anxiety—some physical troubles—but *don't* let it upset you, i.e., don't react to your reaction—don't fight it! Suffer a bit—it's okay. They say it's part of life—and all that shit! As a matter of fact, it might be good for you —I'm trying to tell you something when I throw all the shit to you. Feel man! Feel it! Don't ask me why—just do—or else be anesthetized. If you ever want to get married—(ha)—to love—you'll have to feel *both ways*—but that's another story.

The main value of making this homework, instead of working it out only in a therapy session, is that this man did it himself. He allowed his expression to flow freely on his own. Furthermore, the specific content was important to him, too, because the confrontation between these two intrapersonal factions went beyond mere obsessionalism into a negotiation for a genuine interrelationship and a recognition that integration made sense and had even already been reached in some areas and was essential in the total function of the one person.

Homework is an almost inevitable development of therapy because the mobilizations occurring in therapy always have implications for the world beyond. Otherwise therapy may remain only entertainment, exciting—even intriguing—but set apart, like a book or play. When this happens, the therapy may actually prove a deterrent to growth rather than its agent.

The concept of homework is consistent with the concept of self-therapy. Two of the early reports concerning self-therapy

are those of Horney* and Perls, Hefferline, and Goodman.**
In the latter book, a series of experiments was suggested and
many people who engaged in these experiments reported reactions which showed a profound self-exploration. Recently, commercial programs have been produced which give instructions
for self-exploration at home, large encounter groups are designed with minimal leadership, and there are promises of
increased use of TV, films, records and tapes which will help
people to make their own therapeutic explorations. These are
all a natural extension of the experiment and of homework.
They orient people to try out behaviors and feelings for themselves. Through the new technical innovations which have already been developed and which promise to be invented, the
spread of therapeutic impact can be multiplied beyond any
level which we have yet been able to reach. The prospect for an
authentically populist movement exists, where the psychotherapeutic ethos will become relevant for the population-at-large
rather than only for the growing but limited group of explorers
who have been affected so far.

In summing up the experiment, it is important to remember
that there is a practically limitless range and the value depends
on the skill and sensitivity with which it is employed. What it
provides is a diverse body of techniques which help make
therapy a live, current experience rather than one where someone may excessively talk *about* his life. The experiment must
flow freely from the patient's own expressions and awarenesses.
Every expression and every awareness has a direction which—
when interrupted—produces tension and prevents the individual from reaching closure. When we become interested in that
direction, we start a search to free this movement so that it
moves through the barriers and comes to its natural resting
place. The resting moment emerges from the arrested moment.

---

* Horney, Karen. *Self Analysis.* New York: W. W. Norton &
Co., 1942.

** Perls, F. S., Hefferline, Ralph and Goodman, Paul. *Gestalt
Therapy.* New York: Julian Press Inc., 1951.

10

Beyond One to One

My people are gray,
　　pigeon gray, dawn gray, storm gray.
I call them beautiful,
　　and I wonder where they are going.

CARL SANDBURG

Recently, a brochure from one of the country's well-known growth centers included this description of gestalt groups:

A gestalt leader generally works with one volunteer at a time, while other members observe or participate as auxiliaries to the main leader-member interaction. A "working" member is encouraged to explore his dreams, fantasies, expectations, gestures, voice, and other personal traits by enacting them before the group.

HOT SEAT

This image of gestalt therapy is very difficult to shake. It is true that the concept of the "hot seat"—a popular gestalt

285

term—means that someone volunteers to work individually with the leader. It is also true that Perls—whose demonstrations have been the most famous and dramatic presentations of gestalt therapy—worked almost exclusively with the "hot seat" technique. When the master works, it is hard to discriminate between what is his *style* and what is the theory which supports his style. Even further, it is true that the intensity which characterizes gestalt does move into making a particular individual *figural* against the ground of the group. Nevertheless, it is not fundamental in gestalt therapy to rely exclusively on a one-to-one methodology.

Before describing the gestalt possibilities for group interaction, however, it is worth noting that there *are* some great advantages of one-to-one work *in a group* as distinct from a private session.

First, the person who is on the "hot seat," in the center of the action, experiences an enhanced sense of community because the very presence of other people deepens the implications of what the figural person is doing, even though the action may be only between him and the leader. Accumulations of people are natively exciting; remember the vibrancy of a circus, a football crowd or a political rally.

Beyond this native excitement, there is also an opportunity for the person on the "hot seat" to reveal himself not only to an experienced professional but also—in a sense—to people at large, where social acceptance or rejection is more than a hypothetical risk. Mowrer* has observed that we are our secrets. While this may seem overstated, there *is* inherent power in the recovery and public statement of what has been concealed, representing, as it does, an expansion of one's bounded sense of self.

Furthermore, the therapy-experience-in-community takes on the condensed power of an Everyman drama, depicting not

---

* Mowrer, O. H. *The New Group Therapy*. Princeton: D. Van Nostrand Co., 1964.

only individual but universal concerns, heightening the common sense of humanity among people. Witnesses to the dramatic one-to-one interaction may learn from it what is applicable to their own lives, opening new vistas, a basic power of all drama that transcends entertainment.

Finally, when a group is present, there are many purposes to which it can be put, even though the interaction may be mostly one way—directed from the figural individual toward the group. Suppose, for example, the one-to-one interaction reveals a compulsively modest person who has compressed himself into an image of smallness. Suppose also he needs to try boasting so that he can push out the restrictive I-boundary that he has constructed. He can do this in a group, bragging to them, recounting a particular exploit, swaggering, etc. By doing this in a community of people, his action takes on substance and dimension beyond boasting privately to the therapist.

FLOATING HOT SEAT

Going beyond the hot seat and including the spontaneous *participation* of the rest of the group broadens the dimensions of interaction—well *within the range* of gestalt methodology:

> The group becomes an adventure because (of) interactional conflict. There is a concerted effort to maximize contactfulness and to identify all possible sources of deflection from contact. The therapist must give attention to the specific ways barriers to contact are set up. He (and the group, too) must see that certain (people) look away when talking, ask questions when they mean to make statements, use lengthy introductions to simple observations, compulsively tell both sides of all stories, sit in statue-like positions, use mannerisms and expressions which reflect disinterest, play for sympathy, use submissive words when their tones are hostile, and so on, endlessly. These resistances are approached frontally, in the belief that with their resolution good contact will naturally follow.*

* Polster, E. Encounter in Community. In Burton, A., Ed. *Encounter*. San Francisco: Jossey-Bass Inc., 1969.

Given contactfulness as a guiding orientation, the gestalt leader expects that group interactions would provide a solid source of discovery about people's characteristic ways of engaging with each other. Furthermore, exploration of these habits and the resolution of internal contradictions preventing good contact in a group would lead to immediate and palpable confrontations.

Jay, a most sincere man, took the bull by the horns one day and began at last to reveal his deepest secret, that he was a female impersonator. Al began interviewing Jay bombastically, asking leading questions which, in spite of Al's gauche style, were helpful in getting the story out. The group, however, was dismayed that Jay's revelation, tender as a bud, might lose out because Al was playing therapist. Finally Ted could stand the performance no longer and screamed in fury that he was interested in *Jay* and *not* in Al's bull-in-the-china shop interrogation. Other people chimed in with agreement and Al, shaken, retorted that even if the rest of them were all going to be silent as zombies *he* wasn't going to let Jay flounder! Al had been confronted with his dominance and his intolerance for just letting things develop. Some of the others came into touch with their passivity. Jay learned that he had been heard and that sympathy and recognition were transparently present. With this acceptance, he was free to describe what it was like for him to play a woman: the relaxation of it, the undemand and the sense of closeness to his warm mother.

Awareness, added to contactfulness as another guideline in group interaction, fosters the exploration of here-and-now experience. People learn to be tuned in to their inner process, to articulate it, and to behave in terms of it. Fury at Al had filled the room. Nevertheless, until Ted expressed it, others remained mute, not acting on their own awareness. Paradoxically, while Ted's expression of anger also unleashed theirs, one other person said *he* was pleased about what Al had done.

Jay, himself, surprised the others by saying that Al's questions had been helpful to him!

Almost invariably there is support somewhere in a group for whatever behavior anyone may try. The group has a wisdom of its own extending beyond the wisdom of the leader alone. It is as if the group becomes a Greek Chorus speaking in all the different voices and reflecting in its multiplexity all of the human possibilities available in that situation at that moment in time. The compositional nature of the individual, which we described earlier, cannot help but be enriched by this evidence of alternative ways of thinking, feeling and acting. Group awareness becomes the raw data of experience. It is the reciprocal of contactfulness, grounding contactfulness in information from which action can emerge. Through the simple accentuation of awareness, excitement is magnified and the consequent absorption inspires people to give each other the best that is in them.

The opportunity to set up experiments joins contactfulness and awareness, completing the generic triad of gestalt principles applicable to working with groups. Jay, for example, could have been asked to play out his female impersonation right there. Or he might have been directed to "make the rounds" of the group, telling each person something that he liked about playing a woman. Or the leader might have set up a group experiment such as all closing their eyes and fantasying what it might be like for each of them to be of the opposite sex. More likely, though, once one particular person starts into his own personal experience, *he* is the one who will receive considerable individual focus and the experiment will probably be set up to heighten this aspect of the event. Even without an experiment, the natural interactions will tend to unroll sequentially into focuses on one individual or another as his needs become figural.

This movement of the group into concern with a particular person is an organically sound *group* phenomenon. It is quite different from individual therapy in a group because it flows naturally out of the group interaction instead of from the volunteerism of the "hot seat." Individual focus comes then not from exclusion of others but rather because of specific tension systems and their surge toward figural ascendency in the group. This special kind of one-to-one interaction might be called a "floating hot seat." Although the work is with one individual, under these conditions all members of a group have every right and possibility for entering into the action whenever they wish. In fact, their entry is frequently encouraged and enter they do, sometimes at the risk of interrupting a vital process.

This risk regulates free participation naturally—rather than by fiat—because each person must gauge the harmony of his actions with the momentum of the ongoing drama. Such a risk is not confined only to therapeutic interactions in a group. The art of uniting one's needs with an already ongoing tension system is one of the recurrent challenges people face. One is born into an already existing family, to begin with, and gains admittance to an already existing social system as he proceeds through the years. Some people choose to integrate with these systems by influencing them very little or by attempting to dominate them or by taking care of oneself in the face of unfriendly requirements or by abandoning one's needs entirely in the supposed service of the larger and better established system.

So also in the gestalt group. Fritz Perls once asked me why I was so silent in a group he was leading. I replied I didn't want to interrupt the other people. He assigned me the role of interrupter, which I then played to a fare-thee-well, granting my whole free-association system absolute license, speaking up no matter what was happening. Perls became annoyed with me and somebody reminded him that *he* had told me to interrupt. He said, "Yes, but I didn't tell him I would like it!" Undaunted, I continued my activity, and what had started out

as interruption turned into an experience of carefree leadership—one of the most important lessons of my life.

In a recent gestalt training group, people were upset about
what had happened at their previous practicum group meeting
when I had been absent. Some had felt isolated from the rest
of the group, misunderstood, taken advantage of, and left
painfully hanging with unfinished business at the end of the
preceding session. Two weeks later they were still furious.
Dotty spoke with great pique and immediately drew the
attention of the practicum leader who was working under
my supervision. He turned to work with her individually,
affected as he was by her need and responsive to it. I pointed
out that it was premature to work with her individually, there
was too much feeling in the *whole group* that was as yet unexpressed and would be festering while he worked with Dotty.
So he turned to the others and they, too, began to express their
annoyance and sense of injury. Soon a shouting match developed. Two of the women in particular were verbally grappling
with each other. It became apparent that to resolve their
abrasion they would need to come into more poignant—rather
than merely grudgeful—interaction. One of them, Brenda,
saw Dotty as capitalizing on a childish attractiveness which
made her the center of attention. When Brenda was asked to
speak to the child in herself, she discovered that its nature
was very similar to what she was objecting to in Dotty. She
was encouraged to allow herself to be childishly playful—and
her resentment completely disappeared! Dotty became her
companion in delight, and Brenda herself recovered a personal
possibility which she had been severely blocking. Then another
pair, still simmering, confronted each other with their needs
to be recognized and supported. They explored how each might
do it for the other. And so on throughout the evening. By the
time the group was finished, people again felt at home with
each other and were able to be together without mutual grudge.
The focus on *group* process, however, was crucial because

it permitted all of them to contribute to the resolution of the conflict and to a renewal of their sense of purpose together.

Since the gestalt approach lends itself easily to group focus, the gestaltist may see his impact and relevance stretching far beyond the one-to-one experience as it occurs in therapy or in the small encounter group. So he may seek to go wherever people may gather together, voluntarily or accidentally, and deal there with the qualities of contact, awareness or the experimental opportunity to try out new modes of being with each other. Meeting the needs of individual people who may come together in large groups is important in widely diverse settings. For example, this element is important in work organizations—both to bring on a sense of community of interest and to process interrelationship and/or task-solving problems. It is equally valuable in neighborhoods to foster similar results. Ditto in golden-age settings or in churches or in dormitories or in classrooms or among clinic personnel or. . . .

An example of going *to* people instead of inviting them to meet only on the therapist's own home ground is an exploration of the uses of gestalt therapy method in an indigenous setting, a public coffee house.* Here, the groupings of people and their general activities would take place whether the therapist ever came there or not. In this coffee house, conversation and play were what the customers generally came for. Nevertheless, they also wanted some activities which could bring the total group together. Usually poetry readings, musical performances and even occasional lectures served this purpose. So we planned a series of bi-weekly meetings called Encounter which would harmonize with the general style though, of course, the customer interaction would be greater, as we shall see. Our sessions took place during the regular coffee house evening hours when people, 50 to 150, came and

---

* Some of the material concerning the coffee house originally appeared in Polster, E., Encounter in Community. In Burton, A., ed., *Encounter*. San Francisco: Jossey-Bass, 1969.

left as they wished. The coffee house was under repeated har-
rassment by the police, partly because of drug traffic, partly because of supposedly disturbing the neighborhood, and partly
because of prejudice about blacks and whites congregating
together.

There were three purposes in these exploratory efforts. One
was to learn how to activate group participation in a large
group. The second was to restore and work innovatively with
topic-centeredness within the so-called encounter technique.
The third aim was to affect self-limiting attitudes and behaviors.

The first purpose, the activation of group participation,
was haunted by the familiar "spectator" tendency of most
large-group situations. The outsized demands of talking to a
crowd of lined-up strangers are notoriously torturous and only
the best public speakers seem to retain feelings of immediacy
or personal effect. Large audiences, though they promise
magnified liveliness, are frequently unmanageably depersonalized. How could the encounter group style, developed in small
groups, be applied to large groups or conferences? The encounter group often fosters personal interaction by splitting
into smaller units, no larger a group than could permit each
person a chance to unfold in his own way. But the small
group is too small a world to live in and events have a way
of happening when large numbers of people are together. In
the fast action of the coffee house there was no time for the
complex designs normally used in large groups. What was
needed was to experience the contagion of spirit which
stretches beyond the miniature workings of intimate small-
nesses.

Our first meeting was called Hippies and Policemen* and
shows how a participating body emerged. Two people were
selected to role-play a hippie and a policeman in conversation.

---

* The term hippies is outdated now and never was a loving name,
but at the time of these meetings most of the young people who
came to this coffee house were so identified and selected this title.

They started by saying very stereotyped words. The policeman exhorted the hippie to get a job, quit wearing crazy hairdos and clean up. He described him as unruly, dangerous and unappetizing. The hippie on the other hand saw the policeman as a brute—cold, lacking understanding, insensitive, unreachable. At first, no matter what I would say to them, their responses remained stereotyped and cruel. When confronted with the outlandishness of some of his remarks, the policeman at one point was taken aback and began to examine his feelings. He then said that he really had a job to do and could not afford to have much feeling about what he was doing. He just wanted to get it over with. He did not want to have to think about it. Furthermore, he was afraid he might get hurt if he did not stay tough. The hippie did not give any specific recognition to the policeman's change in tone and continued talking as he had before. When this was called to his attention he recognized his unhearing and that it might now be possible to communicate with the policeman. Nevertheless, he did not want to. He *wanted* the policeman to remain impossible so that he could vent his anger and gloat over his superiority. He wanted to stay angry and if he could avoid seeing the difference, he would. It is unwitting commentary on the nature of conflict, even in large social movements, that when a great force of unfinished business builds up it must have its opportunity to emerge. The need to complete the blocked expression remains even after conditions change. One is likely therefore to ignore changes until one's own need is completed. Militant blacks, for example, have unfinished business and must release their fury whether or not improvements happen. Such dysrhythmias in timeliness among parties to a conflict are root troubles. One side may be resolved when the other is not yet resolved. Resolutions must be delayed until the party with unfinished business can complete his accumulated need for expression. The other party, if authentically respectful of the force of unfinished business, will give the injured party some recognition of the rightfulness of his need.

In this coffee house session there were about 125 people present. Unlike an ordinary audience this one actively participated. People questioned the right of the policeman to say what he was saying. They cat-called about the errors of thinking. Then the policeman and the hippie were asked to switch roles, much to the relief of the man who had been playing the policeman. He now suddenly relaxed in the friendly atmosphere. The switch in roles aroused the audience to want to play roles, too, and several pairs of people did. Soon a communal spirit developed. Then, in climax, the last person to play the role of the policeman left the stage and went to the rear of the room to arrest the proprietor, confronting him with certain picayune violations which would make him subject to arrest. The policeman then started the proprietor toward the door. The proprietor did not go altogether willingly but put up only token resistance. The people in the audience, however, began to shout, "Don't let him take him away," leaving their tables to join in a rescue attempt. A wild melee followed. People were swinging their arms, lifting their chairs threateningly, shouting. Anyone entering the coffee house at that moment would have thought that a riot was on. When the force of their aggression had spent itself and the rescue operation had succeeded, the people returned to their tables. What had begun as simple role-playing by two people had ended as a dramatic audience role-playing situation. When all were seated again, there was an aura of hushed awe at what had happened. A large group had walked the line between poetry and reality. Though one could not always tell the difference between the poetry and the reality, the individuals in the group, though fully invested, were apparently aware of their perspective and never allowed the dramatic situation to be an excuse for actual violence. The group then discussed the meaning of the experience and the prevailing sense was the obvious one of having expressed suppressed aggression against the police—acting out in the role-playing situation what they were powerless to do in real life. This powerlessness resulted, said they, in their feeling alienated and the opportunity to act the scene out brought them together into a sense of community.

The second of our purposes was to develop topic-centeredness. In the above illustration the topic was instrumental in orienting people to what they were going to do, yet permitted their own personal needs to be focal. The risk of topics is that they may lead to sterile intellectualism, but obviously people may also get personal, even impassioned, when dealing with topics. Nearly all of the coffee house sessions started out with a topic. Some of the other topics were hippies and straight people, hippies and teachers, sex between the races, listening, building a community, psychedelic trips, how to evade the draft, how to create change, the meaning of war, etc. On the evening we dealt with hippies and straight people, we invited some straight people for the occasion. In addition, others just showed up, having heard about our sessions and become curious about them. What made these people straight was that they lived well-organized lives, dressed conventionally, lived in traditional family relationships and worked in continuing jobs. There were about as many so-called straight people as there were so-called hippies.

The session started out stiffly but it was not long before one of the hippies, Jack, confronted one of the straight people by brazenly accusing him of cowardly silence. Jack became the center of a storm. He was experienced at shoving stereotypes down people's throats. The straight people didn't like it but they were accustomed to politeness and permissiveness and were taken aback by this sudden and stark attack. He had started the ball rolling, though, and a marked polarization developed between the so-called hippies and the so-called straight people. Each side was unhappy to be categorized and did not like being called either hippie or straight. The idea that all people are individual was bandied around a lot. Nevertheless, in spite of these high-minded attitudes, each side was considerably stereotyped about the other and became very defensive about its own position. Some of the straight people finally became so angry that they left their seats and walked toward Jack and some of the other hippies, haranguing them about being individual people. Some said Jack and his companions were presumptuous. Some were especially irate when Jack accused them of coming down to the coffee house to get a respite from their dreary suburban lives. Other statements were comparably confronting. In the beginning there was little effort to find out about other people's lives. Everybody seemed to *know*. After a while support for the straight people arose within the hippie group, some pointing out that they really did care about them and were glad they had come. They *did* want to make contact. One hippie girl said she and her friends were afraid of the straight people because they were older and because they were really afraid of their own parents. They would like to get along with their parents but knew they couldn't. Her own father would never be caught dead in a place like the coffee house and always refused to have anything to do with her views about life. The hippie people wanted to expand their community and their opportunities for talking to people who had "made it" in society. One girl observed that the straight people present were nothing but old hippies.

All of our topics aroused very lively interaction. Frequently these interactions were verbally aggressive, but aggressiveness and directness would almost invariably turn a session into an exciting one. Intellectual discussions, on the other hand, almost invariably toned the room down and resulted in impatience and restlessness. Statements which strongly affected another individual were the ones most likely to pay off in good communication and a sense of unified community. However, whenever intense contact occurred, a support system developed which aided some individuals and also served to unify some of those who had previously been adversaries.

The third purpose underlying these sessions was the effort

to work through self-limiting characteristics of people in the group. One of the sessions faced resistance of some coffee house people to communicating with people outside of their own small groups. There was a common imperviousness among them to relate to matters they didn't readily understand or from which they felt alienated.

One night the topic was religious experience. One group wasn't having any and was even noisily unwilling to be involved. Perceptive cat-calling, yes, but on a hit-and-run basis. It was not long before people in the room became annoyed with them. One woman finally arose, her ire shaking her into remonstrance. She wanted to be heard by them. They said she was belligerent and they did not dig belligerence. But others felt only excessive energy would get through to them, like hitting the donkey with a two-by-four to get his attention.

People came to the support of this exclusive group, some saying they must do what is right for them and the rest of the people should go on about their business. One man, a minister, said they had something very special among themselves—such mutual acceptance and such deep esprit that he felt it was itself religious expression. Another minister, however, said he did not think this was very religious at all. He said they were nothing more than a clique, rejecting any real sense of otherness.

After considerable build-up of tension one of the recalcitrant ones got up imperiously and said, on the tail end of much frustrated communication, "Make it, don't fake it!"—a short sermon in authenticity. He caught me at the end of my rope and I let go, falling right into their midst as my mountainous rage poured out of the lengthy frustrations in communication. I confronted them with my own resentment of their closed system, from which they took potshots outside and then retreated into their own enclave, barriered but crying worthlessness at whoever did not crack into their system. I left the stage and approached them, bellowing my words. Now they listened

to my screams. When I was done they talked as though a
boil had been lanced and we moved from religion to riots and,
after some touchy name-calling, the group came together, not
unified in agreement but as people able to be unitedly contactful. As had been true often before, the entering confrontation
changed wall to flow.

The coffee house events show one approach to the application of basic gestalt practice in an indigenous population. The
development of good contact through confrontation heightened
the encounter among people. Accentuation of people's own
awareness of themselves and their awareness of other people
served to facilitate the resolution of conflicts. Experiments,
such as those in role-playing, dramatized topics and conflicts
requiring resolution. Bringing actual representatives of various
groups of people right into the room rather than only talking
about the issues helped to enliven the proceedings and heightened the sense of reality of engagement. Mere intellectualism
deadened interaction and lively and incisive language cut
through the depersonalizing process. Intellectualism supported
by contact served as orientation for what was important to
these people. Thus, the three touchstones of gestalt therapy—
contact, awareness, and experiment—were all brought to bear
on the conflict resolutions of people in the coffee house.

Another application of the fundamentals of gestalt therapy
to an indigenous scene is in the orientation of college freshmen.
Usually, freshmen are expected to get to know each other on
a catch-as-catch-can basis or in a herd, at teas or equally sterile
social encounters. Many freshmen are just not ready. It is
hard for them to bite into what seems too big either to swallow
or assimilate. A format which will elicit what matters to them
is better than leaving them standing around shifting from one
leg to the other as though waiting for a toilet to appear. Many
of these young people experience the environment as unfriendly
and believe that nobody is much interested in them or anyone
else for that matter. The paradox is that so many of them

feel that way—aching to meet someone else and believing nobody wants to meet them. They need a vehicle for asserting themselves meaningfully to others, where time and attention can be paid to what they have to say.

Here is an approach that worked well at one college. Six two-hour sessions were scheduled over a two-day orientation period, so that people could come to them when they were free. Some people came two or three times, and the groups ranged in size from 12 to 150. We started out with a short talk, exploring what it was like to be there with each other and how our meetings might help them know one another and themselves. After this introductory contact, I asked them to split into pairs and to spend ten or fifteen minutes talking with their partners, discovering enough about each other so that they could introduce each other to a group of people. After doing this, they merged into small groups of six where these introductions would be made. These instructions gave them the opportunity and support for making themselves visible as well as exploring another person—not just "making conversation." For most pairs, these conversations proved very stimulating and formed a basis for an interrelated group where there was support and curiosity for getting to know each other. After a half-hour or so, we got together as a total group and discussed what had been discovered. Other exercises were used to enchance contact between people or awareness of oneself as it might be communicated to an interested "other." For example, each of them named a game and described to each other in what ways they were like that game. Or, they built a "machine" where one individual stood up and began to make a simple repetitive movement and, one by one, was joined by others who fitted a movement of their own devising into the already ongoing operation. There are moments when this exercise has all the flow and expressiveness of dance or the free-ranging humor of a slapstick routine in a silent film.

In another freshman orientation, for an art school, participants were asked to draw a four-part cartoon-like statement about some very important aspects of themselves or their lives and to put it on, placard style, and walk about the room looking at the drawings others were wearing, asking questions, making comments, comparing, explaining, and discovering. Later on, in the total group, they were asked to close their eyes and fantasy a headline in tomorrow's paper which would make a great change in their lives. Then each told the group the headline and what it would mean to him personally.

In an all-day workshop for the students and faculty at a private high school, one activity consisted of an "emotional scavenger hunt" where teams of participants were given lists consisting of words like trust, delicate, suspicion, loneliness, etc. and asked to find objects on the campus that illustrated these feelings. All the collections were assembled in the gym and people moved from one exhibit to another, explaining their choices and how they felt about these human conditions. For the word sadness, for example, one group had brought in a biological specimen of a human foetus; for suspicion, another group had put up a section of portable fencing around a scrawny dead bush; for playfulness, one teacher brought in her two young sons.

In all of these experiences, people observed how much easier it was to get to know others here than in their wanderings around campus or in teas or in dormitories, where talking about what mattered deeply to them was very difficult.

LARGE-GROUP DESIGN

There is a wide range of activities which have become part of the humanistic movement, starting with sensitivity training exercises and gestalt therapy experiments and including inventions conceived by leaders and designers of group encounters. The concept of *design* is itself one of the technical innovations that has extended the application of encounter-group methodology so that it can include very large groups and, in addition, can be relevant to specific topics, purposes or uses. Characteristically, the small-group method permits and even depends on a natural, organic flow of expressions from within the group. There are usually no prior intentions or orientations. The very large group, however, is difficult—but not impossible—to manage this way because when the competition for air time becomes heavy there are just too many people who may lose the opportunity to express themselves. It is important that every participant be at least *able* to speak even though he may choose not to. In the small group, even though some may *not* speak, everybody feels the opportunity is there and can take the responsibility for his own silence.

When designing the large-group encounter, this need can be taken into account by providing the opportunity to divide into groups small enough to encompass the assertiveness of each individual. It is also important, though, to design a rhythm between small subdivision and interaction within the total group so that the dynamic contrast can be heightened and the person who can fend for himself in the small group may be heartened to take his chances in the deeper water of the larger crowd.

We recently set up an eight-meeting large-group encounter series* in which approximately 50 people participated. We wanted to have a group of people joining together, *not* for a one-shot deal as is so often the case in large-group encounters, but for a series of meetings. These meetings were all centered around personally relevant themes like Belongingness, Becoming Known, Approaching and Leaving, etc.**

It was clear to us that, given our format and adding television and a chain of co-leaders, we could have had an indefinitely large group of people, all of them simultaneously engaged in similar activities designed to arouse individual crea-

---

* Sponsored by Case Western Reserve University, 1972.
** An illustrative design of one of the meetings is presented in Appendix B.

tivity, inspire personal awareness and move into contactfulness. With television as a central source of direction for people all acting at one time, the sense of community would be
accentuated, amplifying the significance of the individual's
activities. Any opportunity for individually formed expressions to take on resonance through being aired in a culturally
meaningful setting binds the individual together with his community.

The global culture has been underplayed too long as a factor in human development. It is one thing to learn something in
a group that meets *hostility* outside that group and it is quite
another to learn something in a group that is also *acceptable*
to the larger community. The larger the group—and the more
compatible with everyday existence—the better the chance of
getting harmony between individual needs as exercised in
cloister-like experiences and individual needs as exercised in
the general culture. Even more far-reaching, cultural needs
would themselves be open to new orientations.

Gestalt therapy encourages the individual to search for
moments and experiences of good contact, not only in the
special situations of therapy, but in every moment when the
possibilities for good contact exist. Excellence of contact, of
course, is never guaranteed to anybody. Even under the most
ideal circumstances there will be a range of skill; some people
will be likely to achieve lively and nourishing contact with
others and other people are just as likely *not* to, just as we
know that one person can play the violin better than another.
Nevertheless, in a community where good contact is prized,
more people will be likely to learn to accomplish it well. If
playing the violin and drawing were attributes highly valued in
the community, the common denominator of violin playing or
drawing would be at a much higher level of skill than in a community where the activities were not esteemed or encouraged.

In addition to variations in personal talent, another com-
plication is that there are contradictions among those qualities

our society claims to value highly. Reflect, for a moment, on some of the human values espoused in religious principles and moral codes which have fallen into disuse because of general environmental pressures.

For example, one time when I was exploring the relationship of religion and psychotherapy, I set up some groups in churches and temples. These groups met with the goal of extending the tenets of their religion into the actual experience of the group members. In one temple group we started out with an actual religious service. When this was completed, we moved into group interaction centering around the content of the evening's prayers. One evening, when the prayer had dealt with the expression of gratitude, the group process revolved around our own expressions of gratitude, discovering much unfinished business. People were almost uniformly aware that expressing gratitude had been largely cut out of their lives except for routine thank-you's. Frank couldn't express gratitude toward his father because gratitude would bring the two of them unbearably closer and Frank might have to give up a long-standing grudge. When Frank did speak to the image of his father and stated his actual gratitude, his grudge melted—at least temporarily—and he felt warmed and softened. As it happened, his father had been good to him on many occasions and this expression of authentic gratefulness unfroze a sense of forgiveness for those injuries which Frank's father had also done to him. Comparable experiences occurred for the other people in the group.

What good is it for people of religion to sermonize gratitude and then neither teach people how to grow into it nor change the cultural norms which prevent it? People are, of course, taught to say thank you, and they do express gratitude with smiles, return of favors, statements of pleasure, etc. We are, after all, not totally bereft of gratitude. But these routine habits are not enough for the development of the richer experience which comes when someone moves gratefulness into accentuated awareness, especially when it is done with communal recognition and support. One of the most exciting and warming exercises we have ever devised in our large group encounters is one we frequently use to end our meetings. A person comes to the center of the group, says his name, and the group applauds and cheers for a full minute while he acknowledges the applause in whatever way he feels. On the face of it this sounds like a phony maneuver. It is contrived, of course, since the person hasn't *done* anything specific to merit the applause. Nevertheless, in almost every instance, the applause is experienced as altogether right, even spontaneous and genuine, and moreover it is a mind-blowing delight for both the applauders and the applauded. It is a momentary engagement of love, with nothing to gain but joy. We are profoundly in need of love statements but we have trained ourselves well not to make them except with our intimates, and even then only in "right" moments.

In a class of theology students* each class session started with a student presentation of a worship experience. Then we moved into group to work through the human dilemma presented by the worship experience. One of the students started his meeting by turning his back to the class and speaking directly to God. He was enraged with God's relationship to man and with what He had done to man. His remarks were a lesson in passion as well as projection. Then, after talking to God, he turned around and spoke to his classmates. Here he became boring and trite! We spent the rest of the session leading him into interactions with his fellow students which would be at least as compelling as had been his with God. Some of the intensity he invested in talking with God was not being transmitted into talking with human beings. He couldn't live only with God, though. The lesson with God, if one believes in Him, must be transferable to everyday life and everyday people. Nothing less will work.

---

* Course called Worship & Human Relations, taught at Oberlin Graduate School of Theology, 1968-69.

COUPLES AND FAMILIES

It is a small step from working with groups, of whatever size, to working with couples and families, either privately or in groups composed of these particular units. The basic philosophical underpinning for working with these combinations of people is that they are natural economies where the systems established are seen to be as important as the individuals within those systems. The sum of the parts is indeed different from the whole. John individually plus Mary individually is often surprisingly different from the marriage between John and Mary. These surprises are commonplace. One woman I can hardly stomach when she is with her husband, but I like her when she sees me alone. The clean sweetness of Sid, alone, is lost when his son confuses him and he turns into a crud. Even the addition of a speechless babe-in-arms—when a sitter didn't show up and a young woman kept her appointment with me anyhow —has unpredictable repercussions for "family" therapy. One loquacious patient clams up when his family is present, a happy-go-lucky woman becomes a serious "mother" and so on. Every time I fan out from among the people I have worked with individually and see them in a group, I feel like a fiance whose future in-laws are about to meet his parents. This phenomenon would be even more graphic if instead of seeing people in our offices we were to see them in their homes—as many case workers do, for good reason—or have dinner with them, go to the theater with them, go to the office with them, see them with their mother and father . . .

The principles of working with couples or families are essentially the same as the principles we have been describing throughout this book. The undoing of projections, for example, is at least as valid a process in working with couples and families as in individual work. How better to work at undoing introjection when the source of the introject may be present in the room? And since the undoing of retroflection is the search for the appropriate other, where better to look for him than in one's family? Confluence, with what and with whom, is almost inevitably a family issue in various guises, all of which may be played out with immediacy and force when all the members of the cast are present at the family drama.

The whole range of barriers to good contact needs to be brought into focus, whether they be expressive-barriers, body-barriers, familiarity-barriers, etc., so that the quality of contact may be improved and the awareness of oneself and each other can enrich the familially shared present. Married couples and families need to see each other, hear each other, touch each other, taste each other, smell each other, move toward each other and speak into each other. When they short-cut some of these, they run into trouble because they start lugging along all the unfinished business they have bypassed.

There is a special excitement and emergency in seeing people together in therapy who are also together *outside* therapy. Of course, any therapy worth its salt will have this emergency quality, too. But when an individual comes in with people he's living with, the emergency created by the inescapability of consequence is an additional force to cope with.

For example, after Chuck has told his wife, in couple's therapy, that he never has liked her body much, he is not finished when the session is over. This is just one link in a chain which includes prior hurt and which stretches further into implications running the gamut of hurt feelings, resentment, feeling duped and kindred complications. Imagine that when Chuck says to Tina that he never did like her body, he gets from Tina a bland smile—and nothing more. To allow this exchange to recede and fester would be Tina's habit. So the therapist, not interested in lullabies for sleeping dogs, explores her experience. Soon she says, "I feel taken advantage of because I always thought you liked my body and now I believe you were only tricking me." Suppose then that Chuck feels embarrassed and remembers aloud for the first time how queasy he has been about women's bodies and recalls what it was like to see his mother menstruate and his sister leave a glob of shit in the toilet. So, mostly, he closes his eyes lest he see bodies too clearly and too irreverently. Tina then recognizes that it is not *her* worthlessness that is at stake, but rather Chuck's personal set concerning the purity of bodies. Now, asked to look at his wife's body again, Chuck says he feels a combination of excitement and nausea and his face becomes flushed. Tina says, "You look to me like a very dear little boy right now and I'd just like to take you in my arms and hold you and rock you." He says, "I can't let you do that, but I'm feeling hot inside. I'm too embarrassed to hold you but part of me wants to. Your skin is beginning to look creamy." Tina and Chuck have to learn to transcend the opening remark which appears to characterize their *total* relationship. They can do it best when their responsiveness is immediate rather than delayed. Thus, what starts out as a harsh confrontation, if not interrupted and made focal, could fester and become another marital scab, picked-at and tender, calling for still more covering-up and unawareness.

In designing workshop or group experiences for couples and families, the commonality of problems and the alternative styles of dealing with shared dilemmas become an important part of the group-community. A leader may, for example, ask children to compose an alternative family from among the participants and play out in this "new" family some of the difficulties they have in their real families.* The parents the child chose may then pair off with the real parents and explore what the children see in them and what the children look like to another parent. Or in a couples' group, women and men may have separate sessions by way of exploring the common state of being somebody's "husband" or "wife" or "mother" or "father" and wondering how they meet their internal needs for being "women" or "men" or "lovers" in the face of external

---

* This technique was invented by Virginia Satir.

demands. These exchanges can unstick the logjam of personal habit.

Experiences in the group often lead to new willingness of one member of a conflict to listen to the other, to receive the full impact of what he heard and to follow it through to completion. This is the momentum of conflict resolution: to move beyond the engagement where one party seeks to vanquish the other at any cost into a new relationship which impels a union. Naturally, where there are severe incompatibilities resolution may reside in recognizing these incompatibilities and battling for one's needs. Furthermore, some resolutions may require two people to give up on each other and move in separate directions. But many conflicts which are not powerfully jelled into obsession and premature strategy will not require prolonged battle.

These movements beyond the one-to-one encounter are forays into new territory. When individual developments are contradicted by an antipathetic society, the consequences may be discouragement or clashes where the new learning may ultimately engrave itself into the established system—but not without a few bruises. Still, if people in groups embrace or kiss when they meet, or touch each other when they talk, they must ultimately be free to do this in the larger culture. If people can say they're bored within the small groups, they must also be able to do it elsewhere. If people can be silent in a group until something authentic takes shape within them, they must also be free to remain silent in the general culture without being regarded as incompetent or uninvolved. To speak only when it is organically right in a gestalt group and then, dreading a moment of silence, rattle on in company or at home, is like a devoted churchgoer stealing his business colleagues blind.

Though retreats from the toxicity of the general culture are useful—almost indispensable for recouping the losses people sustain in their everyday lives—integrity requires that what one practices in a therapy situation be practiced there *primarily* so as to make one more skillful in engaging generally, not merely marking time in everyday life until one may retreat and be "real" again.

Correspondingly, there is no point when a person becomes so well endowed with his own powers that he will never again want community attention to his psychological needs. The termination of therapy, for example, is the completion of only one form of communal aid. The traditional view of the terminated therapy is naive and mechanistic, counting on the delusion that once one is rid of his own faulty view of the world, the world will neatly fall into place. Of course, the world has never fallen into place in any age, and surely not in this one. Childrearing problems have existed since Cain and Abel; sexual dysrhythmia since Adam and Eve; environmental cataclysm since Noah; the rigors of paying the price since Jacob and Rachel; sibling rivalry since Joseph and his brothers; dysfunctional organizational behavior since the Tower of Babel. These tales record the many natural tortures which are the by-products of a human system of heterogeneous interests and contradictions. An ageless web forms in the interrelationship between the individual's needs and the group's needs and between two dissonant acts of the same person.

The consequent struggle calls for communal orientation, support and stimulation to guide or arouse behavior too difficult for solo performance. The community serves as a group ethos, providing mores, rituals, and instruction which give ease to the individual, freeing him from personally exploring everything under the sun to determine what is right for him. Pubertal rites facilitate entry into the adult world, mourning rites guide one through loss and orient one to morality, marriage ceremonies are a community witness to a statement of personal union, etc.

What we need now are new rituals, mores, and instructions, sensitive to recurrent need but rooted also in present experience. Psychotherapists are finally beginning to take some responsibility in shaping some of the possibilities for living a good life.

The principles of gestalt therapy in particular apply to actual people meeting actual problems in an actual environment. The gestalt therapist is a human being in awareness and interaction. For him there is no pure patient-ness. There is only the person in relationship to his social scene, seeking to grow by integrating all aspects of himself.

Appendix A

Some Theoretical Influences on Gestalt Therapy

Jung differed from Freud in some ways which are reflected in gestalt therapy. For one thing, he articulated the polar quality of human life. According to Jung, aspects of the overt personality by their very prominence cast into shadow a counterpart aspect. Until this disavowed or unrecognized characteristic was acknowledged and integrated into the personality, the individual remained incomplete. The gestalt view of polarity is more free-ranging than Jung's —not confined to archetype, but springing into life as the opposite of any part, or even any quality, of the self.

Jung also viewed dreams and dream symbolism as creative expressions of self rather than unconscious disguises of troublesome life experiences. Jung held that dream symbols were chosen because they were the richest, most complete way to say what needed to be said. The gestalt therapist also views the dream as creative expression rather than camouflage. This is a natural consequence of our intention to take phenomena seriously for their own sake instead of searching for hidden, "more real" meaning. We do not try to trace the dream back to obscure meanings which may have become obliterated in the inventive richness of the dreamer's imagery. For us the dream is a springboard into the present, a commentary on the current existence of the dreamer. We look for meanings as yet only vaguely formed and still to be discovered in the workthrough of the dream. The original creativity of the dream is respected and leads from one exploration to another until the dream expressions find their full voice. We conceive of the dream in terms of unfinished situations calling for satisfaction and completion.

The concept of the unfinished or incompleted situation leads to another influence: Gestalt learning theory. The early gestalt psychologists believed in the innateness of the human need for organization and integrity of perceptual experience. This meant that the perceiver structured his experience so as to move into wholeness and unity of configuration. We hold that the person cannot move on until he has completed whatever it is he experiences as incomplete in his life but will concern himself with it until the experience is finished off to his satisfaction.

A further legacy from gestalt learning theory is its definition of figure/ground formation, the basic perceptual economy which permitted the perceiver to organize his perceptions into their most compelling unity. We have adapted this concept so that it embodies the basic rhythm between awareness and unawareness. In doing this, we have made this concept our version of a dynamic life process, or as Wallen* puts it, ". . . an 'autonomous' criterion" for good function.

Adler's concepts of life style and the creative self supported the unique and active participation of each individual who—in the course of his personal evolution—carves out his own specific nature. He depicted man as a conscious creator of his own life, even to the extent of providing himself with fictions by which his actions were guided. Adler reminded psychotherapists of the importance of the surface of existence. For gestalt therapy, the surface of existence is *the* plane of preordinate focus, the very essence of psychological man. It is on this surface that awareness exists, giving life its orientation and meaning.

---

* Richard Wallen: Gestalt Therapy and Gestalt Psychology—Paper presented at the Ohio Psychological Association meeting, 1957. Distributed by the Gestalt Institute of Cleveland.

In addition, Adler was a populist therapist who treated people not as stylized pathologies but as unique individuals who were attempting to deal with the action into which such accidents as parental influences and birth order had cast them. He used words which were unjargony and he paid attention to common wishes and needs, preparing the way for a populist approach in psychotherapy which could deal with man in terms of daily moment-to-moment existence. We, too, believe that man creates himself. The greatest energy for this Promethean effort comes from his awareness and acceptance of himself as he currently is.

Two of Rank's directions have special importance in the evolution of gestalt therapy. Although his theory is based on the primacy of the birth trauma and its pervasive influence on all subsequent existence—a moot question—he asserted that the primary struggle in life is for personal individuation, also a preordinate concern in gestalt therapy. This struggle is waged in the individual's efforts to integrate his polar fears of separation and of union. Separation brings with it the danger of loss of relationship to otherness, while union brings the risk of loss of individuation. Constructive resistance to these fearsome alternatives leads to a new creative integration of these classically opposed forces.

The constructive view of resistance and its role in the resolution of disparate parts of oneself is a major theme in gestalt therapy. Gestalt therapy recognizes the power of creative resistance, mobilizing it into a major force moving beyond the mere resolution of contradiction and into a new personal composition.

Finally, Rank's interest in the developing sense of individual identity led to a change of focus in the interaction between patient and therapist. Acknowledgement of the human aspects of this interaction make him one of the major influences toward a humanistic orientation in psychotherapy—an important inheritance for gestalt therapy.

More than anyone else, Reich led Perls to an interest in man's character as distinct from man's symptoms. Instead of remaining fixed in symptom patterns, Reich brought everyday behavior into the analytic scene by attending to linguistic, postural, muscular and gestural characteristics. He believed that embedded within these habitual expressions were the chronic neutralizers of experience and unless these neutralizers were dissolved psychoanalysis would be futile. Reich developed a methodology aimed at the dissolution of these neutralizers and his formulations were concrete and specific. For example, the concept of libido, which had originally been formulated to account for the erogeneity of the infant, had become a mystical abstraction in analytic thought. Reich reformulated libido as excitement, which accounts for current activity without getting bogged down in either instinctual or infantile speculations.

Reich described the creation of the body armor as the habitual residue of the habitual act of repression, which, for him, consisted of nothing more than a person selectively tightening up his muscles. Therapy then was devoted to loosening up these restrictive body rigidities so as to release the excitement for the natural behavior which the individual had buried. This was a tellingly simple view of man, spotlighting such unadorned basics of behavior as sensation, orgasm and the richness of unmediated and undistorted expression.

Reich was indignant about the subtle implications in Freud's theory of sublimation describing adult activities, such as surgery, artistry, athletics, etc., as merely disguises accommodating a society which viewed the underlying motives for these behaviors as objectionable. He wanted to take behavior at face value—an emphasis highly respected in gestalt therapy. Reich's willingness to look at simple actions *simply* led to a more vigorous phenomenology.

Moreno recognized anew the ageless power of art forms to produce change in people. He put art to work in his new form, psychodrama, and opened up the creative possibilities inherent in making an artistic statement about one's own life. Furthermore, perhaps even more important in the framework of its impact on gestalt therapy, is the lesson implicit in psychodrama that one is more likely to make discoveries by *participating* in an experience rather than only by *talking* about it. This acknowledges the force of direct experience and moves beyond reliance on the interpretive function so central to the psychoanalytic ethos.

Naturally, in the hands of the gestalt therapist, the psychodramatic production is quite different from what Moreno had in mind. Essentially, the difference is that in gestalt therapy the drama is more likely to evolve out of the individual's improvisations rather than starting from a given theme or with specified characters. Also, the gestalt dramas may often have the single individual—like Shakespeare's players—playing many roles. Although both Perls and Moreno might disagree, we believe that this is primarily a difference in style rather than in theory. Perls believed that since each of the roles was only a projection of parts of the individual, nobody else could play these parts. Nevertheless, projection or no, there is still a world out there—and it is capable of ever-changing configurations and susceptible to a variety of interpretations. Thus, if someone plays John's grandfather and John plays himself, the requirement for John to face the other guy's version of his grandfather could still be a valid confrontation wherein John can investigate whatever possibilities for action John needs to recover in his life. This does not have to rule out the powerful experiences John might also have in playing both himself *and* grandfather.

Existentialism's primary contribution to psychotherapy has been through the development of a new—and broadly inclusive—ethos. It has brought relativity into the social and behavioral sciences by defining fresh views of authority, truth, participant experience and the application of psychotherapy principles for personal growth, not just for pathology. It has made us more respectful of the importance of the common, daily issues in living: complications of birth, death, absurdity, confusion, impotence, responsibility, etc. Ignoring or denying these problems produces a selective, but costly, security which is paid for by depersonalization, explosive and random violence and second-hand living. Though the existentialists offer little in the way of practical prescriptions, their concepts of experience, authenticity, confrontation and the need for lively and present action, have encouraged psychotherapeutic inventiveness aimed at giving substance to these otherwise abstract goals.

Appendix B

Large Group Encounter and Seminar Case—Western Reserve University Session 2—April 6, 1971

BECOMING KNOWN

1. *Introduction*—Short statement re: the process of becoming known (Group leaders)

2. *My Bag*—Everyone is given a paper bag, some slips of paper, and provided with a pencil. They are asked to write down on the:

   Outside of the bag: "four things about yourself which most people who know you are aware of—either they've told you or have asked or commented about them—these are things about yourself that you are likely to accept or consider accurate."

   Slips of paper inside the bag: "four things about yourself that are not generally known. Although you have no objection to people knowing these things about you, for some reason or another, shyness, lack of opportunity, they don't come up very often—people just haven't seen these things in you or would have to know you pretty well before they would know these things about you."

Now, choose a partner—trade bags, and first of all, read and talk about what is written on the outside of your partner's bag.

Then, take turns pulling one statement out of your partner's bag and discussing these things he has described that are less well known about himself.

3. *Fictional Characters*—Form into groups of four people—don't stay with your partner from the previous exercise.

This time, look at the other people in your group and decide how you would use each of them in a story or novel or play that you might write. Imagine how each of the other people in your group might be a character in such a story. For example:

Whom would you use in an old-fashioned period? Which period:
   in a romantic adventure?
   in a futuristic scientific fantasy?
   in a spy/mystery/melodrama/comedy?
   in a realistic story about the present?

Would they be:
   hero/heroine?
   villain?
   lover?
   wise-cracking, hard-boiled character?
   spy?
   earthy wise man/woman?
   comic relief?
   innocent bystander?
   tragic character?

Take the time to discuss how this person reacts to the kind of character he suggests to you. Try to use what you are aware of right now, so that you can share your reasons for assigning the other person the role that you gave him/her. Discussion in whole group.

4. *Touching,* Part I—Staying in your group of four, one person at a time closes his eyes. The other three people come up to him, one at a time, and put their hands into his. The person with his eyes closed has to find out all he can about the other person

merely by touching his hands; through hand contact alone he is to try to discover what he can know about the other person. Discuss this with your group.

Part II—Choose a partner from your group of four. Take turns with one person closing his eyes and the other touching his face only—no talking—to get a sense of what the other person's face and the structure beneath it feel like What can you know, then, about the person whose face you are touching? For the person whose face is being touched: attend to how you feel about that, what parts of your face are alright for another to touch? What parts make you uneasy when someone touches them? Switch roles without talking. Then afterwards discuss the experience with your partner.

5. *Added Person Fantasy*—Three pairs of people join together to form a group of six. Close your eyes and think back over your life, and in fantasy add a person to your past life who would have contributed something you've missed that would have made a great difference to you. For example, you might add an older brother, or a certain kind of teacher, etc. Tell your group about your fantasy and the differences you imagined such an added character might have made in your life.

6. *Applause! Applause!*—Group gathers together, sitting as a whole with a space cleared in the center of the floor. One person at a time, whoever chooses to do so, goes to the cleared space and says his name aloud. At this, the rest of the group gives him an ovation, clapping, cheering, shouting "Bravo!" if they wish, etc. The person in the center acknowledges the applause in whatever way he wishes. A few others also take turns.

Index